Let's Eat

Let's Eat

Jewish Food and Faith

Lori Stein and Ronald H. Isaacs

ROWMAN & LITTLEFIELD
Lanham • Boulder • New York • London

We acknowledge with thanks permission to include the following recipes:

Avramila, Sour Plum Tart, pp. 221–22, by Janet Amateau. First published in SephardicFood.com, October 1, 2016. ©2016 by Janet Amateau. Used with permission.

Cheesecake, pp. 210–11, from *The World Famous Ratner's Meatless Cookbook*, by Judith Gethers and Elizabeth Lefft. Used with permission.

Kuba, pp. 44–46, and Matbucha, p. 15, *The Kitchen of Savta Aviva*, ©Eliraz Orian, 2016.

Published by Rowman & Littlefield
A wholly owned subsidiary of The Rowman & Littlefield Publishing Group, Inc.
4501 Forbes Boulevard, Suite 200, Lanham, Maryland 20706
www.rowman.com

Unit A, Whitacre Mews, 26-34 Stannary Street, London SE11 4AB

British Library Cataloguing in Publication Information Available

Library of Congress Cataloging-in-Publication Data
Names: Stein, Lori, author. | Isaacs, Ronald H., author.
Title: Let's eat : Jewish food and faith / Lori Stein and Ronald H. Isaacs.
Description: Lanham : Rowman & Littlefield, [2017] | Includes bibliographical references and index.
Identifiers: LCCN 2017017457 (print) | LCCN 2017018478 (ebook) | ISBN 9781442271043 (Electronic) | ISBN 9781442271036 (cloth : alk. paper)
Subjects: LCSH: Jewish cooking. | Food—Religious aspects—Judaism. | Jews—Food—History. | Holiday cooking. | Fasts and feasts—Judaism. | LCGFT: Cookbooks.
Classification: LCC TX724 (ebook) | LCC TX724 .S733 2017 (print) | DDC 641.5/676—dc23
LC record available at https://lccn.loc.gov/2017017457

♾™ The paper used in this publication meets the minimum requirements of American National Standard for Information Sciences—Permanence of Paper for Printed Library Materials, ANSI/NISO Z39.48-1992.

Printed in the United States of America

For all my nieces and nephews
And all my great-nieces and great-nephews
And all the ones to come
LS

For my soulmate Leora
RHI

Contents

Authors' Notes and Acknowledgments

This book is the result of a collaboration that was remarkably efficient, effective, and pleasurable. I want to thank Rabbi Ron Isaacs for his huge contribution to this book, both in the "Reflections" essays at the beginning of each chapter and the enormous trove of information and insight that is embedded on every page. I hope that he enjoyed it as much as I did.

The person responsible for this collaboration, and therefore for the entire book, is our literary agent Joan Parker, and I want to make sure she knows how grateful I am, not only for introducing me to Ron but for shepherding this book through every stage of its existence. Not only was she the agent who said, "Yes, I can sell this," she also helped us craft the outline and was meticulous about reviewing and providing valuable commentary from start to finish.

And I also want to acknowledge Boyd and Julianne Griffin, who suggested that Joan and I get together.

Thank you, Suzanne Staszak-Silva, our editor at Rowman & Littlefield, who saw value in this project. She provided just the right amount of support without ever being intrusive; she allowed us to follow our own instincts while gently guiding us to a better book. We also want to thank production editor Elaine McGarraugh, editor Kathryn Knigge, copyeditor Katy Whipple, and jacket designer Sally Rinehart of Rowman & Littlefield for their expert attention.

Throughout this project, my sisters Deena and Michelle, as always, pitched in whenever and however needed. For testing and tasting, figuring out what was missing from a recipe, proofreading, and telling me the truth—that's what family is for, but they go way beyond. Thank you to my mother, Shirley Stein, who was an artisanal cook before the term was invented. To my sisters-in-law Tzviya and Channah Stein of Rechovot, Israel, who introduced me to the many tastes of Jewish food over forty years ago and provided a lot of the food knowledge that is in these pages—in gratitude for everything you do. To my brothers, Joseph and Rabbi David Stein, who created homes where Jewish food was always plentiful and delicious (and to David for reading the section on kashrut and making sure that the Orthodox viewpoint was represented; I hope he is satisfied with the final result). To Eliraz and Yishai Orion and Chelli and Zvi Stein, who were always there to make sure that the Sephardi side of this book was given full attention. And to all my nieces and nephews, and great-nieces and -nephews (fifty-four of them, with a few more every year) because eating would not be as much fun without them.

Hundreds of books have been written about Jewish food; I referred to many of them, and they're listed in the bibliography. But I have to single out a few of them that were so incredible and full of information that they made my own research possible: Gil Marks, *Encyclopedia of Jewish Food*; Claudia Roden, *The Book of Jewish Food: An Odyssey from Samarkand to New York*; John Cooper, *Eat and Be Satisfied*; Matthew Goodman, *Jewish Food: The World at Table*; and Joan Nathan, *The Jewish Holiday Cookbook*.

I am amazed and grateful that so many people were willing to provide and test recipes and to answer all my questions. I want to acknowledge the contributions of Bonnie Lane Webber, Peg Streep, Henchi Lew, Dick Sandhaus, Beth Lefft, Janet Amateau, Jodi Bogen, Paula Algranati Izenstein, Ann Snyder Benator, and the Bukharan taxi driver whose name I can't find, but who told me about all his families' traditions.

In talking to so many people as I worked on this book, I came to realize that every family has its own traditions and some ideas that were considered universal were known only to a few people. Even within my own family, not everyone agrees; my mother and her sisters regularly engaged in heated arguments over whether Mama put dill in the chicken soup. So I am sure that some people will read some of this and think that parts of it are not true, when actually they are true, just for someone else. The topic of this book is enormous; it touches on just about every other topic in the world. I can't tell you how much fun I had while working on it and how much I hate to leave it because I know it can never be finished. But I hope you enjoy it.

Lori Stein
February 2017
New York

I want to thank Joan Parker, a personal friend and my literary agent, for bring-ing Lori Stein and myself together to learn more about Lori's vision. And I am privileged and honored that Lori, an accomplished writer and owner of Layla Productions, a book production company, asked me to join with her in this project. Not only does she possess a wealth of knowledge regarding the impact of food on Jewish culture and religion, she is also an outstanding cook and recipe tester in her own right. It has been a joy to work with her, and I cannot wait to try out some of her recipes. I have learned so much from her (as I know you will too) about the connection between food and Jewish values, food traditions around the world, and how food, eating, and community are pillars of Jewish culture.

I hope that those of you who read this book will be encouraged to try out some of the recipes in the book, tweak them, and create some originals of your own. You will surely gain a new perspective on just how food and Judaism intersect. And you are in for a culinary treat that will not only whet your appetite but have you asking for more. Enjoy the book! As we say at Passover time: "Let all who are hungry come and eat!"

Ron Isaacs
February 2017
New Jersey

Introduction

They Tried to Kill Us. We Survived. Let's Eat

Judaism is a complex religion. It combines profound morality, intricate law, diverse culture, explosive history, and strong communal spirit. It has existed for almost four thousand years and has spread to most regions on Earth, changing and evolving in each century and region. But there is a thread that runs through it. This thread does not define the values or essence of Judaism—but it provides a lens through which those values, that essence, can be better understood.

That thread is the food that Jewish people have eaten, the recipes and ingredients that have become part of our practice and connection to our faith, culture, and history. Not only is Jewish food comforting and delicious, it's also a link to every facet of Judaism. It turns out that the kitchen is an excellent place to start, or to further, a Jewish education. By learning about and cooking traditional Jewish dishes, we can understand fundamentals such as kashrut, community, and diversity. Jewish history is so connected to food that one comedian said that the story of Judaism can be condensed into nine words: They tried to kill us. We survived. Let's eat.

Our most intense memories and connections to Judaism involve food and cooking. The pure pleasure of braiding a challah with a grandmother, building the perfect pastrami sandwich, standing on a street corner in Jerusalem and nibbling on falafel—these recollections resonate with all of us.

REFLECTIONS: A FORSPEIZ, BY RABBI RON ISAACS

I'll bet that nearly every person remembers their first introduction to tasting a new food. If that experience is a positive one, it will likely result in a continued desire for it. I still remember the celebration of one of my first Passover seders when I ate matzah and was called upon to ask the Four Questions. Just thinking about it brings to life all of those in attendance around the table. Transactions surrounding food are the glue of the social system. Many of my childhood memories revolve around the family dinner table, Thanksgiving turkey dinners, and of course family Jewish holiday gatherings accompanied with a festive meal and foods symbolic of the holiday. As a congregational rabbi for more than forty years, noshing, schmoozing, and dining with congregants and guests was one of the best ways for me to get to better know people and build lifelong friendships with them.

Food is an instrument of both community and identity. Jewish food specifically is difficult to define. There is no question in my mind that Jews love to feed and be fed. If you've ever been in the care of a Jewish mother—whether yours or someone else's—then you must be familiar with the matriarchal words "eat something." Over the centuries Jews have eaten many different types of food, and quite a number of them bear the unique stamp of the socio-economic and migratory patterns of the Jewish community, while also reflecting the Jewish dietary laws and other religious requirements.

The Hebrew word "kosher" is often understood as the word often associated with Jewish ethnic food (kashrut is the state of being kosher). Did you know that the word "kosher" itself has nothing to do with food? It literally means "fit" or "proper," which is why one can ask about a business deal of questionable legality with the question: "Is it kosher?" There are many common misconceptions about kosher food, ranging from the notion that kosher food means that is has been blessed by a rabbi to the belief that the kosher laws are part of an ancient code of health. However, the biblical dietary laws have nothing to do with blessings or health. Simply put, the Bible associates keeping kosher with holiness and forging a Jewish identity. The laws of keeping kosher not only include a listing of the type of animals and fish that can be consumed, but also include ethical laws related to compassion for the animal, such as forbidding the consumption of animals' blood, the prohibition against hunting, and that animals for food must be killed by a special ritual slaughterer with one quickly drawn stroke against its throat in order not to prolong their death.

Although a person needs to eat in order to live and survive, Judaism has always viewed the act of eating as a sanctified act. Rabbinic thinkers have compared the dinner table to the altar that once stood in the Jerusalem Temple. The whole process of eating is thus changed into a richly beautiful ceremony, where ritual washing of the hands and blessings before and after the meal are recited in appreciation of having ample food to enjoy.

Personally speaking, I have often been struck by the many references to food in the Bible. Adam and Eve eat of the forbidden fruit, Jacob offers Esau a pot of lentil soup in exchange for his birthright, the Israelites hurriedly flee Egypt and take with them unleavened bread, and for forty years the Israelites led by their Prophet Moses are showered with heavenly mannah. Not only do all Jewish holidays have symbolic foods, but eating a special festive meal is a religious obligation, part of all Jewish life cycle events in order to enhance and glorify the celebration. Even death in Jewish law requires a meal of condolence, the first full meal that mourners eat upon returning from the cemetery, traditionally provided by the neighbors and friends of the bereaved. In this way, the mourner is given the sustenance of life, figuratively and literally, the "bread" of his/her existence.

There is simply no way that Jews can practice Judaism culturally or religiously without food. Even on Jewish fast days when Jews are required to abstain from food, they are required to eat a meal following the fast. And on Yom Kippur, the Day of Atonement and the most celebrated fast festival of them all, the custom is to end the fast with a Break the Fast meal, which is often celebrated in people's homes or a communal meal in the synagogue.

FOOD AND PHILOSOPHY

The underlying philosophies, values, and character of Judaism are intertwined with the ways that Jews grow, prepare, eat, and distribute food. Many of the more practical aspects of *tikkun olam*—the responsibility for fixing the world that is at the core of a Jew's relationship to the Earth and to other human beings—are food-based. When harvesting a field, Jewish farmers and gardeners are exhorted to leave one corner for the needy. Recalling this practice while preparing fresh vegetables helps us to understand *tikkun olam*, our responsibility to make the world a better place. At just about every special event where food is served—at weddings and other life cycle events, at the feast of Purim and other holiday meals—the needy are invited. There is a custom of tearing off a piece of challah dough before we bake it and burning it—to remind us of the requirement of donating a percentage of our food to the priests of Holy Temple in Jerusalem during biblical times, and the importance of supporting our communities today.

Shmirat Hatevah—guarding nature—is another Jewish value that is manifested in the way we grow food. Agricultural sustainability—encompassing crop rotation, companion planting, and using organic fertilizer—was discussed thousands of years ago in the Talmud, well before being "green" became fashionable (see page 127). The practice of leaving a field fallow every seventh year—called *shmitah,* which means sabbatical—is a sound agricultural practice that prevents the loss of topsoil. Refraining from picking fruit from a tree for three years allows the tree's roots to become strong. The reverence for and understanding of the way soil produces food is the reason that modern Israel is able to produce so efficiently, to make the desert bloom.

The practicality and frugality that are stereotypes of the Jewish character—and sometimes used derogatorily—are also built into the Jewish food system. Jewish law—called *Halachah*—prohibits displays of wealth. Most Jewish books are not illuminated (*Haggadahs,* used for Passover seders, and *Megillah,* scrolls that are read on certain holidays are exceptions). Jews are buried in simple pine boxes, not velvet-lined caskets that cost thousands of dollars. You'll never find even the most revered rabbis in the elaborate outfits that the Pope or Cardinals wear (another exception—the garment that the High Priest of the Holy Temple wore). This may be because the Patriarch Jacob made a fancy coat of many colors for his son Joseph and that turned out badly (see page 149). Some of this frugality was based on poverty rather than philosophy—but it is also an intelligent and practical way to behave.

This freedom from pretension and showiness extends to food. Jews cooked with scraps and less-desirable cuts of food and found the right techniques, spices, and herbs to make them tasty. Gefilte fish (see page 37) and *cholent* (see page 46) are good examples of this. The quintessential Jewish cut of meat—brisket—was originally ignored by most cooks, considered paupers' food. It needed long slow cooking and tenderizing by addition of herbs and spices to turn it into a delicacy that is the showpiece of many Jewish holiday meals.

Traditional Jewish meals are also healthy, using nutritious grains, legumes, and pulses including barley and chickpeas (which contain amazing amounts of protein and other nutrients). God created our bodies and housed our souls in them, so it is our responsibility to take care of them. Another iconic Jewish food, chicken soup, has been proven to be have anti-inflammatory properties (see page 41); Rabbi Moses ben Maimonides, the famed twelfth-century Spanish sage and physician, recommended that every Jew eat it often. Many Jewish writings support the precept of *Shmirat HaGuf,* guarding the body. Instructions for how to eat, dress, wash, and care for babies are sprinkled throughout Jewish writings. For example, there is an exhortation in the Torah, "If you find honey, eat only what you need. Otherwise, you will overdo it, and throw it up" (*Proverbs,* 25:16), and an instruction in the Talmud, "Don't get into the habit of taking drugs, don't leap over a sewer, don't have your teeth pulled" (*Pesachim,* 113a).

The Jewish attitudes toward caring for the environment and for oneself are loosely entwined by another underlying precept: Don't waste (*Ba'al Tashchit*). We live in a world where 50 percent of the food that is grown is thrown away, where we squander our health and our planet because we ignore the practices that would keep our air and water clean, our soil full of nutrients, our bodies healthy. The same mindfulness that eating kosher encourages—whether one chooses to follow every rule to the nth degree or simply note them—is what is needed to protect ourselves and our planet. The great philosopher Wendell Berry said, "The way we eat determines, to a considerable degree, the way the world is used." Every aspect of Jewish food takes that into account (even though the man who said it wasn't Jewish).

RITUAL, SYMBOLISM, AND FOOD

Jewish ritual often involves food. Understanding the complexity of Jewish rules about food brings the intricacy of Jewish law into focus. Holidays have specific foods attached to them: blintzes on Shavuot, jelly doughnuts on Hanukkah, honey cake on Rosh Hashanah. We designate matzah clinging to the backs of fleeing slaves as the symbol of Passover; we commemorate the discovery of one small flask of oil in the destroyed Temple by eating fried foods on Hanukkah; we turn the three-cornered hat of Purim's arch-villain into a pastry (even though he never wore such a hat, see page 135).

Jewish law is both sophisticated and convoluted—both characteristics that Jews are known for. Understanding the rules surrounding what foods we are allowed to eat requires decades of study, if one is interested in truly following every bit of them. In ultra-Orthodox schools, called yeshivas, young men sit for hours every day debating the minutiae with the intellectual zeal of constitutional scholars.

Food also serves as symbolic references to our hopes and fears. On Rosh Hashanah, the first day of the New Year, we eat foods that symbolize prosperity and good health (see pages 59–62). For Tu B'Shevat, the birthday of the trees, kabbalists have organized a seder (order) that helps us celebrate the beauty of nature by tasting foods that symbolize the seasons and our own personalities. At the well-known Passover seder, we use food to remind us of the years the Jews spent as slaves in Egypt.

COMMUNITY, FAMILY, AND FOOD

Food is the glue that holds families and communities together, for Jews and just about every other culture. But food has a more central and multi-faceted role for Jewish communities because the Jewish nation is so diverse. Many countries develop their own cuisines over centuries, and most are based on the ingredients that are available in their region and climate. Though they borrow from neighboring countries, there are boundaries that keep them together. Jews, dispersed to every part of the world, can rely on no such borders. Some Jewish communities (the Bukharans, Ethiopians, and Yemenites, for example) had very little communication with Jews in other countries, and much of their food is adapted from their host country, but certain aspects, based on both Jewish law and tradition, have been retained—the hot stews that must be kept warm overnight because of the rules prohibiting cooking on Shabbat; the sweet foods to herald a sweet new year; the simple, frugal, nutritious foods that hew to Jewish values.

SOME BASICS: A SHORT GUIDE TO JUDAISM

One can't really fully know the basic principles of Judaism without knowing something about Jewish food. But one can't appreciate Jewish food without knowing something about Judaism. So, here are some basic terms and concepts that will make the following chapters understandable even to those with very little prior experience with Judaism. There's not going to be a quiz at the end, but we're not going to define these terms each time they come up in the book. If you come to a term that you don't understand, you can check either this section or the Index on pages 247–255, which will list the page where it is defined.

The rule books: Judaism comes with several users' manuals, holy books that explain what the rules are. The first, and most important, is the **Torah** (also called the Old Testament of the Bible). One of the main principles of Orthodox Jewry is that the Torah was given to Moses, the leader, who, under God's aegis, brought the Jews out of slavery in Egypt, by God himself on Mount Sinai (see page 193). Other Jewish scholars believe that Moses received the Torah orally and that it was not transcribed until many centuries later. The Torah consists of the Five Books of Moses, plus many later writings that tell the story of the creation of the world, the origin of Judaism, and the conquest of the Promised Land; for more information, see page 132.

The **Talmud** is a more detailed explanation of the laws and spirit of Judaism, a transcription of the Oral Torah that was relayed to Moses on Mount Sinai and passed down from generation to generation through memorization. The Talmud was written over several hundred years, from before the destruction of the First Temple to 500 CE. It is a collection of writings from thousands of scholars on everything from *Halachah* (Jewish law) to philosophy, history, and practical matters (including agriculture, construction, how to dress, and how to eat). The Talmud is written in Aramaic and stretches over six thousand pages, divided into sixty-two tractates. It consists of two sections: the *Mishnah*, which is a transcription of the

Oral Torah (written about 200 CE), and the *Gemarah*, elucidation and commentaries (written about 500 CE). The **Midrash**, written around the same time as the Talmudic tracts, was a further elucidation of the material in the Talmud.

Over the next thousand years, rabbis wrote thousands of treatises debating many points in the Talmud, to the point that no one could really know just what they were supposed to be doing. Then, in 1563, Rabbi Yosef Caro of Safed gathered these all together in a book called the **Shulchan Aruch** (the set table). To this day, its conclusions about *Halachah* are accepted by almost everyone.

Language: The primary language of Israel is Hebrew, the language in which the Torah was written and which was spoken by Jews during the time that the Temple stood. But Hebrew was not the most commonly spoken language after the Jews were exiled. Instead, Aramaic, a language used by many nations in the Middle East, was used for both conversation and writing. A modern version of Hebrew was brought back into use in the nineteenth century, when pioneers began to move back to Palestine; the fledgling language was advanced when Eliezer Ben-Yehuda created a modern Hebrew dictionary. Today, Hebrew is spoken by about nine million people, including about six million who live in Israel.

Jews also picked up languages from the countries to which they were exiled. Yiddish is a combination of German and Hebrew and was used throughout central Europe starting around 1300. There is an incredible trove of Yiddish literature and theater, including works by Nobel Prize–winning novelist Isaac Bashevis Singer, Scholem Aleichem, and I. L. Peretz. Although it is not used by the majority of Jews anymore, the ultra-Orthodox community still speaks Yiddish and teaches it to their children, scholars still study the literature, and theater groups present Yiddish plays. Ladino is a combination of Spanish and Hebrew, used by Jews in Spain and their descendants, many of whom settled in North Africa and other countries in the Middle East after they were expelled from Spain; it too has a rich collection of literature and songs that are still cherished. There are other local dialects used by small groups of Jews.

ALL KINDS OF JEWS

Jews have divided themselves into several groups based on how and to what level they practice the rituals of Judaism—some groups strictly adhere to the *Halachah* that was created two thousand years ago and others have re-interpreted the rules to adapt them to modern times and philosophy.

Orthodox: The term "Orthodox" is a retronym, like rotary phone and analog clock. It did not exist until the nineteenth century—there was only one kind of Jew, so the term did not need a qualifier. If you were Jewish by birth, you were either connected or you weren't—and most people were, because most societies did not condone much mixing. The term "Orthodox" was used only after the period known as the Enlightenment, when some Jews challenged the strict adherence to *Halachah* that marks Orthodoxy. Orthodox Jews keep kosher and don't work on Shabbat and all the holidays. They remain segregated from the general population and usually send their children to schools called Yeshivot. In the last century, Orthodox Jewry has split itself into two overlapping segments: Modern Orthodox Jews still keep the *halachot* but interact with both non-Orthodox and non-Jewish people. They also wear modern dress and educate themselves (after high school) in secular universities, often achieving high positions in business, medicine, law, and other professions. Women are still expected to sit in separate sections in the synagogue and are not allowed to serve as rabbis, though that is very slowly changing as they are given more and more responsible roles. Ultra-Orthodox Jews (called *haredim*, or tremblers, in Israel) want to keep everything exactly the way it was in the Middle Ages, dressing in the garb that was worn by noblemen in medieval Europe, covering every part of their body and staying away from everyone else as much as possible. Between the most modern of Modern Orthodox Jews and the most ultra of Ultra-Orthodox Jews, there are subtle gradations of rigorousness. While most Orthodox Jews follow the rules of kashrut (see pages 198–203), they are somewhat flexible. Ultra-Orthodox Jews consider it necessary to follow higher standards, requiring much more supervision and sometimes demanding foods (such as dairy or wheat) that have been monitored only by Jews at every stage of production. Airlines often offer two levels of kosher food: one standard and one "*mehadrin*," or super-duper.

Hasidim and Mitnagdim: The ultra-Orthodox segment is also split into two segments: Hasidim and non-Hasidim (the latter are known as Mitnagdim [Protesters] or Yeshiva people). The Hasidic movement was founded in the middle of the eighteenth century in Ukraine by Rabbi Yisroel Iserles, also known as Baal Shemtov (Master of the Good Name), in reaction to the rigid, intellectual way that Judaism was practiced in that time. A few, usually wealthy, Jews learned in academies (yeshivas) and were close to the rabbi, who made all the decisions. The peasant class was removed from most aspects of religion other than following the rules; there was little enjoyment for them. Baal Shemtov went out into nature and felt the spirit of God and relayed that passion to his followers, who responded with fervor that is still a mark of Hasidism today. Incorporating elements of the Kabbalah, Hasidim (the word means pious and shares a root with the word *hesed*, which means loving kindness) seek closeness to and profound, spiritual understanding of God. People sang and danced as they prayed, experiencing this closeness. Each group rallied around their rabbi, or Rebbe, who was revered in an almost cultlike fashion; many Hasidim thought that these Rebbes had mystical powers. The Hasidic movement spread throughout eastern Europe and Russia, with groups adhering to minor and major Rebbes (such as the Satmar in a town called St. Mary's in Hungary, the Belz in Ukraine, the Gerer, the Puppa, the Breslover). When Hitler decimated eastern European Jewry, many of these groups, having lost large percentages of their members to camps, moved to the United States and Israel, where they still live apart from society in segregated neighborhoods. Some groups, however, actively encourage secular Jews to join them, such as the Lubavitch who send *Mitzvah* mobiles around cities and nudge people to eat matzah on Passover, shake a palm branch on Sukkot, say a prayer, or join them for Shabbat. The Breslov hold a mass reunion in their original town every Rosh Hashanah, where tens of thousands of their followers and other seekers of truth gather to pray in the woods.

As the Hasidic movement gained strength, the Yeshiva crowd looked down their noses and mocked them for their lack of scholarship and decorum. The Yeshiva crowd is every bit as religious (and reactionary) as the Hasidim, they just approach religion in a very different way. When they left Europe, they set up Yeshivas all over the United States and Israel; there are major Yeshivas in Lakewood, New Jersey, in Baltimore, Cincinnati, and Cleveland. Both the Yeshiva people and Hasidim monitor Kashrut and affix their specific seals to foods; many people in each group do not trust the others' foods.

The Enlightenment: By the end of the eighteenth century, the segregating limitations on Jews in eastern Europe were beginning to lift. Jews were allowed to join guilds and attend universities; they became prosperous and educated. And many began to wonder if it was possible for them to explore the world outside Judaism. Individual secular Jewish philosophers and writers such as Bernard Spinoza and Heinrich Heine in the early eighteenth century laid the groundwork and by the middle of the nineteenth century there was an established movement that sought to move Judaism away from its all-encompassing roots and move it into the outside world—without losing the culture, values, and history of Judaism. The movement was called the *Haskalah* (which means wisdom) or the Enlightenment.

Reform Judaism: According to a recent Pew study, the Reform movement in the United States constitutes 35 percent of Jewish Americans that affiliate with a denomination (30 percent have no affiliation according to the study).[1] Reform Judaism arose in Germany in the early 1800s both as a reaction against what some Jews regarded as Orthodox inflexibility and as a response to Germany's more liberal political climate that seemed to be more open to Jews who were willing to drop traditions that isolated them from their German neighbors. For Reform leaders Judaism was seen as a developing, evolving religion, one that would disappear if it were not kept up-to-date, one which needed constant reform and change. Such changes included use of instrumental music on the holy Sabbath, an abridged prayer service with less Hebrew and more English, and an abandonment of the kosher dietary restrictions. The liberal spirit of early America encouraged freedom of religious expression, and this was the perfect soil in which Reform Judaism could grow. The first Reform congregation was in Charleston, South Carolina, formed in 1824. Baltimore established its first Reform Temple in 1842, and New York City's Congregation Emanuel followed in 1845. Then Albany, Cincinnati, Philadelphia, Chicago, and other cities joined the movement.

In 1883, Isaac Mayer Wise opened the Hebrew Union College in Cincinnati to train Reform rabbis. In 1885, the Reform movement produced its Pittsburgh Platform, which declared among other things that all of the biblical and rabbinic laws pertaining to regulating diet are apt to obstruct rather than to further modern spiritual elevation. The few non-Reform Jews in the United States in the 1880s came together to take steps to combat the increasing Reform influence, and in 1887 a new rabbinical school called the Jewish Theological Seminary opened its doors in New York City. Today it continues to serve as one of the homes of the Conservative movement's rabbinical, cantorial, and school of education. There is a West Coast school called Ziegler that has a graduate program of study leading to ordination as a conservative rabbi. This school is an arm of the American Jewish University in Los Angeles.

THE TREYFE BANQUET

In July 1883, a banquet was held to honor the first graduating class of Hebrew Union College in Cincinnati. It was a night of great pride and pomp, but when the first course was served, many of the participants were appalled to find what they assumed was shrimp (it turned out to be littleneck clams on the half shell) on their plates. A group of rabbis, some of whom observed the rules of kashrut, stood up and left, assuming that this was a deliberate attempt to once and forever sever ties with *Halachah*. The hosts insisted that the shellfish was the caterer's mistake, which was hard to believe because a printed menu listed not only clams but actual shrimp, softshell crabs, frogs' legs, and ice cream to conclude a meat meal. Despite the reaction of the more traditional guests, the hosts, including Rabbi Isaac Wise, declared the banquet an unqualified success and used it to herald a new Judaism that was not founded on the stomach or the kitchen.

The treyfe banquet was certainly a pivotal event. A segment of Reform Jewry condoned and praised Rabbi Wise's break with traditional Judaism. Another group of rabbis was not ready to discard all connection to *Halachah*. By 1889, the Central Conference of American Rabbis was established to represent the more traditional voices of Reform Judaism and the Union was split forever into Reform and Conservative branches.

Conservative Judaism: Conservative Jewish affiliation in the United States is 18 percent. Like the Reform movement, Conservative Judaism had its beginnings in Germany. Many thought that Reform had gone too far in discarding and changing traditional practices. They sought a middle ground that eventually became known as Conservative Judaism. Its early leader was the famous rabbi and scholar Zachariah Frankel of Prague. Along with a group of moderate reformers, he founded the Jewish Theological Seminary of Breslau in 1854 and began to teach a new version of Judaism. His group did not enjoy wide success in Europe. Like the Reform movement, the great victories of Conservative Judaism would be won in America. The first important Conservative movement leader in the United States was Isaac Leeser, who served as rabbi of Philadelphia's Mikveh Israel Synagogue. The Jewish Theological Seminary in New York opened in 1887. Solomon Schechter, the renowned Romanian scholar, was chosen as the school's first president.

Conservative Judaism's original motto was "tradition and change." It was founded on the belief that Jewish tradition is vital and must be preserved. It is therefore important to study the historical growth of Jewish laws, customs, and institutions. Thus along with tradition there is the possibility of change.

Reconstructionist Judaism: The founder of this denomination is Mordecai Kaplan, who in 1922 formed his own synagogue in New York, called the Society for the Advancement of Judaism, which became his laboratory for developing his ideas about reconstructing Judaism and Jewish values. With the opening of the society the Reconstructionist movement was born. Kaplan's main thesis is that Judaism is an evolving religious civilization, one in which religious teachings, ritual observances, peoplehood, and culture all play a part. Kaplan also rejected the doctrine of Jews as the chosen people and also rejected the notion of God as a personal deity. In 1968, the Reconstructionist Rabbinical College was founded in Philadelphia. Reconstructionists often feel that Orthodoxy relies too much on its belief in a personal God. They are critical of the Reform movement because it neglects the religious meaning of peoplehood and the value of ritual. It also posits that Conservative Judaism is too concerned with the past and with its attempts to remain true to Jewish law, while at the same time changing it.

Jewish Renewal: The term Jewish Renewal refers to organizations of those who are dedicated to reclaiming the Jewish people's sacred purpose of partnership with the Divine in the inseparable task of healing the world. Jewish Renewal groups seek to bring creativity, relevance, joy, and an all-embracing awareness to spiritual practice as a path to healing one's body and mind. One of the most important Renewal rabbis is the late Rabbi Zalman Schachter-Shalomi, a charismatic rabbi trained in the Hasidic movement who later left to found his own institution. The Aleph: Alliance for Jewish Renewal organization is the outgrowth of P'nai Or Religious Fellowship, founded by Reb Zalman in 1962. Many of the Jewish Renewal groups and synagogues put their emphasis on direct spiritual experience and kabbalistic mystical teaching. They are known for their creative liturgy and often use meditation, dance, and chanting. According to a recent Pew study, Jewish Renewal and Reconstructionist Jews in America constitute 6 percent[2] of those affiliated with a particular branch of American Judaism.

JEWISH GEOGRAPHY: THE DIASPORA

There is another way to classify Jews, one based on geography rather than the way they practice religion. Geography is a huge issue for Jews. For several hundred years after they settled in the Promised Land, most of them stayed put; there were small groups of traders who settled communities in places like Turkey or Syria, but Jews had a home base. But then their country was conquered by others and they were exiled—twice. Without a land of their own, Jews set down roots all over the world, as they were pushed from one country to another. This disconnection from their homeland is called the Diaspora (*Galut* in Hebrew) and has had a profound effect on Judaism.

The first exile, by Nebuchadnezzar, King of Babylon, was in 586 BCE—and from then on, there were Jewish settlements in different regions. In each case, some Jews stayed in the place to which they were exiled, some returned to Israel, some moved to other places. And that is the source of the amazing diversity of the Jewish people. There are few corners of the world that don't have at least a trace of Jews living in them, and in dozens of places, there were large communities with synagogues and schools.

The history of Jews in all of these places is similar. In most cases, they were welcomed and given rights to join society, industries, and universities, either when they first arrived or soon after. Under those conditions, they flourished and were valued for their intelligence and skills; they became doctors and scientists, and were prominent members of the intelligentsia. And then a new government would take over and decide that the Jews were the cause of all their problems; Jews were typecast as scapegoats from early on. They suffered from persecutions as brutal as death or as devastating as not being allowed to practice their religion or enter society professionally, academically, or socially. In some cases, they found other ways to prosper; Jews became bankers and traders, traveling all over the world on the spice and silk routes. And in many other cases, they fell into poverty and depression, losing their schools and houses of worship so that their children were no longer educated, bringing them down even further. The change—in either direction—usually took a couple of hundred years.

Ashkenazim and Sephardim: Many Jews identify themselves—and cook—according to whether their ancestors came from eastern or western Europe

(Ashkenazi Jews), from the people who moved to the Ottoman Empire and other countries in the Middle East after the Jews of Spain were banished during the Spanish Inquisition (Sephardic Jews), or from communities that settled in Middle Eastern countries many centuries earlier, when the Jews were exiled from Israel (Mizrachi Jews).

Mizrachi Jews and others: In the sixth century BCE, the Jews were exiled from the Promised Land when Babylonian King Nebuchadnezzar destroyed the First Temple in Israel. The exiled Jews established communities in the region where Babylon was a major city; this region is now Iraq and borders on the region that is now Iran; Syria was also a neighbor. Most of these Jews returned to Israel when Cyrus the Great lifted the exile in 538 BCE, but pockets remained in what is now Iran, Iraq, and Syria, and some moved to Uzbekistan, Kurdistan, Afghanistan, India, and Pakistan. Over 50 percent of the Jews who now live in Israel have some Mizrachi roots, though most consider themselves Sephardim. A few of these communities, including the Yemenites of the Arabian peninsula and the Bukharans of central Asia, stayed apart from the rest of Jewry and established their own cuisines, but most melded with groups who came later, after the Spanish Inquisition.

Sephardim: Although a great percentage of the Jews who call themselves Sephardim probably did not descend from the Jews of Spain, their name comes from the Hebrew word for Spain. Though there is some evidence that there were Jews in Spain during biblical times, the first large group of Jews first arrived in Spain after the destruction of the First Temple in 586 BCE and many more ended up there as exiles from Israel after the Roman conquest wandered through Europe looking for a home. For many centuries, Jews were reviled and when Spain became a stronghold for the Catholic church in the early Middle Ages, many were forced to convert. The Council of Toledo passed many draconian laws against them, including one in 633 that said that if a Jew refused to convert, his children should be taken away.

Then the Moors conquered Spain; they were much more accepting of Jews, recognizing that they could make a contribution. The Golden Age of Judaism in Spain—a period when Jews were accepted in society and became influential in arts, science, and business—dated to the invasion of the Moors in the eighth century. Rabbi Moses Maimonides, known as the Rambam, is one of the best known figures of that period; in addition to writing revered commentaries, he was also a respected physician. The Golden Age ended in the eleventh century, when the Moors were replaced by more fundamental Muslims; a massacre in the city of Grenada was a turning point. For the next few hundred years, Jewish life deteriorated and things got even worse when the Catholics returned to power. In 1492, a royal edict gave Jews three choices: conversion, expulsion, or death. Many converted, and some of the converts (called Anusim) practiced Judaism secretly for hundreds of years. But a large number—estimates range from forty thousand to a hundred thousand—dispersed throughout north African countries and others under the influence of the Ottoman Empire, including Morocco, Libya, Egypt, Tunisia, Syria, Iran, Iraq, and Turkey. There, they connected with existing Mizrachi groups and melded their religious practices and cuisines. The vast and various Sephardi cuisines include elements from Spanish and Middle Eastern cooking, using spices and sauces that the original emigrants brought with them and those they found in their new homes.

SEPHARDI FOOD

In every country where they settled, they adjusted and adapted ingredients and techniques, so that today Sephardi cooking is a treasury of tastes from both Europe and the Middle East. It has recently begun to take its rightful place as one of the great cuisines of the world.

Sephardic meals often start with mezze, sometimes called meza—small plates of intensely flavored cooked salads and other appetizers. Some are as simple as plates of cooked beans with salt, pepper, and a splash of olive oil or spiced nuts; others require hours of preparations, such as stuffed grape leaves or fried pancakes. For a major meal, either on a holiday or just Shabbat, a dozen mezze might be prepared, including oranges with black olives, celery with artichoke and fennel, mashwiya (roasted vegetables such as tomatoes and peppers, popular in Tunisia and Libya), zaaluk (a Moroccan salad of mashed eggplant and tomatoes), homemade pickles of pink turnips or tiny eggplants, fava bean salad, preserved lemons, celery root salad, beet and chard salad, steamed leeks with lemon, Jerusalem artichoke salad. Spreads made with sesame paste (tahini), ground chickpeas or fava beans (hummus), and garlicky, spicy tomatoes (matbucha) were also served as mezze.

Vegetables stuffed with grains, meat, or cheese were often served as main dishes, and several kinds of dough were stuffed with many different fillings and fried or baked; they're called borekas or sambuseks. Grains such as rice, lentils, or chickpeas were served as side dishes. Meat was usually lamb, often grilled. All of these were taken from Turkish, north African, or Iraqi-Iranian-Syrian traditions.

Sweets were served at both the start and the end of the meal. In some countries, guests were welcomed with a tavola di dolci, an elaborate tray of marmalades, marzipan, and baked goods soaked with honey and sprinkled with chopped nuts. Many different cookies and cakes were served as dessert.

Sephardic food is rarely simple and bland and usually is flavored with spice mixes and intense sauces.

Just a few of the signature sauces of Sephardic Jews are presented here.

HAWAIJ (YEMENITE)

Combine three tablespoons each of coriander seeds and cumin seeds, two tablespoons of peppercorns, one tablespoon of coriander seeds, and one teaspoon of cloves. Toast the mixture in a heavy skillet for a few minutes until they begin to pop; let them cool. Bring in a spice grinder or mortar and pestle, then add one teaspoon ground nutmeg and one tablespoon ground turmeric. Mix well, and store in a tightly covered glass jar.

SCHUG

Seed and dice ten hot peppers. Wear gloves! Remember that the more seeds you leave in, the hotter the final product will be—you may want only one seed. Add three cups chopped cilantro, eight peeled garlic cloves, a teaspoon each of salt, ground cumin, cardamom, grated lemon rind, and salt. Pulse a few times, then add two tablespoons of olive oil and process until almost—but not quite—smooth. If it's not hot enough for you, add cayenne pepper. If it's too hot—too bad, just use it sparingly.

Harissa is served with every type of food. Prepared jars are available in Middle Eastern stores. **Za'atar** is also readily available; its main ingredient is a wild hyssop (called za'atar) that is mixed with coriander, sesame seeds, sumac, and other spices.

MATBUCHA (NORTH AFRICAN)

This garlic-tomato sauce is often served as mezze.

Makes 1 cup

INGREDIENTS

¼ cup olive oil
6 large garlic cloves, minced
1 small hot pepper, diced (remove all or most of the seeds depending on how hot you want the final product to be)
1 small bell pepper, diced (optional)
2 pounds tomatoes, peeled (if you wish), seeded and diced
Salt to taste
Cayenne pepper (optional)

Heat the oil in a saucepan. Add the garlic and hot pepper and sauté over medium heat until they are very soft. Add the minced bell pepper (if you are using) and the tomatoes and sauté until they begin to lose their shape. Reduce to low heat, add a quarter teaspoon of salt, and simmer until thickened; watch it carefully and stir frequently if not constantly. Cook for at least fifteen minutes, more if you have patience. Taste, adjust salt, and if it is not spicy enough, add cayenne pepper. Serve hot or cold with bread, vegetables, over anything, or on its own.

PRESERVED LEMONS

Turning regular lemons into preserved ones deepens the flavors and adds a silky texture to whatever you're making. Some people add spices and herbs to the marinade, but those may interfere with your recipes.

INGREDIENTS
6 to 8 lemons
¼ cup kosher salt

Quarter four of the lemons vertically from top to bottom, but don't cut all the way down so that they are still attached on the bottoms. Rub the exposed flesh with salt, then close them up. Pour about one tablespoon of salt into a one-pint jar with a tight lid; you'll probably fit only three or four. Pack as many of the closed lemons into the jar as will fit. Squeeze them as you pack so that they release as much juice as possible. The juice should cover the tops of the lemons, but doesn't have to fill the jar. If the tops of the lemons are exposed, juice the rest of the lemons to fill. Close the jar tightly and place it in a warm place. Shake the jar and turn it over each day to move the salt and juice around. After about thirty days, the lemons will be preserved. Open the jar, remove what you need, and reseal. You can keep opening and resealing for six months or more. Rinse the lemons before using—use rind and all.

ASHKENAZIM

By the time the Roman Empire conquered the Promised Land, there were Jewish communities all over the world; some were leftovers from the Babylonian exile, living in Persia and the lands surrounding it, others were started by traders who moved through the silk and spice routes to north Africa, Europe, and India. No one is sure how many remained in Israel to be expelled, but historians estimate that over a million were killed during the revolt that preceded the expulsion and over a million lived outside of the Jerusalem area. There is no number given for the Jews who ended up in Europe in the first century CE or exactly where they settled. But we do know that there were settlements in the Mediterranean countries—especially Spain, France, and Italy—in the early Middle Ages (from the fifth to the eleventh centuries). There was very little Jewish presence in the region that is now Germany and eastern Europe; that area was ruled by the Visigoths, who were not very tolerant hosts. Despite the fact that the word "Ashkenazim" refers to Germany, the people who that term refers to lived in the region that is now Germany for a relatively short time.

Jews slowly moved northward as things began to fall apart for them in the Holy Roman Empire; religious proclamations led to persecution and exile, and although there were thriving Jewish communities in southern and western Europe—the Golden Ages of Judaism in Spain and France—some rabbis went east and north. Around the tenth century CE, the German king invited some rabbis from Italy to settle in the region. He knew that the Jews were a stable society. Several groups moved and over the next few centuries, they grew exponentially. It is estimated that only a few hundred Jews lived in central and eastern Europe in the tenth century; by the time World War II broke out, there were almost ten million. (This is a great boon for researchers studying genetics, who can trace genes back to a very limited gene pool.)

Rabbi Kalonymus ben Meshulem, a member of an important French-Italian rabbinical family, moved back and forth between France and Mainz, a town in what is now Germany; he is credited with making the region hospitable for Jews. By the thirteenth century, when the Crusades were over and many Jewish communities had been decimated in western Europe, Germany was a full-blown Jewish center and Poland's Jewish scene was expanding rapidly. By the nineteenth century, central and eastern Europe held by far the largest population of Jews ever collected in one region—about ten million people, about 60 percent of world Jewry (estimated at about fifteen million to seventeen million people).[3] Then, by the end of World War II, only a fraction were left.

The word "Ashkenaz" comes for a term for Germany, but the food we think of as Ashkenzi originated in western, central, and eastern Europe. Jews in the region were almost uniformly poor and crafted their meals from the poorest of ingredients. They ate the heavy vegetables that were available to them—cabbage, onions, carrots, with potatoes coming much later, plus plenty of barley and lentils. Fish and meat were for holidays and Shabbat. Spices were expensive and few of them were used; they were lucky if they had salt, and in Hungary a bit of paprika. But they did find enough fine white flour to bake challah for Shabbat and used a common braided form for it. They also partook of the heavy goulashes and stews that were popular in the region.

Nevertheless, a set of Jewish favorites emerged in each region. Gefilte fish, chicken soup, and cheaper cuts of meat such as brisket were most common. For most dishes, if you look for a reason why it was adopted by Jews, the answer is because it was cheaper. But two things that Jews had were time and ingenuity. Jewish housewives learned to get the very best out of any bit of food they could find, turning chicken livers into a delicacy, cooking tough brisket long and slow to make it tender, using scraps of chicken for chicken soup and scraps of beef for *cholent*. When they began to prosper and were able to afford better ingredients, these foods were favorites that they retained.

Ashkenazi food has a bad reputation; it is considered bland and heavy, to be used only for sentimental reason. That's at least partly because many of the Ashkenazi dishes that we know are mass-produced, without regard for freshness and taste. But there's a renaissance going on, and many cooks are finding that making these foods the way they were made before jars and freezers are actually quite delicious. As Jeffrey Yoskowitz and Liz Alpern stated in their "Gefilte Manifesto"[4] (and showed in the cookbook that resulted from it), "We need not accept the extinction of this tradition, or the robust, colorful, fresh flavors of Ashkenazi cuisine. We know that gefilte—and borscht, kvass, and so many Old World foods—is excellent when done right."

So—you'll find fresh looks at Ashkenazi food in this book—at chicken soup made with quality ingredients and matzah balls that float and latkes and kugels that are full of flavor. You'll be inspired to consider baking your own challah, rugelach, and hamentashen, looking for kuchen and babkas, learning how to make a brisket that's the opposite of tough and tasteless. Some of these dishes are extremely simple—kasha varnishkes are just bowtie noodles with buckwheat and butter; for others, like pickled herring or bagels, you're probably better off finding sources that make them professionally. But Ashkenazi food, like Judaism, is not going to disappear—not because it's been around for a long time, but because it's intrinsically wonderful.

JEWS IN THE WORLD

Although there are rumors that Christopher Columbus was Jewish and that he found America while searching for a homeland for the Jews (he started his expedition just a few days after the edict of expulsion from Spain was issued), there is no proof of that. But small contingents of Jews settled in Brazil and in other South American countries in the fifteenth century and twenty-three of them landed in the colony of New Amsterdam, now New York, in 1654, when they fled persecution in Brazil. They founded Shearith Israel, a congregation that still exists (though in a different building). Other groups of Jews came to America from Europe; there were Jews who owned plantations in the South before the Civil War, especially in Charleston, South Carolina. There was a Sephardic synagogue in Newport, Rhode Island (1658), and in 1795, the first Ashkenazi synagogue was founded in America, in Philadelphia.

But great waves of Jews did not come to America until the 1850s, when German Jews joined the small number of Sephardim who were already here. Then, in the 1880s, when economic difficulties hit Europe, millions of Jews packed themselves into steerage class to come to "The Golden Land." They had heard rumors of streets paved with gold and unfettered opportunity, and they were willing to vomit for two weeks to find new lives there. By 1924, there were over two million Jews in America. Most of them lived in New York, but others looked for opportunity in big open spaces. There were Jewish synagogues in southern New Jersey, in South Dakota and Louisiana. A concerted effort to relieve crowding in New York Jewish neighborhoods led to a settlement in Galveston, Texas. In the 1930s, when hundreds of thousands of Jews tried to come to America to avoid the growing threat of Nazism, most were turned away because President Roosevelt and many Americans felt they could be clandestine Nazis and therefore security risks. But after the war, the gates opened again and a good percentage of the survivors of the Holocaust moved to North and South America. Today, estimates of Jewish population range from five to eight million people. According to the American Jewish Yearbook of 2014, there are just over seven million Jews in the United States today, about 3 percent of the country's total population. The largest centers are New York (1.6 million), California (1.05 million), Florida (847,000), New Jersey (484,000), Massachusetts (347,000), and Illinois (400,000). The smallest are North Dakota (800) and South Dakota (1,200).[5]

American Jews enjoy all the typical Ashkenazi and Sephardi foods from Europe and the Middle East, but they have also developed a set of their own favorites, which have crossed over into the general population. Bagels (with lox or cream cheese, see pages 19–68); pickles (including pickled cucumbers and pickled herring); bialys; deli meats such as corned beef, pastrami, and tongue; and egg creams (which are made with neither eggs nor cream) are the foods most closely associated with Jews. If you look for a connection between them, you'll find that most of these foods are cheap and long-lasting; they use ingredients that might go to waste and preserve them. Many of the first immigrants kept kosher and looked for kosher food, which was hard to find and store, especially when there were no refrigerators; by curing and pickling meat and fish, they made cheap cuts taste better and last longer. American Jews did not invent all these foods—pastrami is from Romania, lox is from Russia and Scandinavia, bagels are from Poland—but they did bring them here and exalt them.

American Jews love their food and make sure there are places where it is served all over the United Stated and Canada. The Milesend neighborhood of Montreal is known for its deli and bagels; Zingermann's Deli in Milwaukee is known as one of the best restaurants (not Jewish restaurants, not deli restaurants, but best of any restaurants in the country). Chicago and Miami—the cities with the largest Jewish population—are meccas for lovers of Jewish food. Cincinnati was home to the first matzah factories. The West Side of New York is home to upscale kosher restaurants; Forest Hills, Queens, in New York City, has a slew of Bukharan restaurants.

But no neighborhood is connected to Jewish food as closely as the Lower East Side of Manhattan (which, by coincidence [or not] is the neighborhood where one of the authors of this book grew up). The Lower East Side is very near the port where most Jews disembarked after the frightful journey from Europe. It was full of cheap tenement housing, synagogues of every ilk, and other Jews; and most new immigrants walked over and stayed there. Food was everywhere, from the pushcarts that lined the streets selling fresh produce to cafes and delis that became gathering places. And one of the quintessential Jewish foods, the egg cream (made by combining chocolate syrup, milk, and seltzer), was invented right on those pushcarts (some Brooklyn enthusiasts beg to differ), possibly by fortuitous accidents.

MORE JEWISH COMMUNITIES

These are just a fraction of the Jewish communities that exist now and in the past. There are Jews in India (three solid communities, in Calcutta, Cochin, and Bombay), in China (a small group in Kaifeng whose members don't know how they got there, but avoid eating the sinew of cows and keep a sacred book that looks like the *Megillah* of Esther), and in Ethiopia (a large community that may be the remnants of the lost tribes that disappeared from Canaan during biblical times, and has largely been relocated in Israel). There is also a large Jewish population in South America, most of them started by refugees from Hitler's Germany—combined, South America's Jewish population is the third largest in the world, after Israel and the United States. Each community has its own special dishes that combine the core of Judaism with the traditions of the country in which they live, connecting them to their homeland and to their current homes.

TIMELINE

This timeline covers multiple millennia and the whole world, which made it necessary to be selective in its coverage of events.

BCE

1900–1700: Age of the Patriarchs; Abraham worships one God, the children of Jacob go to Egypt.

1450: The Ten Plagues; Pharaoh releases the Hebrew slaves, God parts the Red Sea.

1410–1050: Israel conquers Canaan, settles down in tribes led by Judges.

1200–1000: The Iron Age; iron tools are used for agriculture and construction.

1050–933: The Kingdom of Israel: Saul unifies tribes; David enlarges the Kingdom. Solomon builds the First Temple.

928: The Kingdom splits in two, Israel in the North, Judea in South. Prophets try to teach people to heed God's word.

722: Assyria conquers northern kingdom and takes its people captive. Later, the ten tribes that form Israel disappear, possibly ending up in Ethiopia.

586: Babylonians conquer Judea and destroy Temple. Babylonian exile begins.

538: King Cyrus permits return to Judea. Second Temple is built.

Fifth century BCE: Queen Esther saves her people from Haman's plot; the date is debatable, and some scholars believe the story is fiction.

322: Jews become immersed in Greek culture (Hellenism).

168–164: Assyrian King Antiochus driven out by Maccabees; Temple cleansed. Hanukkah is declared a holiday.

63: Romans conquer Judea.

c. 30: Hillel the Elder becomes leader of the Sanhedrin, the ruling body in Israel. He created the bitter herb sandwich that is still eaten during the Passover seder.

CE

30: Romans kill Jesus. His followers begin to spread Christianity throughout empire.

66–73: Jewish revolt against Rome; last Jewish rebels die at Masada.

c. 130: The practice of eating poultry with dairy, which was permitted until then, is forbidden.

132–135: Second Jewish revolt against Rome. Jews continue to pray and study in secret.

200: Center of Jewish study shifts to Babylon. *Mishnah* edited by Rabbi Yehuda HaNasi.

400–500: Babylonian Jews build academies. *Gemara* is completed.

622: Muhammad founds Islam in Arabia.

631: Arabs conquer Jerusalem; most Jews are treated well under Muslim rule.

711: The Moors conquer Spain.

740–970: Judaism spreads as far as Russia.

950–1391: Spain is the new center of Jewish life. The period from 755–1146 is known as the Golden Age of Judaism in Spain.

950–1100: Jews settle in England, France, and Germany, where Gershom and Rashi study and comment on Jewish law.

1096–1320: Crusaders drive Muslims out of Palestine and destroy many Jewish communities.

1200–1400: Jews persecuted in western Europe; Jews are sometimes accused of using the blood of Christian children in matzah.

1254: Jews are expelled from France; centers of Judaism move to Central Europe.

1270: First mention of dairy being used for Shavuot in a commentary on the Torah by Rabbi Avigdor Tzarfati.

Early thirteenth century: Rabbi Kalonymus ben Kalonymus suggests special foods for Hanukkah and Purim.

1348–1349: The Black Plague, increased oppression.

1492: Expulsion of Jews from Spain.

1500–1600: Spanish and Portuguese Jews flee to Italy, north Africa, and the New World, find welcome in Turkish Empire and Palestine.

1516: The first Italian ghetto is established.

1562: Code of Jewish Law (*Shulchan Aruch*) written by Rabbi Joseph Karo in Safed, Israel.

Early seventeenth century: Pri Etz Hadar, the guide to the Tu B'Shevat seder, is written.

1610: Bagels appear in the Krakow Jewish community. They were originally used as gifts for expectant mothers and midwives, and may have been inspired by a circular bread from Central Asia or by a boiled Spanish bread called escaladadas. The word could be derived from a German word for ring (bougal) or from a Yiddish word for bend (beigin). By the end of the seventeenth century, they were popular in Jewish communities throughout eastern Europe.

1400–1648: Jews live peacefully in Poland, governed by Council of Four Lands.

1648–1658: Cossacks in Poland revolt and destroy hundreds of Jewish communities.

1500–1700: Anusim (Spanish Jews who practiced Judaism in private after the expulsion) move north to Holland and France to practice Judaism freely. Jews begin to return to England.

1654: Twenty-three Jews come to New Amsterdam from Brazil.

1750s: Hasidism emerges as a religious revolt.

1787: U.S. Constitution promised religious freedom to all. France gives equal rights to Jews.

1800–1900: Equal rights spread to western Europe; pogroms in eastern Europe.

1840s and 1850s: Crop failures and famines in eastern Europe; potatoes, which had come to Europe a few centuries earlier, become more popular because cabbages and turnips are not available.

1840s: Jaffa oranges, formerly known as Shamoutis, become popular in Israel and are exported to Europe.

1878: Petach Tikvah, the first modern agricultural settlement in Palestine, is founded.

1881: Pogroms in Russia; Jews begin emigrating to western Europe and America.

1882: Fourteen Russian university students, under the aegis of an organization called Bilu, go to Palestine and set up an agricultural settlement.

1888: The Breakstone Dairy is opened in Manhattan, bringing European dairy products like sour cream to the New World.

1894: Dreyfus falsely accused of treason in France.

1897: First Zionist Congress.

1900–1914: Pogroms drive more Russians to western Europe and Palestine.

1903: The Jewish National Fund is established to collect money to plant trees in Palestine.

1909: The first kibbutz, Degania, is established in Palestine.

Early twentieth century: Rabbi Behr Manischewitz improves machinery for making matzah in his Cincinnati factory; square matzahs are produced.

1917: Britain issues Balfour Declaration: More Jews settle in Palestine.

1922: The first recorded Bat Mitzvah in America is made for Judith Kaplan Eisenstein.

1923: The Union of Orthodox Congregations certifies its first kosher product, Heinz Vegetarian Baked Beans.

1926: Tnuva, a food cooperative, is founded in Israel.

1933: Nazis gain power in Germany. Jews persecuted.

1939–1945: World War II. By 1945, six million Jews are killed.

1939: Simcha Blass, Israel's "Water Man," noticed that a tree growing near a leaky water pipe is taller than others nearby and conceives the notion of drip irrigation. Twenty years later, he starts a company that spreads drip irrigation throughout Israel and the world.

1948: State of Israel established.

1949 through 1950s: Ingathering of Exiles begins with Operation Magic Carpet for Yemenites, bringing hundreds of thousands of immigrants (and their foods) from north African and Middle Eastern countries.

Early 1950s: During a period of austerity and food shortages, David Ben-Gurion asks Osem, a food manufacturer, to come up with a cheap, fast food. Ben-Gurion's rice, an extruded pasta that resembles rice and Israeli couscous, another pasta product, are the result.

1956: Supersal, Israel's first supermarket, opens; Agrexco begins to market Israeli food products outside Israel.

1967: Israel wins Six-Day War; Jerusalem reunited.

1973: Yom Kippur War.

1979: Egypt and Israel sign Camp David Accords.

1980s: Mass exodus of Ethiopian and Soviet Jews.

1

Shabbat

Food for the Body, Food for the Soul

S habbat is one of the best ideas ever. Whatever you're doing—whether it's thrilling and wildly successful or depressingly dull and at the brink of failure— stopping for a day of relaxation and reflection will invariably improve your state of mind and ability to function. The root of the word Shabbat is connected to stopping—but even more valuable is what starts when the whirl of everyday life stops, when pleasure, contemplation, and spirituality have space to thrive.

Shabbat and food are connected in two ways. First, the rules of Shabbat (which prohibit many of the tasks required in cooking) make it difficult to prepare food in the usual ways. Whether you follow these rules strictly or just note them as traditions, they've had a deep effect on the foods that are associated with Shabbat. Second, the heart of Shabbat is pleasure, and food is a fundamental part of pleasure. The taste, fragrance, and satisfaction of a good meal fuels not only our bodies but our spirits—especially when the foods we eat connect us to our past and symbolize our spirituality.

And so, the foods of Shabbat have become a compendium of our best memories of being Jewish. When we think about the foods of Shabbat, we think about our families, friends, and neighborhoods, about good times. Many of the foods we eat on Shabbat date back to the time of the Bible but have been customized by different communities and families.

REFLECTIONS

That Sabbath is a Queen whose coming changes the humblest home into a palace.—*Talmud Shabbat*, 119a

Since ancient times, Shabbat has been singled out as the most important of all the Jewish festivals. It is the only festival included in the Ten Commandments: "Remember Shabbat to keep it holy. You shall not do any work."

But Shabbat is not all about prohibitions. Its spirit is imbued with the positive rabbinic commandment to honor the holy day through special preparations and to enjoy the occasion with praying, festive meals, singing, and celebration. Everything is focused around *Oneg Shabbat*—the joy and delight of Shabbat.

By enjoining every member of the family to remember and observe Shabbat, the Torah gives a family focus to its observance.

When and how the seventh day of the week became the holy Shabbat has never been determined with complete certainty. The Torah mentions the number seven more than five hundred times. Some trace the emphasis on this number to the prominence of the sun, moon, and the five planets observed in antiquity. Another to the Babylonian division of the lunar month into four seven-day periods and the designation of the day of the full moon as *shappattu*. Whatever the origin, in the *Book of Genesis* Shabbat becomes the official divine seal of creation, when God blesses the seventh day and makes it holy (*Genesis*, 2:3).

According to the *First Book of Maccabees*, Shabbat was once observed so strictly that on one occasion during the Maccabean revolt, the Jews allowed themselves to be killed rather than resist on Shabbat (*I Maccabees*, 2:31–38). Later it was decided that Shabbat laws may be transgressed in order to save a life (*I Maccabees*, 2:40–41).

The Rabbis of bygone years wax eloquent on the value of Shabbat observance, writing that "If Israel keeps one Shabbat as it should be kept, the Messiah will come" (*Exodus, Rabbah* 25:12). Although the Rabbis added many restrictions to Shabbat in order to keep it from being violated, they also promoted activities that were intended to transform the day into a day of delight and physical pleasure, intended to promote holiness, happiness, tranquility, relaxation, domestic harmony, and intellectual stimulation.

The earliest rabbinic enactment designed to enhance the Shabbat atmosphere dates from the beginning of the rabbinic era. The prophet Ezra (fifth century BCE) was said to have decreed that the family laundry be done on Thursdays, instead of Fridays, to make certain that clean clothes were prepared for Shabbat (*Talmud BabaBatra* 82a). A next step in the development of Shabbat was the introduction of the use of ritual wine for its sanctification (the *Kiddush*). The custom of lighting Shabbat candles is said to have emerged in the first century, and by the second century the custom emerged of eating at least three meals on Shabbat, instead of the two meals normally eaten on weekdays.

Despite the emphasis on the aesthetic and culinary aspects of Shabbat, the rabbis never overlooked the opportunity for intellectual stimulation. They delivered discourses that were open to the public on Friday nights and Saturday afternoons.

During the rebirth of Jewish mysticism in the sixteenth century, new Shabbat customs arose in the city of Safed in northern Israel and eventually spread to other countries. The great mystic Isaac Luria would go out of Safed into the fields on Friday afternoon to greet the Shabbat, singing the psalms and hymns that are today part of the *Kabbalat Shabbat* welcoming service on Friday night. The Kabbalists chose six psalms (*Psalms* 29 and 95–99) to introduce Shabbat eve service, said to symbolize the six days of the week. A seventh psalm (92) was also added, as it begins with the words "a song for Shabbat."

BORROWED CUSTOMS

Derekh Eretz—literally, the way of the land—is an important feature of Judaism that promotes good behavior and politeness. The Talmudic tractate by the same name includes advice on how to be a good guest and a good host. One way that Jews respect the customs of their hosts is to incorporate the local culinary habits of each region in which they lived. So Shabbat foods, while the same the world over in many ways, also exhibit the marvelous diversity of the Jewish people.

Food is an essential element of Shabbat meals, but not its only or most important one. Freed of work—and today, unplugged—we have time to join with friends and family to talk and sing as we share our food and focus on enjoyment and appreciation of this day. The meals of Shabbat sustain us throughout the week—and we know that the next Shabbat will be there when we need it.

WHAT IS WORK?

Traditional Jews agree that keeping Shabbat means not working. But here's the big question: What is work? Is it digging ditches, going to an office, working on a computer? Is riding in a car work—or does it take more effort to walk? Is work the same for everyone?

The prohibition against working on Shabbat is one of the Ten Commandments. During the time of the Talmud, the rabbis came up with a list of thirty-nine tasks, called *melachot*, that were considered to be work. All of these tasks were performed in the Jerusalem Temple. These included activities such as planting seeds, digging holes, threshing, weaving, and building. Some of these tasks were related to cooking: baking, kneading, and lighting or putting out a fire are all on the list. But let's not forget that at the time this list of *melachot* was made, the world was a different place. If you wanted to light a fire, you had to gather wood, create a spark, and then fan it—it was work, really hard work. Today, we turn a knob or flip a switch, and voila—fire!

Some people stick with the old ways. They don't do any cooking at all on Shabbat, not even lighting a flame under a pot (though most will take cooked food off the stove). Some extend the original *melachot*, declaring that using electricity in any way constitutes lighting a fire. Many Jews create their own definitions of work and how to make a work-free day.

PREPARING FOR SHABBAT

All over the world, the meals of Shabbat have always been elaborate and joyous, a time for poor, overworked peasants to feel like kings and queens. In order to achieve that freedom, they prepared in advance.

In the *shtetls* (Jewish villages) of eastern Europe, Shabbat was on everyone's mind all through the week. People ate very little during the first days of the week. On Wednesdays and Thursdays, housewives shopped the markets for the best food for Shabbat; they bought fish on Thursday and kept it in the bathtub. On Thursday night, they made the challah dough and let it rise slowly overnight. On Friday, they cooked all day.

Shabbat loomed large in the Middle East as well. In Turkey, employers paid their workers on Thursday night or Friday morning so that they could buy their Shabbat meals early. The best foods were cooked on Friday and saved for Shabbat. These included large trays of borekas (pastries stuffed with meat and vegetables), which were baked in communal ovens.

KIDDUSH AND CREATION

And the heavens and the earth and all their hosts were completed. . . . And God blessed the Seventh Day and made it holy, for on it He rested from all His work.—*Genesis*, 1:31

Friday night dinner usually begins with reciting the words of the *Kiddush* (the word means both sanctification and separation), the blessing over the wine. Its words are meant to serve as a reminder of creation: in six days, the world was created; on the seventh, God rested and blessed the day. We drink a little wine, made from the fruit of the Earth—and a touch of sanctity is added to the evening as we separate ourselves from our weekday lives. This custom of remembering Shabbat and keeping it holy by drinking wine was established by *Anshei Knesset Hagedolah* (the Men of the Big Assembly), a group that governed Jews from about 500 to 300 BCE. The particular passages from the Torah that we recite today were formalized by Talmudic rabbis between 200 to 500 CE.

Sweet wine is not part of the ritual; it's just the kind that many Jews in Europe preferred. Sweet wine was also cheaper than aged dry wines, another reason that it was used. Families that could not afford even the cheapest wine sometimes made the blessing over raisin wine and if that was not available, over challah. The cup was filled to the brim, symbolizing an abundance that was usually absent. In many families, everyone from grandparents to infants tasted from the cup, instilling intimacy (and germs) to start the evening.

Viniculture always was and still is an important industry in Israel. Grapes and wine have been grown since biblical times and were a key religious symbol—there is a phrase in the Torah about each person living under his "*gefen*" or grapevine. In Roman times, wine made in Israel was prized and exported to Italy. When the state of Israel was established and agriculture became more sophisticated, technology was used to improve the type and quality of grapes. Today, Israeli wines are respected throughout the world.

CHALLAH AND MANNAH

The traditional table setting for Shabbat is as formal as the ones in British manor houses. The candelabra, which is lit with a special blessing that marks the beginning of Shabbat, is at the center. Wine and a silver goblet (*becher* in Yiddish, *gaviah* in Hebrew) are placed near the person who will recite *Kiddush*. And challah—usually two of them, the plural is challot—have a place of honor, covered with a decorative cloth. After *Kiddush*, we uncover the challah and connect to ancient history, remembering the mannah that nourished us as we wandered in the desert for forty years after leaving Egypt. We place two challot on the Shabbat table because God provided two portions of mannah on Friday so that no one would have to gather food on the day of rest. On all the other days, the mannah that was not collected by the end of the day spoiled. But on Friday, Shabbat's mannah stayed fresh for two days.

The challot also represent bread that was displayed in the Holy Temple; twelve challot were placed in the Temple each Friday night and the challot that we serve on Friday often have six braids each, a total of twelve, to commemorate them. As we say the blessing over the challah, we confirm that we know where our food is coming from.

The tradition of baking a special loaf for Shabbat originated in Talmudic times. At that time, loaves were usually round or rectangular. The custom was carried to Europe in the diaspora, and each community had its own type of challah; some used poppy seeds or egg washes. The braided challah originated in the region that is now Germany; it was a local specialty that the Jews incorporated and is now primarily Jewish. Rectangular loaves, sometimes baked in large loaf pans, were used throughout the Middle Ages and are still almost as common as braided loaves; they are sometimes called sandwich challahs. Round loaves, made by twisting the dough into a spiral shape, are more popular on Rosh Hashanah.

In some families, it is customary to tear off pieces of challah instead of cutting it with a knife, so that a knife, a symbol of violence and war, is not used on the challah, a symbol of the peace of Shabbat. In many traditional households, salt is sprinkled on the challah. This salting alludes to the Temple sacrifices. In lieu of a sacrificial system, our dining tables become an altar and we salt the challah.

TAKING CHALLAH

At the time when the Holy Temple stood in Jerusalem, when people baked challah, they saved a portion of it for the *Kohanim* (priests; direct male descendants of Aaron) who were in charge of the Temple. The *Kohanim* did not own any land or have other jobs, so this was a way for the community to support them.

When baking challah today, some people remove a small piece of the dough, set it aside, and burn it—a symbol of Jewish commitment to support the community. This reminds us, as we prepare a bountiful meal, that not everyone is lucky enough to do so. So our enjoyment has another level: an awareness of other people that is carried through every celebration in the Jewish religion.

And to bring up another Jewish characteristic—there are many ways to use left-over challah, never any need to waste it. It makes the best French toast and can be sliced for sandwiches. Or slice it thinly, toast it, rub it with garlic, and use as croutons.

CHALLAH

Traditional challah is rich and delicious, made with fine white flour, eggs, oil, and sweetness. Though it is entwined with historical and ritual significance, it is also a joy to eat.

Including a bit of cinnamon and/or vanilla adds new flavor to a traditional challah; some people love it, but some traditionalists find it sacrilegious.

It's important to achieve a soft, pliable dough. Creating a "sponge" by adding some of the flour to the yeast as it proofs and allowing it to begin its rise before the rest of the flour is incorporated helps with this. But you don't want the dough to be too soft, or it won't retain its braided shape as it bakes.

The amount of flour you use depends on many factors, including the size of the eggs, the temperature and humidity in the room, and your ability to handle stickiness. The more flour you use, the heavier your challah will be. Start with the lower amount; add more as you stir and knead until you can handle the dough; keeping your hands dusted with flours helps.

• • • • •

Makes one large or two small loaves
(about twenty to twenty-five portions)

INGREDIENTS

2 cups warm water
4 teaspoons active dry or instant yeast
2 tablespoons sugar, divided
1 tablespoon salt, divided
7 to 8 cups all-purpose flour, divided
⅓ cup sugar or honey
6 large eggs, beaten (reserve ½ an egg for eggwash)
½ cup vegetable oil, plus one tablespoon for oiling
½ teaspoon each cinnamon and vanilla (optional)

Put the warm water in a large bowl. Add the yeast, 1 tablespoon sugar, and ½ teaspoon salt; mix well. When the yeast is dissolved, add a cup of flour and mix well. Cover with a damp cloth, put in a warm place, and leave it for about forty-five minutes; it should be actively foaming by that time.

Add the rest of the sugar, salt, eggs, and oil to the yeast mixture. Beat with a spoon until combined. Add the flour, half cup at a time, along with the cinnamon and vanilla if you are using them. Mix until a shaggy dough forms. Dump the contents of the bowl—some of the flour probably won't be incorporated yet—on a generously floured board.

Knead the dough by hand for ten minutes. Push it with the heel of your hand, fold it over, and push again. You don't want to overwork it, but you want to make sure it holds its shape; if the creases remain when you fold it over, you have to keep kneading (you can also use a dough hook attachment on a food processor for six to eight minutes, which is much easier, but much less satisfying). If the dough is too sticky to work, add a little flour, but not too much or the challah will be dry—a little sticky is okay. Finding the right balance between heavy dryness and unmanageable stickiness is tricky, and you might not get it right the first time. Learning the art and skill of making challah requires experience, but it's worth the effort.

Once the dough is smooth and elastic, form it into a ball. Let it sit on the board for a few minutes while you wash, dry, and oil the mixing bowl. Place the dough in the bowl and turn it so that it is coated with oil. Cover with a damp cloth and leave in a warm place to rise until it's doubled in bulk, about two hours. Punch down, and let it rise again for another half hour. Or, put the dough back in the bowl after punching it down, cover it with a damp cloth, and put it in the refrigerator for eight hours or overnight, then remove it and let it rest at room temperature for an hour before braiding.

Preheat the oven to 350°F before you begin to braid the challahs. Line a large cookie sheet with parchment and oil it lightly.

Dump the dough onto the floured board again. Separate the dough and roll into six long ropes. You can braid them into two three-rope braids or one six-rope braid. Three ropes can be braided just the way you'd braid your hair. If you're braiding six ropes, lay them out as in the image on the left; create an "x" with the two center ropes, then move the outer ropes into the x repeatedly until the entire challah is braided. Pinch the tops and bottoms and fold them under to seal.

Challah braiding.

Place the braided challah on the baking sheet and let it rest for about twenty minutes. Mix the reserved half egg with one tablespoon of water and brush all surfaces of the challah, using about half of the egg wash, taking care to get into all the crevices.

Place the challah in the preheated oven. After about twenty minutes, remove and brush with the rest of the egg wash. Turn the baking sheet when you return to the oven, and bake another fifteen to twenty minutes until it is nicely browned all over.

Allow the challah to cool completely before slicing.

Variation: You can substitute one or even two cups of white flour with whole wheat; the challah will still be fairly light; the more whole wheat flour you use, the denser the challah will be.

● ● ● ● ●

MORE SHABBAT LOAVES

Most modern Sephardic families bake European-style challot. But in past generations, a flat bread called *khubz* was the choice for Shabbat in Moroccan homes. It uses only a bit of sugar and no eggs at all. It is sometimes flavored with *za'atar* (a combination of Middle Eastern spices) or sesame seeds. Ethiopian Jews' Shabbat bread is called *dabo*; it is a round yeast bread, made with wheat flour and honey and seasoned with turmeric and black caraway seeds, and made in a frying pan. In Yemen, *jachnun*, a flaky bread that is baked for hours until it caramelizes, is eaten on Friday night. *Chubanah*, the egg-free bread eaten on Shabbat morning, is also baked for a long time and incorporates lots of butter or margarine. *Chubzeh*, an anise-scented bread prepared for Shabbat, is used in Iran as well as in many north African countries. In Iran, *noon shabbati*, a flat bread, is baked. In the Bnai Israel community of India, flatbread *chapatis*, which are eaten during the week, are made special by adding coconut milk on Shabbat.

FISH FOR THE SEVENTH DAY

Shabbat without fish is like a wedding without dancing.—Yiddish saying

Fish has been an important part of the Shabbat meal since biblical days; during the time of the Talmud, it was sometimes the only dish served. Fish was a delicacy in most parts of the world and its great taste would make it a natural choice for a pleasurable meal. But historians have found other reasons. The numerical values of the letters in the word *dag* (the Hebrew word for fish spelled with two Hebrew letters, *daled* and *gimmel*) add up to seven (*daled* is the fourth letter in the Hebrew alphabet, *gimmel* is the third). Others point to several texts that mention that Jews will eat fish at the banquet that follows the coming of the Messiah, and since Shabbat is a hint of what life will be like after the Messiah, it gives us a taste of the future. Fish are a symbol of innocence—they were not killed during the great flood because they had not sinned—and fertility.

Every region had its own fish and fish dishes. In Mediterranean countries such as Spain, salt cod was used. In the Middle East, tomato sauces spiced with cumin, ginger, and coriander were added, and the fish was often eaten cold. This recipe is still used in Sephardic homes today. In Turkey, parsley, dill, and chives were added to sautéed fish patties; in Salonika, a Greek city with an ancient Jewish population, the flavorings were oregano and thyme.

After Jews established themselves in Europe in the Middle Ages, Jewish traders journeyed to the Far East on the silk and spice routes and introduced a large, easy-to-raise fish called carp into Europe. Jews in Poland controlled the carp industry, and carp became the most popular fish on Jewish menus. It was mentioned as far back as 1758 as having been cooked in beer, sometimes with onions and spices.[1] A dish called jellied carp was a delicacy in France and still appears on menus today.

In Jewish homes in medieval England, Shabbat fish was fried in oil; this was an improvement over fish fried in lard, which was more available but congealed and made the dish messy and unappetizing. This "Jewish fried fish" became popular throughout the country. In 1847, in England, a Jewish merchant named Joseph Malin added fried potatoes to the meal, and fish and chips were born.[2]

But the best-known Jewish fish today is the gefilte, at least in the West. No one is quite sure when the term gefilte—which means "stuffed"—was coined, when the dish was created, or by whom. Some historians date it back to Talmudic times, others insist that there is no solid evidence for it existing until the nineteenth century. By 1350, there are reports of Jewish cooks mincing fish[3] and stuffing it into fish intestines for Friday night dinner, but the first recipes for gefilte fish that is much like that cooked today appeared in a German cookbook in 1867 and in Esther Levy's *Jewish Cookery Book* in 1871.[4]

By the beginning of the nineteenth century, cooks realized that dealing with fish intestines wasn't necessary; they could shape the minced fish into patties and poach them gently. At the time, carp was the main ingredient in gefilte fish. White fish and pike were added, and each community developed its own mixture and spices.

Gefilte fish served many purposes. It was made from scraps of the cheapest varieties of fish and stretched by adding even less expensive ingredients (bread crumbs, eggs, onions), so even the poorest Jews—and the Jews of eastern Europe were rarely well-off—could afford at least a little. It was made in advance and served cold, so the prohibition of cooking on Shabbat could be observed. It was pre-ground, so removing bones—which is considered work under the Talmudic rules of Shabbat—did not have to be done.

WASTE NOT: THE JEWISH PRINCIPLE OF AVOIDING WASTE

Today, in a world where half of the food that is produced is never eaten, it is important to note that avoiding waste is not only a practical matter for Jews—it's a religious principle. The theory of *ba'al tashchit* (literally, don't destroy) was derived from a commandment in *Deuteronomy* that forbids an army from cutting down fruit trees to make fighting easier. Jewish leaders extended the idea to other forms of waste; it's a spiritual foundation for the frugality that Jews are known for (though poverty played a part as well).

Shabbat foods are excellent examples of this sustainable practice. Gefilte fish is made from scraps and bones of the cheapest fish available, extended with eggs, bread, vegetables, and other ingredients. *Cholent* (see page 46) uses bones, tough cuts of meats that needed long cooking, and filling, nutritious, easily available barley. Instead of serving whole, perfect vegetables—and throwing away the ones with spots and bruises, a major cause of food waste—Jews cut away bad parts and grind up what's left in kugels. *Ba'al tashchit* is the basis of Jewish environmentalism, connecting Judaism with respect for the planet.

GEOGRAPHICAL SWEETNESS: HOW TASTES DIFFERED AMONG EUROPEAN COMMUNITIES

Some Jewish communities like their fish sweet and add copious amounts of sugar to their gefilte mixtures; others like it spicy and add pepper. Historians attribute the taste for sweetness to a Hasidic tradition that equated sweet food with enjoyment. The distinction is geographical; in western Europe and countries such as Poland—where the Hasidic movement took hold—gefilte fish recipes are the sweetest. Further east, in Lithuania and Russia, pepper is the main spice. Historians say that a geographical line can be drawn, separating team sweet from team pepper. The sweetness extends to other foods, particularly challah.

Another taste that was added was sharp horseradish, called *chreyn* in Yiddish. This was a popular condiment in Germany and is still used on gefilte fish today.

MAKING YOUR OWN GEFILTE FISH

Many people buy jarred or canned fish, and most of them don't like it because it is vastly inferior in taste and texture to homemade. There isn't a standard of excellence for gefilte fish; most people just want it to taste as it did when their grandmothers served it to them—those grandmothers usually didn't work from recipes on printed pages, and they weren't in a hurry.

The lengthy process starts with making a rich fish broth; bones, fish heads, and skin are boiled in many quarts of water for hours, along with salt, sugar, celery, carrots, and onions. Use all the bones and other scraps that your fishmonger will give you—it will improve the broth and create a beautiful aspic when you're done. The basic ingredient for gefilte fish is ground, boneless fish. You probably won't find it anywhere but a good fish store that has a Jewish clientele. A fifty-fifty mix of whitefish and pike is most common; some people add some carp, which makes the fish darker. Salmon adds a pink tint and a different flavor as well. Grinding fish fillets at home in your food processor is not impossible, but you're likely to get fish all over the place and your food processor will never be the same. Ask the fishmonger for roe (clumps of fish eggs) as well; although the roe of some fish is prized as caviar, the eggs of the cheaper fish that is used for gefilte are often thrown away. If the fish that is ground for you happens to have roe in it, you can usually get it for free. If the fishmonger argues, this is a good time to practice your *hondling* (bargaining) skills. Just slide the clump into the broth about half an hour after you start poaching the rest of the fish and remove them at the same time you remove the fish. It's an acquired taste, but it is nutritious, it's usually free, and some people (including a lot of children) adore it—so why waste it?

While the broth is brewing, mix the ground fish with eggs (one large egg for a pound of fish) and a quantity of salt, sugar, and pepper that varies according to geography and acquired tastes. Some people mix minced onion, carrots, garlic, and other fillers into the fish batter; matzah is also used as a filler or to make the batter hold together.

Since you probably don't want to taste the fishy batter, it's hard to know when the proportions are correct (unless you've done this hundreds of times). To avoid spoiling the whole pot of fish, keep the additions of salt and sugar on the low side (say two tablespoons of sugar and one teaspoon of salt, a pinch of pepper per pound of fish); poach a tiny "test ball" of fish in the boiling broth, remove it after ten minutes, refrigerate it (because warm gefilte fish is awful), taste, and adjust the seasonings; if the mixture is too loose, add a tablespoon of matzah meal. You can also add salt and sugar to the broth. You may have to do this two or three times before you get it right, which is why making gefilte fish is not for busy nights. When your mixture is to your liking, form large balls (about a cup of batter in each) and drop them carefully into the broth. Simmer for about an hour, then remove carefully with a slotted spoon. Remove the carrot that's been boiling in the broth as well—some people think a plate of gefilte fish needs that bit of orange to make it complete.

Now that your fish is done, the real test is ready to begin: Will your fish soup gel? It's the gelatin in the bones and skin that turn your broth into aspic, so this is the part where using all that slimy stuff pays off. The fish broth, after hours of simmering, is packed with salt, sugar, vegetable, and fish flavor. Strain it a few times until all the bones and other detritus are gone, return it to the pot (after washing the pot), and simmer until it's reduced by about half. Let it cool, then refrigerate it. It should gel into a soft aspic that's a fine bed for serving gefilte fish and can be sopped up with challah. If it's too firm (and if you don't like it that way), reheat, add water, and try again. If it remains totally liquid, there were probably not enough bones or they were not strong enough; better luck next time.

SHABBAT FISH DISHES FROM AROUND THE WORLD

Most Jewish communities developed one or a few favored fish dishes that made use of local seafood, spices, and sauces, choosing and/or adapting them so that they worked with the rules of Shabbat. The Jewish community of Italy developed a recipe called *pesca al 'ebraica* (Jewish fish) to preserve fish in vinegar so that it could be cooked ahead of time and served on Shabbat. They added sweet raisins, onions, and pine nuts to counteract the strong flavor of the vinegar. This combination was first used in the Middle East; Jews in Sicily learned it from Middle Eastern traders who stopped there.

CHRAIMY FISH: BAKED FISH IN SPICY TOMATO SAUCE

When the Jews were expelled from Spain after the Inquisition of 1492, many fled to north Africa and set up vibrant communities in Egypt, Libya, Tunisia, and Morocco. Chraimy (rhymes with Hymie) fish incorporates the spicy sauces of that region into a dish that is often served on Friday nights in Sephardic homes. Chraimy sauce is a variation of harissa, a chili paste used in north African cooking—you can substitute packaged harissa for the spice mix below.

This version of chraimy fish is baked; the fish fillets can also be breaded and pan-fried before the sauce is added. The sauce is also a zesty addition to gefilte fish balls, for a fusion of Ashkenazi and Sephardic tastes.

Note on fish: Any kind of fish—including salmon, whitefish, trout, tilapia, and cod—can be used in this recipe. Adjust the baking times depending on the thickness of the fillet.

• • • • •

4 servings

INGREDIENTS

Spice mix (see below)

3 tablespoons olive oil

2 to 3 garlic cloves

1 small onion

12 ounces fresh tomatoes, peeled if you wish, cut into ½-inch chunks (canned diced tomatoes can be substituted)

6 ounces red or green bell pepper, cut into strips (optional)

½ preserved lemon (see page 16), chopped; or zest and juice from 1 small lemon

¼ cup chopped parsley, cilantro, or a mixture of both

Salt to taste (not needed if you are using preserved lemon)

Cayenne pepper or red pepper flakes to taste

1 pound fish fillets, washed, patted dry, and cut into 4 servings (see note on fish)

Spice Mix:

1 small chili pepper

½ teaspoon ground cumin

½ teaspoon paprika, sweet or smoked

½ teaspoon caraway seeds

½ teaspoon ground coriander

2 cloves

1 bay leaf

1 large clove garlic

    Prepare the spice mix. Remove most of the seeds from the chili pepper—consider how hot the pepper is and how hot you want the dish to be when deciding how many seeds to leave—and dice it. Combine all the ingredients in a mortar and pound to a paste with a pestle. Or, put it all in a food processor or mini-chopper and whirl until combined.

    Preheat oven to 350°F.

    Heat the oil in a medium saucepan over medium heat. Add the garlic and onion, and sauté until they are softened and start to brown, two to three minutes. Add the spice mix and stir until evenly browned and fragrant, just a minute or two.

    Add the tomatoes and peppers to the saucepan. Lower the heat and stir until the tomatoes lose their form and the peppers soften, about five minutes. Add the lemon and stir for another minute; the tomatoes should now be a thick, chunky sauce. Add the parsley/cilantro, reserving one tablespoon for garnish, and stir to combine. Taste and adjust seasonings; add salt as desired. If you want more heat, add cayenne pepper or red pepper flakes—but remember that the sauce will become spicier as it cooks.

Spoon half of the sauce on a rimmed baking dish large enough to hold the fish. Arrange the fish fillets over the sauce and top with the remaining sauce. Bake for five to eight minutes, depending on the thickness of the fillets, then turn over each fillet and return to the oven for another five to six minutes. The fish is done when it flakes easily when prodded with a fork.

Garnish with remaining parsley/cilantro. Serve hot, cold, or at room temperature.

• • • • •

CHICKEN SOUP: JEWISH PENICILLIN

In almost all Jewish communities, a soup course was served after Friday night fish, and the soup was chicken. As far back as the twelfth century, Jews knew that chicken soup is good for you. Maimonides (Rabbi Moshe ben Maimon, also known as Rambam, who was the physician to the King of Spain) said that eating chicken soup would cure many illnesses.[5] Medical research agrees; several studies have found that chicken soup alleviates cold and flu symptoms more than placebo or other hot liquids. One study by Dr. Stephen Rennard, a pulmonary expert at the University of Nebraska Medical Center in Omaha, showed that chicken soup has anti-inflammatory properties.[6]

There are many kinds of chicken soup: put a bunch of chicken parts in a pot and cover it with a lot of water; add vegetables, herbs, spices, and other foods, and cook for a long time. In eastern Europe, the soup was made with carrots, celery, parsley, and dill, and usually spiced with just salt and pepper. In Middle Eastern countries, lemon juice, mint, and coriander seeds were added. In countries near the Mediterranean Sea, chopped tomatoes and Mediterranean herbs like basil, rosemary, and garlic were included in the chicken soup. In Curacao, a Caribbean island, Friday night chicken soup is chock full of vegetables like potatoes, tomatoes, carrots, and corn, and is flavored with lime.

Chicken soup is another thrifty food, made from bones and scraps that would otherwise be thrown away. It's one of several iconic Shabbat foods—including chopped liver, kugel, and cholent—that make the most efficient use of food, following the precept "don't waste" (see page 37).

In many Ashkenazi homes, Friday night's chicken soup is served with noodles (*lokshen* in Yiddish) and matzah balls (*knaidlech*, pronounced kuh-neye-dluch or kuh-nay-dluch). Matzah balls and noodles are distinctly Western. In the New Orleans Jewish community, matzah balls are made with Cajun and Creole seasoning. And creative cooks make new kinds of chicken soup all the time, adding new ingredients to matzah balls or coming up with whole new ways of serving soup.

An iconic dish in Iranian-Jewish homes, these chicken and ground chickpea dumplings date back thousands of years to the Jewish ghetto in Tehran (other Iranian-Jewish cities also claim them). Like matzah balls, they are a test of cooking ability. There are hundreds of variations—choose the herbs and spices you prefer.

Iranian Jews made chickpea dumplings called *gondi* by mixing chickpea powder with ground chicken and onion and spices like coriander, turmeric, and cardamom. Italian Jews put pasta in chicken soup. *Gondi* are served in chicken soup that includes boiled chickpeas and is flavored with lemon and lime juices (or with preserved lemons or limes, see page 42). The *gondi* are usually prepared in clear broth to keep them clean, but they can also be boiled in the soup as it is cooking.

KUGEL AND OTHER SIDE DISHES

After challah, fish, and soup, most people don't need more food. But on Friday night, the meal has just begun. A main course of chicken or meat is usually served, accompanied by one or several kugels in Ashkenazi homes and a variety of vegetable and grain dishes in Sephardic communities.

Kugel means "ball" in German; early kugels were round like balls. Now they're made in all shapes and from every food imaginable—carrots, squash, sweet potatoes, chickpeas, rice, tomatoes. Some are sweet, and some are peppery or spicy. Some people say that only potato kugels are genuine, some insist that noodle kugels are much better. Hasidim consider kugel to be sacred; one Hasidic rabbi insists that noodle kugel was ordained as the official kugel on Mount Sinai.[7]

The first kugels were made from bread and flour, then from cheese and other dairy products. Potatoes and other vegetables were latecomers to the kugel repertoire.

The invention of the food processor has turned making a kugel into a fifteen-minute task. Put all the ingredients except the potatoes into a food processor—for two pounds of potatoes, use two eggs, a quarter cup of vegetable oil, two tablespoons of matzah meal or bread crumbs, one small chopped onion, and salt and pepper to taste. Process for about a minute until smooth and frothy. Then add the potatoes, peeled and cut into cubes. Pulse several times; you want the mixture to be pureed, but still a bit chunky. Pour into a generously greased baking dish and bake at 400°F for about forty-five minutes until the top is dark brown.

Kugel variations are endless, any vegetables can be incorporated—carrots, broccoli, summer squash, and kale are some possibilities. But it's hard to make a tasty potato kugel in which at least half of the vegetables are not actually potatoes.

About eight hundred years ago, German cooks began to incorporate noodles into their kugel mixtures; soon thereafter, they added eggs. In some countries, pasta shapes other than long, thin *lokshen* were used. Refugees from the Middle Eastern countries added raisins, almonds, and honey—staples of Moroccan cooking.

A simpler kugel, based on the Lithuanian love of pepper and avoidance of sweetness, uses only noodles, eggs, oil, salt, and pepper. To make it, mix eight ounces of cooked noodles (any thickness from fine to extra-wide can be used) with a quarter cup of vegetable oil and one beaten egg; add salt and pepper to taste, transfer to a small baking dish, and bake at 375°F for thirty to forty-five minutes until the edges are brown and the top becomes crispy.

JERUSALEM KUGEL—KUGEL YERUSHALMI

Jerusalem kugel actually originated in Europe. Some sources say that it was created in the kitchen of the famous Vilna Gaon (the Sage of Vilna); others say it was first made by eastern European Hasidim. It was brought to Jerusalem in the eighteenth century, where it became a Shabbat staple. It tolerates long cooking—it can be left on a low flame over a *blech* overnight after it's baked. The tricky part is caramelizing the sugar; it must be taken off the flame as soon as it begins to darken or it will turn into a black, gooey mess.

To make a truly impressive kugel, double (or triple) the recipe and bake it in a large, well-greased Dutch oven. Unmolded, it's like a piece of sculpture that tastes and smells divine.

• • • • •

4 to 6 servings

INGREDIENTS

8 ounces egg noodles
¼ cup vegetable oil plus more for greasing
⅓ cup sugar
2 large eggs, beaten
1 teaspoon salt, more or less to taste
¼ teaspoon pepper, more or less to taste

Preheat oven to 350°F.

Cook the noodles according to package directions in a large pot; drain completely. Return the cooked noodles to the pot.

Heat the oil in a small frying pan for about a minute; it should be quite hot, but not smoking. Add the sugar, stirring constantly. In about a minute, the sugar will dissolve almost (but not quite) completely. Keep stirring. In another minute or two, the mixture will begin to turn brown. Remove from heat immediately and keep stirring. It will darken more for the next minute or so; it may separate a bit.

Pour the caramelized sugar into noodles and stir to coat. If the caramelized sugar begins to harden in clumps, turn on a low flame under the pot and stir until the mixture softens. Allow to cool slightly, then add the eggs, salt, and pepper, and stir until the noodles are completely coated and the salt and pepper are distributed.

Generously grease a nine-inch round or square baking dish. Spoon the noodles into the baking dish and smooth the top slightly; noodles that stick up will become slightly burned (which is not necessarily a bad thing). Bake for thirty minutes or until the top is completely browned. Allow to cool, cut into wedges and serve hot or cold.

Variations: Add a quarter cup of toasted slivered almonds and/or a quarter cup of plumped raisins when you add the salt and pepper. Or, for something different, add candied pineapple or mango and chopped macadamia nuts.

To increase the vitamin level, add a half cup of chopped kale, chard, or spinach to the noodles while they cook.

For a more flavorful kugel, add your choice of spice mix (see page 15); start with a tablespoon, and add to taste. Remember that some of the spice mixes are super hot.

There's an alternate method for making this dish. Instead of cooking the noodles beforehand, add them to the caramelized sugar (before you add the eggs) along with a quart of water. Cook, stirring constantly, until the water is absorbed and the noodles are fully cooked, then proceed with the rest of the recipe. This means there is one less pot to wash—and the noodles absorb more of the oil and sugar.

• • • • •

SEPHARDIC SIDES

Side dishes are not limited to kugels on the Sephardic Shabbat table. There are many complex grain and vegetable dishes to follow the many mezze, the spicy fish and the soup, including couscous with meatballs, borekas, and sambuseks. Sephardic Jews also eat stuffed vegetables on Shabbat, symbolizing mannah, which was "stuffed" between two layers of dew. Vegetables such as peppers, eggplant, squash, and tomato are both stuffed and serve as stuffings, sometimes mixed with ground meat.

KUBAH

One favorite is a shell of dough or pressed bulgur filled with meat, vegetables, or a combination. This dish appears throughout the Middle East, often on the Shabbat table. It goes by many names: Iraq's *kubah* and Syria's *kibbeh* are probably the most renowned. Some versions are baked instead of fried, and some people layer the filling over the starch, lasagna style, rather than stuffing. The filling can be pretty much anything—vegetables only, fish, ground lamb, even nuts and honey for Rosh Hashanah. But these delicacies, shaped like eggs or torpedoes, are always welcome—and once you get the hang of it, they are not nearly as difficult to make as they seem, especially when you consider how delicious they are.

• • • • •

6 servings
INGREDIENTS

Fillings:
Choose a filling or fillings from pages 141–142.

Batter for outer layer:
1 pound fine bulgur
1 medium onion
Salt and pepper to taste
Herbs and spices to taste
1 cup flour
Oil for deep frying

Make the batter for the outer layer. Put the bulgur in a large bowl, cover with water and let it soak for an hour. Drain in a sieve and let it drain completely; save about a half cup of the soaking water.

Chop the onion coarsely and put it in the bowl of a food processor; pulse to chop it. Add the bulgur, salt and pepper, herbs, and spices. Process until you have a fairly smooth paste. Add the flour and pulse until you have a heavier paste. Transfer to a bowl, cover, and refrigerate for at least one hour.

Meanwhile, make your filling or fillings. Cook them until they are a bit drier than usual because you don't want them to leak through the outer layer.

Prepare a large, shallow saucepan and a plate lined with paper towels. Add oil to the pan until it reaches about one inch up the sides. Heat the oil on low until it reaches about 200°F, then turn it very low until your kuba are ready.

Scoop up about a quarter cup of batter and shape it into a small egg shape. Using your finger, create a crater in the top; shape it so that the walls around the crater are about a quarter inch thick. Fill the crater with about a tablespoon of filling, then close the crater by reshaping the filling. If there are breaks in the kuba, patch them with more batter. When you have a few kuba ready, raise the flame until the oil returns to 200°F. Drop the kuba into the oil and fry for about two minutes, then turn them over and fry for another minute until the whole thing is uniformly brown. Use a slotted spoon to remove them to the paper-lined plate to drain. Continue making and frying the kuba until they're all done.

Serve with your choice of sauce; yogurt is great, and so is matbucha (see page 15).

• • • • •

A HOT POT FOR SHABBAT

Most Jewish communities have a recipe for a hot dish that can be prepared on Friday afternoon, cooked all night long and served hot on Shabbat morning after synagogue. Because cooking was prohibited on Shabbat, the only way to have a hot meal was to prepare it beforehand. In eastern Europe, this stew is called *cholent*. When *cholent* is on the menu, no one can forget for one second that it is Shabbat. The aroma—warmth, earthiness, soul—fills the house and everyone in it; people have been known to knock on doors of strangers when they smell *cholent* from blocks away.

No one is sure where the name "*cholent*" comes from. Some say it's a contraction of the words "shul" and "ende" because it was eaten after synagogue (*shul* in Yiddish) services were ended (*ende* is the German word for end)—say shul-end fast three times and see what comes up. Others say it comes from the French words *chaud* (hot) and *lent* (slow)—it's a hot dish that is cooked slowly. In Israel, *cholent* is called *hamin* (from *ham*, the Hebrew word for hot).

Each region adjusts this hot dish by adding its regional specialties. In Hungary, *cholent* is spiced with paprika; in Italy, small pasta shapes are added. Moroccan *scheena* includes chickpeas, hulled wheat, and hard-boiled eggs. Bukharan *oshi sabi* (literally "hot Shabbat") is made with rice instead of potatoes and includes fruit and honey. Iraqi t'bit makes use of chicken skin filled with rice, meat, and herbs. *Cholent* served in the Bnei Israel community in Calcutta is spiced with turmeric, ginger, cinnamon, and other curry flavors. *Sanbat wat*, an Ethiopian Shabbat stew, is infused with fenugreek, chilis, cloves, and cardamom.

THE BLECH: A LOOPHOLE

Adhering to the rules of the Torah, in their strictest sense, could lead to considerable deprivation. For example, the prohibition of lighting fire on Shabbat would mean that only cold food could be eaten all day. But deprivation is not part of the

Shabbat spirit—and early rabbis found ways (some of them just a bit contrived) to keep Shabbat pleasurable. Although cooking was prohibited, placing pre-cooked food on a hot surface and then removing it on Shabbat was permitted. The *blech* was born: a sheet of metal that can be placed over an open flame and pots of food for Shabbat morning are set on top of it before Shabbat begins. The flame keeps the food warm; if the food begins to overcook, the pot can be moved to a cooler spot further from the flame, still on the *blech*. A slew of recipes—*cholent, hamin, scheena*—were created to take advantage of this loophole.

COMMUNITY COOKING: SHARING OVENS FOR *CHOLENT*

The tight bonds within Jewish communities—often necessary because Jews needed to stick together to combat persecution—were often forged over *cholent* pots. In communities throughout Europe, bakeries provided ovens where people kept their *cholent* cooking overnight. Fires could not be lit on Shabbat, and keeping a fire burning overnight—and while all members of the family were in the synagogue—was expensive and dangerous. So on Friday night, each family brought their pot to the communal oven and found a spot for it. On Shabbat morning, after shul was over, families streamed in to pick up their pots and take them home. Usually, a child was designated to tote the pot home because of the rules about carrying objects in public places (children were exempt). The heavy pot, steaming and fragrant, would be carefully lugged and the streets would fill with families on their way home to enjoy the meal that they had cooked together.

This community activity, so intrinsic to Judaism, was also common in the Bnei Israel community in India, in pioneer communities in western North America, and in Aleppo, Syria, where Jewish bakeries turned the furn (oven) into a communal bakery on Friday afternoons.

ASHKENAZI CHOLENT

Meat, potatoes, barley, and beans are the main ingredients in the *cholent* served in most Ashkenazi homes. Much of the flavor comes from fatty marrow bones that would otherwise be discarded; when allowed to simmer overnight with the grains and potatoes, they add a rich, heady flavor and aroma.

Cholent first appeared in twelfth-century France.[8] It bears a passing resemblance to cassoulet, but was adapted to conform to the no-cooking-on-Shabbat rule. The

ingredients are pre-cooked, which makes it permissible, even in the most rigorously orthodox homes, to be kept warm until the Shabbat morning meal. When
Germany and other eastern European countries opened their cities to Jews, the
immigrants brought the recipe with them.

• • • • •

4 to 6 servings

INGREDIENTS

1 cup dry beans; any mix of cannellini, kidney, pinto, or other small dry beans
Salt to taste
1 tablespoon oil, for coating the bottom of the pot
½ cup barley
1 pound of fatty meat; flanken or short ribs work well
1 or 2 marrow bones
1 pound of potatoes, peeled and cut into chunks if large
Pepper to taste (optional)

Put the beans in a large bowl; cover with water and allow them to soak overnight.
Don't skip this step, even though the *cholent* will cook all night, the beans won't
be tender unless they are soaked first.

Drain the beans; place them a large pot with about four quarts of water and one
teaspoon salt. Bring to a boil and boil for about ten minutes. Then turn them off
and let them sit for at least an hour.

Grease a large, oven-proof pot or Dutch oven with oil (even if you won't be baking this dish, you want to use a pot that can take an oven's heat). Drain the beans
and add them to the pot. Add the barley, meat, bones, and potatoes, in that order.
Cover with about one quart of water; it should extend about two inches above the
potatoes. Add salt—start with about one teaspoon, more can be added later. Add
pepper, if using.

Bring the pot to a boil, then turn down the heat, cover the pot, and allow to simmer for about two hours. At that point, the *cholent* is partially cooked.

To continue cooking the traditional way, place a *blech* on the oven top over a
low flame. Cover the pot tightly and place it over the flame. Let it cook overnight;
check it when you pass by, adding water as necessary. If the water has not evaporated, uncover the pot for several hours before serving. Do not stir.

Cholent can also be baked in the oven. Transfer the pot to an oven pre-heated
to 300°F and bake for two to three hours, until all the liquid has evaporated. Keep
the pot covered for the first hour or two, then remove the lid if the liquid has not
evaporated.

Cholent is ready when the meat is falling apart, the beans and barley are soft, and the potatoes are golden brown. You'll know when it's done—the aroma is intoxicating and the ingredients have melded. Serve hot, making sure each portion has some of each ingredient (and that the marrow bones go to the most deserving person).

Variations: **Crockpot Cholent**: *Cholent* works beautifully in a crockpot, and after much debate most rabbis, even orthodox ones, agreed that food prepared in crockpots on Friday afternoon could be eaten on Shabbat. Prepare the same way as for stovetop or oven-baked *cholent*. Cook for at least twelve hours on low or ten hours on high.

Hungarian Cholent: The Jews of Hungary added some ingredients to their *cholent*. To make the Hungarian version, sauté a small chopped onion and two cloves of minced garlic in a tablespoon of oil until soft. Add a diced celery rib, a large carrot and/or parsnip cut into discs, and a diced large tomato; stir until the tomato loses its shape. Add a tablespoon of sweet paprika and mix well. Add this to the pot along with the meat and continue as for standard Ashkenazi *cholent*. Some Hungarian families also add a quarter cup of white rice to their *cholent*. If you add rice, increase the water by one cup.

Italian *Hamin*: Italian cholent is stuffed with ingredients that are common in Italian-Jewish cuisine. Chicken meatballs, spiced with sage and oregano, small pasta shapes, goose sausage, and hard-boiled eggs appeared in different versions.

Kishka: A mixture of carrots, onions, and celery (which are also the ingredients in classic French mirepoix), mixed with fat, was stuffed into cow intestines (*kishka* is the Yiddish word for intestines) and usually cooked in the *cholent*. As with gefilte fish, most cooks don't use the intestines anymore.

Scheena/Adafina: In Morocco and other Middle Eastern countries, meat is combined with wheatberries, chickpeas, beans, rice, and dates; whole hard-cooked eggs are added to the stew.

Indian Cholent: Chicken replaces meat and rice replaces barley in the hot dish served in the Jewish community in Mumbai, India. Curry spices—ginger, turmeric, cardamom—connect the dish to its host country.

Ethiopian Sambat Wat: Wat, or stew, is the national dish in Ethiopia. The Jews there—almost all of whom now live in Israel—created a special stew for Shabbat (*Sambat* in their language). They left it cooking over a fire, then ate it on Shabbat morning, scooping it onto their *dobi* bread with their fingers.

• • • • •

SWEET ENDINGS

We're all pretty full by the end of each Shabbat meal. Dessert is sometimes just cooked fruit compote or a light cake (sponge cake, anyone?). In Sephardic countries, dried fruit and honeyed cakes are served, as well as a few special Shabbat cake, such as King's Cake (*Torta de los Reyes*). A complex semolina pudding called *sutlach*, requiring a special set of pots, ended Greek and Turkish Friday night dinners; it's also a Shavuot specialty (see pages 206–07).

SEUDAH SHLISHLIT

The third meal of Shabbat is called *Seudah Shlishit*, which means "third meal." The custom of eating three meals started with the rabbis of the Talmud; on most days, people ate only two meals, and the third meal made Shabbat special. For us, it's a chance to get together again and eat a lighter meal. *Seudah Shlishit* is usually made up of salads, cheese, sometimes fish, and sometimes leftover kugel. In Sephardic homes, people eat tuna, fruit, and a spicy-hot sauce called harissa for *Seudah Shlishit*. The table is often spread with small salads called *mezze* (see page 14); *mezze* are served at everyday meals, but there are special ones for *Seudah Shlishit*. Several of these small plates, mostly salads and dips, make up *Seudah Shlishit* in Sephardic homes. They are also served on Friday night as appetizers.

SHABBAT TRADITIONS AROUND THE WORLD

Iran
In Baghdad's Jewish community—which thrived from the destruction of the First Temple in 586 CE until the twentieth century—Jews ate fried fish and chicken soup with rice on Friday night and a chicken-and-rice dish called *tabyit* for breakfast on Shabbat. On Shabbat afternoon, they ate on their balconies or took picnics to river islands. Some of the foods they ate on Shabbat were mango pickles, fried eggplants, and an okra stew with meat dumplings called *kibbe* (see page 45).

India
Bene Israel, the Jewish congregation of India, does not eat fish on Shabbat because fish is so plentiful that no one thinks it is special enough for Shabbat. The Calcutta Jewish community serves a curry dish called *Harikebab* on Friday night.

Cuba
There was a small Jewish community in Cuba during the 1940s and 1950s, made up mostly of people who had fled the Nazis. On Friday night, they often ate frijoles negroles, a black bean dish.

Yemen

Jews from Yemen, called Taymanim, eat grilled meat with many spicy sauces on Shabbat. Before and after each meal, they eat a mixture of dried fruits and nuts, and make blessings to thank God.

France

Jews in Alsace, a province on the border of France and Germany, were known for raising geese during the Middle Ages. They figured out how to make the goose liver bigger, and chopped goose liver became a popular Shabbat dish. This later became the fancy *pate de fois gras* as well as the chopped chicken liver we eat today (though the chicken livers we eat today are not created by tortuous force-feeding).

Bukhara

The Jewish community in Bukhara, near what is now Afghanistan, was isolated from the rest of the Jewish world until the eighteenth century and their meals were different from those in Europe. On Friday night, they ate salads made with eggplants or tomatoes and cucumber and *Khalti barsh*, rice and chopped meat cooked in a linen bag.

Curacao

In Curacao, where a small group of Jews moved when they left Spain after the Inquisition, a favorite recipe for Shabbat dessert is a thin cake, similar to shortbread, called Pan Levi.

2

Rosh Hashanah and Yom Kippur

Days of Awe and Honeycake

The idea that Jews are neurotic worrywarts may be a stereotype, but Rosh Ha-shanah (literally the head [*rosh*] of the year [*shana*]) and Yom Kippur (the day [*yom*] of atonement [*kippur*]) show that it's at least partially true. Other cultures celebrate the new year with champagne and parties. Jews assume that they are being judged for their past actions by a God who is ready to declare them unworthy.

And so we pray, asking over and over to be forgiven. The liturgy, assembled in thick prayerbooks called *machzors*, is unremittingly lugubrious. We are sinners and have done terrible things; on Yom Kippur, we're called upon to literally beat our breasts as we confess to a pre-written list of sins that we barely understand and have probably not committed. Throughout the service, we repeat that we can avoid a harsh decree only through *teshuvah* (repentance, or in a more literal translation, a return to innocence), *tefilah* (prayer), and *tzedakah* (charity).

To give us strength for all that praying, and to counter its depressing quality, we eat. The Days of Awe come with a menu of awesome foods and the celebration of Rosh Hashanah, once we leave our synagogues or temples, takes place at the dinner table. From the very beginning of Jewish law, rabbis suggested what we should eat to improve our lot, and luckily the foods are delicious. Different communities adapted them to conform to the availability and customs in or of the countries in which they lived, but there are similarities that run through all of them.

REFLECTIONS

Forgive us, pardon us, grant us atonement.—High Holiday Prayerbook

The *Zohar* (the Book of Jewish Mysticism) tells us that Adam, the first human being, was created on Rosh Hashanah. On that day, Adam stood before God the Judge and repented for all his mistakes. God forgave him and said to Adam: "So it will be with your children. They will stand before me in Judgment on Rosh Hashanah, and if they truly say that they are sorry, I shall forgive them." Rosh Hashanah, the beginning of the Jewish new year, provides a second chance. It is a time for self-renewal and an opportunity to resolve to become better people.

Unlike the other historical-national Jewish festivals, which begin in the spring with Passover and close in the fall with Sukkot, Rosh Hashanah (and Yom Kippur soon to follow) are characterized by special solemnity and referred to as the *Yamim Nora'im* (Days of Awe), when all people stand before the Divine throne for judgment.

In the Torah, the name Rosh Hashanah is found only once, in the *Book of Ezekiel*, 40:1. In this passage it appears that Rosh Hashanah is meant simply to refer to the beginning of the year, and not the actual festival of Rosh Hashanah itself. This was likely the beginning of the economic year, when crops of the late harvest began to be sold. It is therefore plausible that the biblical Rosh Hashanah originally marked the beginning of the agricultural year. The Bible scholar Sigmund Mowinckel advanced the possibility of the existence of a pre-exilic autumnal New Year festival of the Israelites on which God was "enthroned" as King.[1] He bases his claim on having found marked traces of the ancient festival in many of the psalms.

One powerful instrument used to motivate repentance during Rosh Hashanah is the *shofar* (ram's horn). The sounding of the ram's horn is a highlight of the Rosh Hashanah liturgy, and its shrill sounds are intended to awaken worshippers to repent and change their ways. The philosopher Maimonides describes the goal of the piercing cry of the *shofar* as "an allusion, as if to say, 'Awake, O you sleepers, awake from your sleep. Search your deeds and turn in repentance.'"[2]

Many important moments in the history of the Jewish people came to be associated with Rosh Hashanah. Adam was said to have been born on this day, as were Abraham, Isaac, and Jacob. Moses appeared before King Pharaoh on Rosh Hashanah. Today many Jewish people like to think of Rosh Hashanah as the birthday of the world itself.

The ten days between Rosh Hashanah and Yom Kippur are known as the penitential days. The holiday day of Yom Kippur is the culmination of the ten days of repentance. Its basic focus is to encourage people to do their part in repairing the world by repairing themselves. Jewish mystics believe that God actually descends through the spheres of heaven in order to dwell among the people during Yom Kippur. It is at this time, say the mystics, that God is the most accessible.

Unlike Jewish holidays when eating food is mandated by their celebration, Yom Kippur is known more for its lack of food. Prayer and fasting force the Jewish people to suspend their daily existence and physical abstinence, deepening them spiritually with greater appreciation for daily life. Yom Kippur is one of the few occasions during which the individual is invited to stay in the synagogue throughout the entire day. Some people wear a *kittel*, a white robe that is also used as a shroud at traditional Jewish funerals. The whole world is suspended in judgment on Yom Kippur—who shall live and who shall die?

Rosh Hashanah and Yom Kippur together affirm the chance for positive change and the hope for new and better days ahead. And the traditional slice of apple dipped into honey at the beginning of the first meal on Rosh Hashanah eve affirms this spirit of optimism. The blessing that is recited states: "May it be Your will, O God, to grant us a year that is good and sweet."

EATING FOR THE FUTURE

There's an underlying theme to the foods we eat on Rosh Hashanah: That eating the right foods is going to determine our fate for the year to come. Sweet, light foods that look like or whose names sound vaguely like health and prosperity are going to make us healthy, prosperous, and able to beat our enemies to a pulp.

Judaism is not the only religion or culture that attaches symbolic meanings to food. The thirty-three layers of baklava, the Balkan pastry, are supposed to represent the thirty-three years of the life of Jesus. Chinese dumplings slightly resemble currency; Chinese philosophers suggest that eating them will make you wealthy. Three-lobed pretzels were created by French monks in the seventh century to look like children in prayer and thus propel those who ate them to pray more. Muslims eat dates at the conclusion of Ramadan to honor the prophet Mohammed, who had a custom of eating three dates to break a fast. And of course there's the wafer that is supposed to turn into the body of Jesus.

On Rosh Hashanah, eating symbolic foods reaches a fever pitch. There are dozens of foods that have been declared lucky and even though very few people believe in actual cause and effect, menus in most Jewish homes—Ashkenazi, Sephardic, or Mizrachi, ultra-orthodox to casually cultural—revolve around these traditions. There are practical reasons behind the traditions as well—most of the foods involved are plentiful around Rosh Hashanah time in most of the world, so they're readily available. And they are delicious, so creating a menu around them is far from burdensome.

Most common among the food, and words, associated with Rosh Hashanah is sweetness. *Shana Tova u-metuka* is the common greeting: may our New Year be not only good (*tova*) but sweet (*metuka*). And though many sweet or sweetened foods are used to ensure that result, honey has become a prime symbol of the holiday.

TWO KINDS OF HONEY

Honey (*d'vash* in Hebrew) is one of Israel's seven signature agricultural varieties (the *sheva* [seven] *minim* [varieties]): wheat, barley, grapes, figs, pomegranates, olives, and honey. You'll note that the other six varieties are plant-based, and in fact, the honey that's included in the *sheva minim* is made from a plant as well. It's actually made from dates and is called *silan* in Hebrew and *rubb* in Arabic. The land of milk and honey should really be called the land of milk and date syrup. Like honey, *silan* is supersweet and sticky and is used to flavor all sorts of desserts and baked goods.

But bee honey was also an important commodity in ancient Israel. The oldest known commercial apiary in the world, dating back three thousand years and capable of handling millions of bees in clay cylinders, was recently discovered in Tel Rehov in the Beit Shean Valley in Israel. The bees were probably imported from Greece or Turkey, where bees were less aggressive and more productive than those in the Middle East. Both date and bee honey were prized as sweeteners in ancient times, until the process for turning sugar cane into sugar was discovered by Arabs in the seventh century. Even then, sugar was rare until Caribbean plantations began to grow and distribute it.

But honey never lost its advocates, and bees have always been protected both for the honey they provide and the critical role they play in pollinating plants; it's estimated that half our crops would disappear without bees to pollinate them. Since 2007, beekeepers all over the world have been challenged by a baffling phenomenon known as Colony Collapse Disorder, in which thriving hives suddenly lose up to 80 percent of their inhabitants. Many theories about causes have been advanced, including use of pesticides, general pollution, and viruses. Scientists in Israel are at the forefront of explaining and curing this devastating trend. They have discovered a parasitic mite that may be responsible for the decline and are working on ways to control the mites' reproduction. The Israeli system of monitoring every hive has led to higher production, a much lower rate of colony collapse, and some of the tastiest honey in the world.

The first mention of sweetness in connection with Rosh Hashanah came in a speech in the *Book of Nehemiah*. Nehemiah was a prophet who was also an assistant to the Persian King Artaxerxes in the fifth century BCE and got permission from the king to rebuild the walls of Jerusalem. On the first day of the seventh month, all the Jews gathered in the town square to hear the words of Nehemiah and his mentor Ezra: "Go and enjoy choice food and sweet drinks, and send some to those who have nothing prepared. This day is holy to our Lord. Do not grieve, for the joy of the Lord is your strength" (*The Book of Ezra*, 8:10).

Over the next centuries, the sweetness in food and drink was provided by honey, sugar, and dried fruit. In the fourteenth century, Rabbi Jacob Molin (known as The Maharil) a scholar who organized the customs of German Jews into a book called *Minhagim* (Customs), first mentioned the apple dipped in honey.[3] Honey found its way into many other foods. A special round Rosh Hashanah challah was sweetened with more honey than the regular Shabbat challah studded with raisins; it's still found in bakeries and supermarkets in every Jewish neighborhood around the High Holy Days. From the beginning of the meal, when apples and challah are slathered with honey, to the end, when a honeycake called *lekach* is served, we pound home the point that we're planning to have a sweet year.

TZIMMES (STEWED CARROTS)

The Yiddish word *tzimmes* means fuss and bother; all the chopping, slicing, and sautéing that are required for this dish show where it got its name. It's an Ashkenazi dish, a variation of the vegetable and meat stews, such as goulash, that are popular in central Europe. It's served on many holidays and often on Shabbat, but it's particularly appropriate for the High Holy Days.

Honey is not the only way that tzimmes fits into the Rosh Hashanah traditions. The carrots are cut into golden coins (orange coins actually, but close enough)—so they symbolize wealth. And the Yiddish word for carrot is *mirren*, which sounds a lot like mirrin, the word for multiply, which is what at least some of us want to do.

Tzimmes recipes are flexible; they can include meat; other vegetables; fruits such as apricots, apples, and currents; sweet flavorings such as honey, brown sugar, and maple syrup; and different herbs and spices. The constants are long, slow cooking, and sweetness.

• • • • •

Serves 4 as a side dish

INGREDIENTS

2 tablespoons vegetable oil
1 large onion, diced
½ pound beef, cut into cubes (optional)
1 pound of carrots, peeled and cut into coins
¼ cup honey, more or less to taste
½ cup dried fruit—prunes, apricots, raisins
Salt and pepper to taste
½ cup water or stock, optional
½ teaspoon cinnamon and/or nutmeg

Heat the oil in a large, heavy-bottomed skillet. Add the onions and sauté over medium heat until soft. Add the beef, if using, and brown on all sides; continue cooking for a few minutes, then remove the beef cubes with a slotted spoon and reserve. Add the carrots and cook, tossing with the onions for several minutes until they are soft. Add the honey and the dried fruit if you are using it; toss and stir for several minutes until fully combined. Return the beef to the pan, add salt and pepper, and toss. Turn the heat to low, cover and cook gently for one and a half to two hours until all is very soft. If you are not using fruit, the meat may turn leathery at this point; if it does, add a little of the stock or water. If you're using spices, add them in the last fifteen minutes. Adjust seasonings and serve hot.

Variation: Replace some of the carrots with chopped turnips, sweet potatoes, or winter squash.

• • • • •

Sweetness is not the only attribute that we strive for when we eat on Rosh Hashanah. Many communities take the word "*Rosh*" (head) literally and choose foods that will put them at the head of the pack, as leaders, rather than the tail end. Fish heads are the usual choice; they are cooked with spices, and the tender flesh is pulled from the bones and eaten. In some families, children actually fight over who gets to eat the squishy eyes. In addition to the "head" metaphor, fish are considered an important part of the Rosh Hashanah tradition because of their fertility and longevity—fish survived several mass extinctions, including the one that wiped out the dinosaurs.

Bukharan families go one step further, boiling, roasting, or grilling a ram or lamb's head and setting it right on the table; the fur is removed, but the teeth and eyes remain. This tradition is still widely practiced in Israel and even in North America; specialty gourmet Jewish markets make the heads available around Rosh

Hashanah time, all cooked and ready to become a lucky centerpiece for a non-squeamish family.

Fertility is another desired trait, so foods with lots of seeds are eaten on Rosh Hashanah. Sesame, pumpkin, and fenugreek seeds are incorporated into traditional dishes. Most appealing of the seedy foods is the pomegranate, *rimon* in Hebrew. There's a legend that says that all pomegranates have exactly 613 seeds, which is the number of *mitzvot* (commandments) in the Torah. The legend has never been confirmed, because most people stop counting and go wash their hands before they get to 613. In any case, the pomegranate, native to the Middle East, is one of the seven varieties for which Israel is famous and was an important image in ancient times; it was engraved on coins and embroidered into the garments of the *kohanim*. The handles of Torah scrolls are called *rimonim* and are shaped like pomegranates. Some Torah scholars believe that the fruit that Eve ate in the Garden of Eden was a pomegranate and not an apple.

Round foods are also common—the round challah, round dumplings served in soup—because we want a full and rounded year. And foods that are stuffed—stuffed cabbage (*holopches*, see pages 79–81), stuffed peppers, ravioli-like kreplach, and Sephardic favorites (see pages 66–77, which are also eaten on Sukkot and Purim, see pages 82–83)—are also typical, because we want a year stuffed with joy.

But dark, bitter foods—black olives, eggplants—are avoided. Some avoid nuts, because the numerical values of the letters in the Hebrew word for nut (*egoz*) is seventeen, the same as for the word for sin (*chait*)—but only if you misspell both words. It happens that the word for good (*tov*) also has a total numerical value of seventeen. But nuts also cause thirst, so there's a less ridiculous reason to avoid them.

SIMANIM: BECAUSE SIGNS HAVE REALITY

The Rosh Hashanah meal, in many families and communities, goes way beyond simple nostalgia. Many people believe that certain foods have a positive effect on our lives in the year to come—that eating these foods is not baseless, mindless superstition but, as Rebbetzin Chana Bracha Siegelbaum (the Dean of Midreshet Bat Ayin, a center of holistic Torah study for women in Israel) calls them, "an opportunity for spiritual elevation."[4] These foods are called "*simanim*," which means signs, omens, or portents, and their consumption has been organized into a "*seder*," or order, that rivals the one that is performed on Passover.

The source of the custom is the Babylonian Talmud (written in the third to fifth century CE), which posits that "a sign has reality" and states, "Now that you have determined that omens are significant, at the beginning of every year a person should accustom himself to eat gourds, fenugreek, leeks, beets, and dates" (*Kritot*, 6A). Over the next few hundred years, a ceremony evolved around these, and several other, foods that seems to rely on a rare show of humor, or at least wordplay, among the rabbis. For each food, a blessing is made tying the food to a desired outcome. The connections are a bit fragile, relying on translating the words into several different languages and accepting variant spellings. Nevertheless, Rebbetzin Sigelbaum believes that "Conducting a traditional Rosh Hashanah Seder is an amazing gateway for drawing down within ourselves and our world, the blessed influence from above."[5] So whether you do it because you think it will work or because it provides a symbolic connection, or just because it's fun—here are the elements of the Rosh Hashanah *simanim*.

A group of foods is gathered; there are variations in different families and communities. As each is passed around and tasted, blessings are recited; first, the general blessings over fruit, vegetables, and bread, then a blessing that starts "*Yehi Retzon*" (may it be the will of God that . . .). followed by a specific request that is connected to the food. Some people call the foods the "*Yehi Retzonim*." There is an order to the tastings, but again, it varies.

Dates are often the first sample; the word "date" in Hebrew (*tamar*) is similar to the word "end" (*tam*); the blessing includes a request to "end" our enemies. Next up for tasting are white beans, called *rubia* (similar to the word "*rabba*," which means many) or *lubia* (like *lev*, heart); we ask that our good deeds be many and that our hearts be strengthened. Then we eat leeks (*karat* in Hebrew, close to the word for cutting), we ask that God cuts our enemies to pieces. Then comes beets or Swiss chard, which are the same plant (some varieties are grown for their roots, others for their leaves). In Hebrew, they are called "*selek*," which is like the word *le-salek* (to depart). We suggest that these enemies just leave (which is better, for them, than getting cut up from the leeks). Then we try pumpkin or winter squash (*kra'a* in Hebrew, similar to the word *le-kroa*, to cut), and we're back to cutting up the enemies.

Pomegranates are usually included in the Rosh Hashanah seder, with a blessing that asks that our lives be fruitful and filled with good deeds, like the pomegranate is filled with seeds. Eating challah or apple with honey gives us a chance to ask for sweetness. For those who have placed a ram's head on the table, this is a good time to remind God of the time that Abraham offered to sacrifice his son at God's suggestion—and to ask that we live as heads and not as tails. If we've used fish heads instead, we skip the part about the sacrifice of Isaac.

Black-eyed peas are commonly substituted for white peas as "*rubia*." They originated in Africa or the Far East, but were imported to the Middle East in ancient times; they grew well and were incorporated into the Rosh Hashanah seder, especially in Syria. When Sephardic Jews moved to the New World, many of them ended up on Southern plantations, where black-eyed peas were a staple, and they used them on Rosh Hashanah. Though usually used as cattle fodder, some Southerners, especially poor African slaves and frugal Jews, recognized their high nutrition and delicious flavor and included them in their own meals. Black-eyed peas ended up as New Year good luck signs in both Southern and Jewish kitchens, particularly in African soul food. One theory for their use on New Year's by Southerners is that when Yankee armies pillaged the South after the Civil War, they stole all the crops—but left the black-eyed peas which they considered suitable only for animals. The starving Southerners considered that to be a stroke of great luck, since it saved them from death. But other sources connect the luck-and-pea connection to the Jews who lived in the South in the eighteenth and nineteenth centuries and used them in their Rosh Hashanah seders.

Simanim are discussed in the Talmud, well before Jews split into Ashkenazi and Sephardi cultures and cuisines. But the Ashkenazim let them fall away; fish heads and challah or apples with honey were often the only good luck charms that were used. The tradition was preserved and followed mostly by Sephardim, though today, it's become wildly popular again because of its spiritual appeal and its tinge of wackiness.

The *simanim* are based in three languages—Hebrew, Aramaic, and Yiddish—so there's no reason not to add English to the mix and to come up with our own version of the ancient signs. Squash and beets are naturals, with names that allow us to call calamity on our enemies. But, since we're already in the area of puns, this is good place to be creative, and especially to work seasonal foods into our Rosh Hashanah meals—turnips (so that wealth and health should turn up in our lives); lettuce (let us all be happy); kohlrabi (let us listen to the voice [*kol*] of our rabbis). One rabbi eats celery-raisin salad in the hopes that salaries will be raised; another serves yams and everyone says "I yam going to have a great year."

At the first Rosh Hashanah seders, the *simanim* foods were eaten in their pure form, unadulterated. But in modern homes, they are incorporated into more elaborate dishes, so that the first part of the Rosh Hashanah meal is a group of small plates, such as bean salad, broiled spiced winter squash, swiss chard dumplings, or honey-glazed beets. One very popular dish is a leek fritter served in many Sephardic homes: boiled or sautéed chopped leeks are mixed with eggs, mashed potatoes and/ or matzah meal, and then fried in oil. These are called *keftes de prassa*—fried pancakes that are known also known as *pitzitzim* or *levivot* in Hebrew and croquettes or fritters in English—and are a staple in Sephardic cooking. Their name is adapted from *koftes*, meatballs that were common in the Ottoman Empire, but Jews who arrived in the Ottoman territories after the Spanish Inquisition adapted the meatballs to include vegetarian versions. All kinds of *keftes* show up at everyday meals as well as on holidays; their oil content makes them especially appropriate for

Hanukkah. They can be made with vegetables or legumes (*kefte de spinaka, kefte de patata, kefte de lentejas* contain spinach, potato, and lentils), fish (*kefte de poisson*), or ground meat (*keftes de karne, kefte de pollo*).

Leeks are the vegetable of choice for Rosh Hashanah because the Yiddish word for leek (*karas*) is similar to the word for cutting (*kerisa*), so we can cheerfully ask God to cut our enemies to shreds as we eat the delicious pancakes. If we want to update this tradition, we can request that our enemies all be hacked and exposed by Wikileeks.

There's one more treat before the main dish is served on the second evening of Rosh Hashanah: the ritual of the new fruit. The exact reason for serving the new fruit isn't clear. Some say it's simply a way to drill down on the newness of the new year. Others say it's a way to avoid a blessing made in vain; blessings include God's name, which should not be uttered without a good reason. On the first night of Rosh Hashanah, we say a blessing on lighting the candles for the new year—"Blessed art thou, our Lord, King of the Universe, who has given us life, and maintained us and brought us to this time"—it's the standard blessing for new things (those we haven't done for a year) and clearly applies because we haven't lit Rosh Hashanah candles since last year. But on the second night—should we say the blessing or not? If the blessing is not appropriate, then we shouldn't be invoking God's name—and there's really no one to ask. So, to avoid any possible misuse, we taste a fruit that we haven't eaten in a year and make the blessing a two-fer. If we weren't supposed to make it on the candles—no problem, we needed it for the fruit anyway. It's a perfect example of the hairsplitting that early rabbis engaged in.

And it's a great excuse for trying new foods, the more exotic the better. Visit a fruit store in a Jewish neighborhood and you'll find fruit you may never have seen before: ten-pound jackfruit, rambutens in their spiky peels (similar to lychees), dragonfruit, cactus pears, star apples, starfruit, sapote. In many cases, they are more interesting than delicious—there's a reason why apples, oranges, and peaches have made it and these didn't, and it's not just climate. Adding these bright new tastes to the meal takes a bit of the sting away from the fact that we've been praying for our lives all day.

THE MAIN MEAL

Once all these blessings—on wine, on the special round challah, on *simanim*, on new fruit—have been made—and the foods eaten, it's time for the full meal. Many communities have specific dishes attached to Rosh Hashanah and most have some connection to the symbolic foods. Soups are served with rounded dumplings or tiny meatball, especially in Hasidic homes (triangular *kreplach* are usually saved for Yom Kippur). Lamb is often the main dish, to remind God that Abraham was ready to sacrifice his son to God before God intervened and accepted a ram instead (Abraham pulled one of the ram's horns off, which became the *shofar* we use as a similar reminder).

In north African countries, there is a popular dish of chicken braised in tomatoes and honey that is often used by Sephardim on Rosh Hashanah. Potatoes are usually replaced by sweet potatoes. Dried fruit—apricots, raisins, pears—add a touch of sweetness to many holiday chicken dishes and vegetables. Noodle kugels are usually the sweet variety, with added sugar and dried fruit. Italian Jews sometimes serve fish in a sweet and sour sauce, followed by honey-sweetened chicken accompanied by sweetened winter squash; dessert might be a hazelnut sponge cake or a quince in honey syrup. Iranian Jews serve a classic Persian chicken dish call *Fesenjan*, made with pomegranates and walnuts. To further the head-and-not-tail imagery, brains are used in many Sephardic homes, in dishes such as calf-brain fritters; Italians use brains in ravioli.

Dessert is, of course, sweet. Many desserts make use of quinces, which were harvested around Rosh Hashanah time and require copious amounts of sugar or honey. In north African homes, fresh dates, figs, and pomegranates are sprinkled with sugar and soaked in rose water for a simple dessert. *Teiglach*, balls of dough that are baked then boiled in a honey syrup, have been eaten since Roman times. They appeared in western Europe as a dessert for special occasions, especially Rosh Hashanah. There are also several popular honey cookies. But perhaps the most common dessert is the honeycake known as *lekach*.

LEKACH

The word *lekach* comes from the Yiddish word for licking. Although there are many recipes, from light, airy cakes to dense loaves, most of them are based on Lebkuchen, thirteenth-century eastern European gingerbread. There were even earlier versions of honeycakes, called *basbousa*, in ancient Egypt—some of them have been found in the tombs of Pharaohs, probably a bit stale.

• • • • •

6 to 10 servings

INGREDIENTS

4 tablespoons (½ stick) butter or margarine, softened, plus more for
greasing the pan
¾ cups all-purpose flour
2 tablespoons ground walnuts or almonds
1 teaspoon baking powder

pinch baking soda
1 teaspoon ground cinnamon
1 teaspoon ground ginger
pinch ground nutmeg
½ teaspoon salt
¼ cup white sugar
2 tablespoons brown sugar
2 eggs, beaten
¾ cups honey
1 teaspoon vanilla extract
¼ cup orange or apple juice or water
¼ cup applesauce
2 tablespoons liqueur (any flavor)
2 tablespoons raisins or other dried fruit
Confectioners' sugar for dusting

Preheat oven to 325°F. Generously grease a nine-inch loaf pan or square pan, or a small bundt pan.

In a large bowl, combine the flour, ground nuts, baking powder, baking soda, cinnamon, ginger, nutmeg, and salt. In another bowl, using an electric mixer, cream the butter, both sugars, and eggs. Add the rest of the ingredients except the dried fruit and confectioner's sugar; beat for two minutes until smooth.

Make a well in the flour mixture. Pour in the half the wet mixture and mix with a spoon until combined; add the rest of the wet ingredients and beat until thoroughly combined, about two minutes. Fold in the dried fruit.

Pour the batter into the greased pan; if there is any batter left over, bake it separately. Bake for forty-five minutes or until a toothpick inserted into the center comes out clean. Cool completely, then dust with sugar if using, before serving.

• • • • •

LET'S NOT EAT: YOM KIPPUR

On most Jewish holidays, food is a main event; on Yom Kippur, it's banned entirely. That doesn't mean that there are no Yom Kippur foods—pre- and post-fast meals are carefully prepared. But on the day of Yom Kippur itself—and the day begins at sunset and ends on the following sunset—there's nothing at all to eat. No coffee, no water, not even the brushing of teeth. Exceptions are made when avoiding all food or liquid will harm someone's health: expectant and nursing mothers, children under bar- and bat-mitzvah age, and people who must take medications or must eat to maintain their health are exempt.

Fasting is a common religious and political practice. Muslims fast from sun up to sun down during the holy month of Ramadan. Hindus fast frequently, often choosing one day a week to avoid food. Buddhists and Christians often engage in partial fasts, removing a particular food from their diet or eating only before or after noon. There are six fast days in Judaism. Five of them commemorate calamities or near-misses. The tenth of Tevet, the seventeenth of Tamuz, and the ninth of Av connect us to the suffering that the Jews experienced in the lead-up to the destruction of the Temple in Jerusalem—the ninth of Av, the day when the Temple was actually breached by the Babylonians, is the second most significant fast day on the Jewish calendar. The other two—the Fast of Esther on the thirteenth of Adar (see page 132) and the Fast of Gedaliah on the third of Elul—are also related to crises; fasting makes us more aware of them, more thankful that we survived. (The fast of Gedaliah commemorates the assassination of a Jewish leader who ruled at the time of the destruction of the First Temple; some people now call it the Fast of Gedaliah and Yitzchak, to honor Yitzchak Rabin, a more recent political martyr.

Fasting on Yom Kippur has a very different purpose: it's meant to remove distractions and help us focus on and repent for our sins. Refraining from food gives us more time to pray and to think about material things (though many people who fast spend a lot of time thinking about what they are going to eat when the fast is over). Many Jews who observe none of the other ceremonies and rituals of Judaism attend services and even fast on Yom Kippur.

But though Yom Kippur itself is the opposite of a foodie day, the day before (when we eat enough to be able to hold out for the next day) and the night after (when we finally get to eat) double down on culinary creations. Both of these meals are crafted around the fast and the ways our bodies react to it.

The meal that we eat before the fast (called *Seudah Mafseket*, the end meal) has to be substantial enough so that we're not hungry an hour later—but not so heavy that we feel bloated. Certainly, it should be bland and not too salty or spicy—nothing to induce a thirst that can't be quenched. We're urged to eat until we're full and then some; many authorities say that eating on the day before Yom Kippur is as important as fasting the day of.

The meal starts much as the Rosh Hashanah meal—a round, sweet challah, dabbed with honey, and a simple fish dish.

Eating chicken soup (see pages 41–42) after the fish is fairly universal. Greeks and Egyptians serve lemon-flavored soup with rice. Although most pre-fast dinners shy away from highly spiced foods that may make a drink of water necessary a few hours later, Yemenite high holy day soup embraces the strong, hot flavors that are a hallmark of Yemenite cuisine. It includes chicken and lots of vegetables, plus four different spice mixes (*Hawayij*, a curry-based mix; fiery *Schug*; complex *Harissa*; and *Hilbeh*, a mixture with fenugreek as its main ingredient [see page 15])—so the soup is the very opposite of bland. This stew-like soup is not eaten right before the fast; Yemenites serve a big meal early in the day, before noon, and then a smaller one right before sunset. The soup is rich enough to be a main dish.

Harira is another deviation from the bland chicken soup tradition. It's a well-known soup made with lentils, tomatoes, and lots of spices; it originated in Morocco but is eaten throughout the Middle East, especially in north Africa. The lentils provide protein and carbs that keep us full for the fasting to come.

Ashkenazi Jews also include chicken soup in their pre-fast meals. They fall back on their standard matzah balls but often add *kreplach*.

KREPLACH

The name *kreplach* is derived from the Latin root *krespa*, which is also connected to French crepes. These filled dough dumplings have been around since the twelfth century. They follow in the world-wide tradition of stuffing wrappers of dough (tortellini, ravioli, Chinese dumplings, borekas, empanadas); in the case of the Ashkenazi Jews of eastern Europe, they were a way of extending bits of meat into a meal. They are almost always eaten in soup, and with their symbolism of fullness, they are a favorite on Rosh Hashanah and Sukkot. They are also eaten on Purim, because they contain a hidden ingredient, which fits in with a Purim theme (see page 143).

• • • • •

6 servings
INGREDIENTS

For the dough:
1 large egg
½ teaspoon salt
2 tablespoons vegetable oil
1½ to 2 cups flour

For the filling:
1 tablespoon vegetable oil
1 clove garlic
2 tablespoons finely diced onions
½ pound ground meat (turkey, chicken, beef, or lamb)
½ cup cooked rice
Salt, pepper, and whatever spices or chopped herbs you prefer
Oil for frying (optional)

Crack the egg into a medium bowl and beat it; reserve and refrigerate one table-spoon for the filling. Add the other filling ingredients, and stir vigorously with a wooden spoon to combine (it's not worth using the food processor for this). When the dough is smooth, dump it onto a floured board and knead for a minute or two. Then roll it out to about quarter-inch thickness and cut it into two- to three-inch squares.

For the filling, heat the oil in a frying pan, add the garlic and onions, and sauté until soft. Add the meat and toss until the meat is completely brown. Pour off any fat or oil. Add the rice, salt, and spices, and stir to combine. Allow to cool—so that the eggs should not cook—then fold in the reserved egg.

Place about a teaspoon of filling (for a two-inch square) or two teaspoons (for a three-inch square) in the center of each square. Fold to triangle shape. Crimp the edges with a fork or with your fingers, then seal with water.

Put them in a big pot of boiling chicken soup or water and cook for twenty to thirty minutes. Or heat oil in a frying pan and fry them in batches until they are brown all over. Serve in chicken soup.

Variations: Substitute any non-dairy filling from pages 142–143; ground meat, and especially liver, are traditional. And though dairy ingredients are usually not mixed with chicken soup, cheese *kreplach* are used in vegetarian soups or as side dishes.

●　●　●　●　●

This is usually followed by a dish made with chicken, a custom that arose be-cause there was usually some dead chicken somewhere in the house around Yom Kippur time. This was due to of the ritual of *Kapparah*, or absolution; people would hold a live chicken above their heads, swing it around a bit, and ask God to lay all their sins on the chicken instead of themselves. The newly sinful chicken was then slaughtered—and by Yom Kippur, it was time to eat it. Today, some people in Hasidic communities still perform *Kapparah*, though animal activists point out that it's not a very nice thing to do to a chicken. There is an alternate ver-sion, in which people swing a handful of coins above their heads and then donate them to charity, which causes much less squawking all around.

Moroccan Jews sometimes use the *kapparah* chicken in a tagine. Bukharian Jews have a special dish called *osh pulao*, a spicy casserole of rice, carrots, onions, and meat (usually lamb) that is cooked on top of the stove. And some families opt for a grain-filled, high-carb dairy or vegan meal, eating roasted vegetables, pilafs, blintzes, and the like. Dessert is usually simple—poached fruit or fruit compote, or a plain cake or cookies.

BREAKING THE FAST

After a day without any kind of nourishment and hydration, the first thing most people want is a glass of water and a toothbrush. After that, the fun begins. Yom

Kippur is a day of solemnity and prayer, but once it's over and you've lived through another fast, most people stop worrying about their fate for the coming year and starting thinking about what to eat. In many cultures, the break-the-fast foods are similar to breakfast, which makes more sense than loading a heavy meal into an empty stomach. Omelettes, quiches, noodle kugels, and salads are usually on the menu; they can be prepared in advance or in just a few minutes, a benefit when you're starving. In Europe, though, the meal sometimes included chicken.

Sephardim break their fasts with small savory and sweet pastries like borekas (see page 140) and cigars, served with anise-flavored tea. Many have a second meal that includes chicken an hour or so later. Sometimes, this includes Harira, a hearty soup that is also eaten before the fast and by Muslims as they break their Ramadan fasts. Syrian Jews include *ka'ak* in their break-the-fast meal; it's a yeast-based, pretzel-like ring that is served at many festive occasions. Many flavorings are used, including anise, cumin, and coriander.

For Jews in America, breaking the Yom Kippur fast is often a social occasion and an excuse to indulge in the Jewish obsession for smoked fish and its close relation, salt-cured lox. Humans have been smoking fish since the Stone Age; it was one of the first ways that people were able to preserve food. There is evidence that a facility for high-volume smoking existed in Poland in the seventh century; by the Middle Ages, smoked fish was popular in Scandinavia, eastern Europe, and Russia. In the nineteenth century, Jewish immigrants brought smoked fish to England and America. Like stone-age humanoids, Jews needed a way to preserve fish (home refrigeration was not available until the middle of the twentieth century) because kosher fish was not always available. Several types of preserved fish—lox, whitefish, sable, kippered herring—became popular foods for Shabbat and celebrations. When Jews began to prosper in cities like New York, Chicago, Toronto, and London, large appetizer stores (they sold fish and dairy products, as opposed to delicatessens that sold meat) sprang up to cater to their love of these foods. On Yom Kippur, a day when even people with the most tenuous ties to Judaism feel the need to connect to their roots, bagels and lox become a good way to celebrate the end of fast. Zabar's, the venerable appetizing store on the west side of Manhattan, sells so much lox on the day before Yom Kippur that they send airplane tickets to retired lox-cutters who have returned to their native Caribbean islands and bring them back to their posts behind the fish counter.[6]

As the break-the-fast parties come to an end, Jews begin preparations for the next phase of the fall holiday season. It's a tradition to start building a sukkah to celebrate the next holiday right on the night after Yom Kippur; so put that last bagel down, wipe the cream cheese off your fingers, and starting building.

HIGH HOLY DAY TRADITIONS AROUND THE WORLD

Mumbai
In the Jewish community in Mumbai, India, the Rosh Hashanah seder includes garlic and bananas. Instead of challah, they eat *chapattis*, a crisp flatbread. Before the meal, slices of halvah are distributed.

Turkey
Turkish Jews replace the traditional *Lekach* honeycake with a sugar-syrup-soaked cake called *Tishpishti*. It's made with chopped or ground walnuts, flavored with orange slices, cinnamon, and/or rosewater. It's a dense, flourless cake that is also suitable for Passover. Similar cakes were made in Spain, and it's assumed that the Turkish version was brought by Spanish immigrants.

Alsace
The province of Alsace was on the border of Germany and France; it frequently changed hands and was controlled by one or the other. It is one of the oldest Jewish communities in Europe, and there are references to synagogues and yeshivas dated back to 1000 CE. To break the Yom Kippur fast, Alsatian Jews eat stewed chicken (*pot au feu*) with tzimmes and several desserts, including fresh and cooked fruit, *teiglach*, and sponge cake.

Central Europe
During the Middle Ages, in some towns in central Europe, men ate a cucumber-like vegetable called *erd epel* that was reputed to curb sexual desire. This allowed the men to focus on their prayers and repentance.

Iraq
Iraqi Jews don't eat fish on Rosh Hashanah because the Hebrew word for fish (*dag*) is similar to the Hebrew word for worry (*da-aga*)—and they don't want extra worries when they start the New Year.

Greece
In Greece, and also in many other Balkan countries, foods flavored with lemon are served to break the fast: lemon tea, bread dipped in a lemon and oil dressing, fish poached with lemon, and *avgolemono*, a chicken soup with egg and lemon.

Bukharia

Palov, sometimes called *plov*, is a signature Bukharian recipe in central Asia, served on holidays and at large gatherings. On Rosh Hashanah, a special version is prepared, adding pomegranates, quince, and barberries to the caramelized carrots, meat, and rice in the standard recipe.

Austria

In Austria, *Apfelstrudel* is served as dessert at Rosh Hashanah dinners and to break the fast after Yom Kippur. It's a sweet, apple-laden version of the popular layered Viennese pastry.

3

❖ ❖

Sukkot Et Al

Holidays of Harvest and Happiness

Sukkot is four holidays in one. It starts with the basic holiday of Sukkot, a remembrance of the forty years that Jews wandered through the desert after leaving Egypt and before arriving in the Promised Land; we eat outdoors in small booths that remind us that we can't always rely on big solid houses. Sukkot is also a celebration of the harvest, and we join with guests in the sukkah to eat the bounty that we have taken from our farms and gardens. The seventh day is called Hoshana Rabba—which translates, roughly, to "many hosannas"—according to legend it is the day on which the fate that was decided for each of us on Yom Kippur is sealed and finalized. Hoshana Rabba gives us one last day to repent. This is followed by Shemini Atzeret, the extra eighth. It's a rather vague festival, allowing us to gather again before we leave the extensive fall holiday season. It's also the day on which we pray for rain in the coming year. Finally, we come to Simchat Torah, the rejoicing of the Torah; it's the day when we finish the annual cycle of Torah readings and start again, and it's marked by frenzied dancing while holding Torah scrolls.

On the Shabbat that falls during Sukkot, we read from the *Book of Ecclesiastes*, written by King Solomon. At first glance, it's the most pessimistic book of the Bible, telling us that "All is vanity" and that "The sun sets and the sun also rises, but there is nothing new under the sun" (Pete Seeger turned to *Ecclesiastes* for the lyrics to The Byrd's hit, "Turn! Turn! Turn!": To everything there is a season . . . And a time to every purpose, under heaven . . . A time to be born, a time to die [chapter 3, verses 1–8]). But reading it more carefully, we see that it is telling us to

71

shed all the vanity, the surface pleasures, and to look for deeper meaning in life—just as we remove life's comforts when we retire the fragile, temporary sukkah.

So, during a long, multi-part holiday, we've celebrated our harvest and the Torah, the source of our identity; we've greeted guests and remembered hardship; we've prayed for absolution and for rain. We've danced, we've sung, we've eaten. And then the holidays are over, and it's time to get back to everyday life.

REFLECTIONS

Moses commanded the observance of Torah; it is the inheritance of the community of Jacob.—*Deuteronomy*, 33:4

Sukkot is one of the most experiential of all of the Jewish holidays. In the Jewish liturgy, it is called *zeman simchatenu*—the time of our rejoicing. There is good reason for singling out Sukkot as the time of happiness. A Jewish tradition mandates that one must never sit alone in the sukkah. Rather, one is always joined by the *ushpizin*, the seven invited biblical guests: Abraham, Isaac, Jacob, Joseph, David, Moses, and Aaron. The custom of inviting seven biblical guests rests on a statement by Jewish mystics to the effect that God's glory shelters the "sukkah" beneath its wings, and Abraham, in the company of six righteous men, enters to participate in the hospitality of the Jew who properly observes the precept of dwelling in a sukkah. This is the Jewish way of teaching that a simcha, a joyous occasion, can only be meaningful when celebrated with others, in community. In the presence of such immortal biblical guests, one should rejoice together with an equal number of needy people sharing one's meals in the sukkah.

Jews around the world are instructed to feel the joy during the festival of Sukkot, which is a festival of thanksgiving for one's bountiful harvest. In many ways, it commemorates themes similar to those of the American celebration of Thanksgiving. In fact, some historians believe that the Pilgrims who came to America modeled their own celebration and feast after the holiday of Sukkot, known to them as Tabernacles, which they knew about from reading the Bible.

The Torah designates four plants as essential for the observance of Sukkot: "On the first day you shall take the fruit of the goodly trees, branches of palm trees, boughs of leafy trees and willows of the brook, and you shall rejoice before God seven days" (*Leviticus*, 23:40). Each of these four plants are explained by the rabbis as being symbolically significant. In one explanation, the *etrog* (citron) has both taste and fragrance, the palm has taste but no fragrance, the myrtle has fragrance but no taste, and the willow has neither taste nor fragrance. Similarly, some Jews have both learning and good deeds, some have learning but no good deeds, others have good deeds but no learning, and still others have neither learning nor good deeds. Therefore God said: "Let them all be combined together, and they will atone one for the other" (*Leviticus Rabbah*, 30:12).

The eighth day of the holiday is known as Shemini Atzeret, whose major prayer is one for rain, since the holiday falls at the beginning of the rainy season in Israel. Rabbi Irving Greenberg, a leading American rabbi and educator, has called Shemini Atzeret "the Zionist holiday" because it kept alive a strong identity between world Jewry and the land of Israel.

Shemini Atzeret is immediately followed by the holiday known as Simchat Torah. Its celebration originated in Babylonia, where the Torah was read over the course of a year, and therefore its completion could be celebrated annually. In the Torah, the Prophet Nehemiah mentions that Ezra read and taught the Torah on the Festival of Sukkot, and so the holiday became associated with the completion of the reading.

Simchat Torah is a most fitting finale for the fall Jewish holiday season. No festival better conveys the Jewish attachment to the Torah than this one. In the diaspora, it falls on the ninth day of Sukkot and is devoted completely to rejoicing. In Israel, where the eighth day is the last day, the practices of Simchat Torah are observed on Shemini Atzeret. For children and their families, no holiday, with the possible exception of Purim, can compare with this one, which celebrates the conclusion of the cycle of the Reading of the Torah, and includes much merriment, singing, and dancing. During the 1960s when Russian Jews were permitted only limited religious freedom, they adopted Simchat Torah as their special day of celebration.

Certain synagogues acquire the reputation of being good places to visit when celebrating Simchat Torah. In some synagogues, Israeli dancing is substituted for the less familiar Hasidic ones, but all Simchat Torah revelry takes its style from that of Hasidim, who lose themselves in ecstatic fervor when carrying the Torah scrolls in processionals.

Simchat Torah is a grand celebration of the Jewish people's relationship to Torah. It is an expression of their love and joy of having the Five Books of Moses as a lifelong companion.

OUTDOOR LIVING

The holiday of Sukkot is named for its central image and ritual, a booth called a sukkah. According to *Halachah*, a sukkah should have four walls (though three walls and part of a fourth is acceptable) and a roof through which you can see the sky. The roof, which is made from plant matter, must be temporary. These booths are erected to follow the commandment in Leviticus, "For a seven-day period you shall live in booths. Every resident among the Israelites shall live in booths, in order that your [ensuing] generations should know that I had the children of Israel live in booths when I took them out of the land of Egypt. I am the Lord, your God" (*Leviticus*, 23:42–43).

The original booths were used during the forty years when the Jews wandered through the desert on their way to Israel. This forty-year trek, which covered only several hundred miles, was not the result of slow walking. The original plan was for the Jews to arrive in Israel, which was called Canaan before the Jews took up residence, soon after they received the Torah; they would quickly conquer the land and proceed to live there in peace. But they misbehaved.

At God's instruction, Moses sent twelve spies to case the Promised Land (an expedition later repeated by the Boss himself) so that they would be prepared for the coming battles. Moses sent twelve prominent citizens—and ten of them returned with startling news. The land was truly flowing with milk and honey; the soil was so fertile that it took several men with poles to carry a single bunch of grapes (Carmel, the Israeli wine company, uses that image as their logo). But the men of Canaan were so big that the spies felt like grasshoppers next to them; ten of the spies believed that there was no way that the Israelites, newly released from slavery, could conquer them. Only two of the spies, Joshua and Caleb, trusted in Moses and God to lead them—and they could not sway the others who thought they would be slaughtered if they entered Canaan.

The people believed them. They cried and grumbled, telling Moses that he should have left them in Egypt as slaves instead of getting them killed in the Promised Land. They looked for a new leader to take them back to Egypt, despite the exhortations of Caleb and Joshua, and the pleas of Moses and Aaron.

Moses realized that the entire population was angering God; after all, God had just pulled off the remarkable feat of bringing them out of Egypt, parting the Red Sea and all that. But he knew that God was merciful and begged for forgiveness. So God compromised. Instead of killing all these faithless Jews on the spot, he required them to wander through the desert for forty years; by that point, everyone over the age of twenty would have died, and their descendants would be the ones who entered Canaan. Only Caleb and Joshua were spared; the other ten spies were killed immediately.

Although the wandering was difficult, God protected his people. He surrounded them with clouds of glory, which are represented by the walls of the sukkah, and kept local tribes from killing them. He also provided them with a remarkable food called mannah to eat.

Mannah is described as being "a fine, flake-like thing" that looked a bit like frost (*Exodus*, 16:14). It was deposited every morning in front of the houses of everyone who was following the rules; it had to be collected and eaten the same day, or it turned wormy and rotten. (On Friday, a double portion was given, so that the Jews would not have to work on Shabbat to gather it—that portion stayed fresh for two days.) Mannah has to be considered the first truly Jewish food, precursor to chicken soup, borekas, and bagels and lox.

There is much conjecture about the consistency and function of mannah. Some believe that it was similar to white coriander seeds, and many think it was so fragrant that it was used as a perfume. Generally, it is believed to be similar to a grain that could be pounded or ground into a flour that was used to make breads and cakes. There are legends that say that mannah was whatever you wanted it to be—it changed according to the desires and imaginations of the eaters.

According to the Midrash, mannah was a natural substance that was brought onto the Earth on the sixth day of Creation. Jews ate mannah exclusively during their forty years in the desert, despite the fact that they also had livestock that could be used for milk and meat. One result of the all-mannah diet was that people did not defecate at all. Eating mannah alone made some people a bit queasy (and possibly constipated) and they argued for meat. God then rained quail down on them, but the quail turned bad quickly, and they went back to mannah alone.

Despite heavenly protection and superfood, living in the desert for forty years was a punishment, not a picnic, and eating in the sukkah for the seven days of Sukkot is meant to remind us of the suffering of the Jews and of the consequences of faithlessness. The sukkah also teaches us humility: when we leave our fancy, insulated homes and eat in a temporary hut, we realize how vulnerable we are to the elements.

But despite its identification with pain, sukkahs are often very pleasant places. Sukkot falls in a season of mild weather, so being outdoors under the dappled sun of a fragile roof is usually delightful. There is a widespread custom of decorating a sukkah; as stated in the Talmud (*Shabbat*, 133b), "Adorn yourself before God in commandments: make a beautiful sukkah in God's honor." In eastern Europe, sukkahs were decorated with birds made of eggshells. In Italy, elaborate art and engravings, some of them made from cut paper, covered the walls. Venetians placed a special arrangement of harvest foods on the Sukkot table. Moroccan Jews brought mattresses, rugs, and silk wall hangings into their sukkahs. In America, schoolchildren spend the weeks before Sukkot folding, cutting, and coloring paper decorations, then spend a day arranging them, along with paper chains, bright banners, and the glitziest, gaudiest baubles they can find. Also included in the sukkah decorations are examples of the seven agricultural varieties—sheaves of wheat and barley, small bottles of honey and olive oil, clusters of grapes, braids of figs, and pomegranates. For anyone who looks at Christmas trees with envy, the sukkah is an even better, bigger opportunity for design fantasies.

HARVEST

The ambience of the sukkah doesn't jive with the theme of deprivation and suffering connected with the wandering in the wilderness, but it's a perfect reflection of Sukkot's second reason for being. Sukkot is also a celebration of the harvest and there's no better way to celebrate than to squeeze ourselves in rickety little booths, exposed to the sun, the night, and the wind, under a roof made of branches or bamboo, with walls hung with samples of the seven species. In biblical times, the ancient Israelites celebrated the amazingly fertile soil of their new land, and we do the same today in whatever land we've ended up.

As the twelve spies found when they visited Canaan, the land was extraordinarily productive, a fact that Moses had predicted: "For the Lord your God is bringing you into a good land—a land with brooks, streams, and deep springs gushing out into the valleys and hills—a land with wheat and barley, vines and fig trees, pomegranates, olive oil and honey; a land where bread will not be scarce and you will lack nothing" (*Deuteronomy*, 8:7–9). We think of the Middle East as a parched desert, but in ancient times, the forests were lush and the soil was full of nutrients—the land may have become desert because of poor management, constant wars, and chopping down the forests for wood and farmland (see page 122).

BIBLICAL SUSTAINABILITY

During biblical times, sustainable practices that we consider the latest best thing were already being followed. The Torah specifically stated that land was to remain fallow every seventh year; the seventh year was called s*hmita*, and is the basis for the term "sabbatical." Even today, *shmita* is observed in Israel; consumers store up produce and buy from sources outside the country, because farmers give their fields a year to replenish, a sound agricultural technique. The Torah also states that fruit trees should not be harvested until their third year, allowing them to become strong. There is evidence in the Torah that biblical farmers used dung as fertilizer, just as organic farmers do today. (The evidence is roundabout; *Jeremiah*, 9:22, describes the result of not following God's orders: "Dead bodies will lie like dung on the open field." If we ignore the unpleasantness of God's vengefulness and the graphic of the open-air corpses, we can take pride and instruction in the use of dung as organic fertilizer.) And the rules for separating crops (called *kelayim*) seem to have some connection to crop rotation and companion planting.

Respect for the land is a prime Jewish value. Careful land management created wealth during Biblical times, though the soil deteriorated over the millennia between then and now. Modern Israel is renowned for the way it has returned the soil to its previous fertility through technological advances and adherence to the organic methods first seen in the Torah and Talmud.

When the Jews entered Canaan and began to farm, the Iron Age was just beginning. Historians date the conquest of Canaan at about 1250 to 1050 BCE. Though the very earliest iron artifacts—nine beads found in northern Egypt—date back to 3200 BCE,[1] creating iron tools required a high smelting point (1,538°C) that was beyond the capabilities of early humans. Some iron tools have been found in Asia and Africa from the third millennium, but it was not until around 1200 BCE that ironmaking became an industry. When the Jews began farming, they had iron tools (imported from other countries, as iron is not found in Israel), such as plows, harrows, and presses used to make wine and olive oil.

The Israelites also incorporated sophisticated farming practices that originated in other parts of the world. They terraced hilly slopes to create flat land and avoid soil erosion; they preserved and directed runoff water from storms and infrequent snow melt to keep the water from eroding soil and to irrigate fields when rainfall was scarce.

These intelligent farming practices led to the healthy harvests that were celebrated on Sukkot. Israel in Biblical times was an agrarian society; not only did they produce enough food to feed themselves, they exported to other countries, bringing money into their coffers that was used for building better lives. And not only was personal health and commerce dependent on agriculture—moral and social health revolved around it as well. The Jews of ancient Israel followed the Biblical precept of donating part of their harvest to those in need and part to the high priests who did not have land of their own. Their calendar revolved around the harvest seasons—three of the ten major Jewish holidays were called the "*shalosh regalim*," or three legs. Different phases of the farming cycle were celebrated on Passover (when the first plants [barley] began to emerge from the earth), Shavuot (when the first fruits were brought to the Temple in Jerusalem), and Sukkot (when the final crops were harvested).

The harvest that was celebrated on Sukkot varied widely. In addition to the *sheva minim* mentioned in God's description of the Promised Land, Jews also grew a variety of healthy pulses—chickpeas, lentils, and broadbeans—and spices and herbs that made their food taste better, including cumin, coriander, and sesame. They also grew radishes, muskmelons and watermelons,[2] leeks, onions, and garlic. Combined with meat from their livestock and fish from the rivers and lakes, they ate well.

Today, we have many other varieties to enjoy as we celebrate our harvests—cabbages, turnips, strawberries, and apples that are native to Europe; chocolate, corn, squashes, tomatoes, and potatoes from Central and South America; sage, nuts, wild rice, and blueberries from North America; eggplants, oranges, and rice from the Far East; and coffee and watermelons from Africa. It has become a tradition for Jews around the world to incorporate all the crops available in Sukkot meals. In North America, we flock to farmers' markets to buy fall produce such as winter squash, kale, broccoli, beets, leeks, apples, and pears. These vegetables find their way into soups and stews served on Sukkot. Sukkot is also a good time to try less-known varieties, such as celeriac, kohlrabi, rutabaga, salsify, and Jerusalem artichokes. Adding some of the foods and flavorings of the Torah—lentils, chickpeas, cumin, and sesame—reminds us of our origin. Combining them with selections from the lands where we live now allows us to enjoy the full range of the bounty that comes from every region on Earth, so that when we celebrate the harvest on Sukkot we show respect for both the land and for all the generations of farmers that have made the most of it.

Sukkot is also a good time to pay attention to the fact that the land is not inexhaustible—that supporting farmers who use sustainable farming practices is the best way to celebrate and respect the harvest. As we read in *Ecclesiastes*, "To every thing, there is a season." Sukkot is the season for understanding how precious and crucial the earth is to our lives.

THE MEALS OF SUKKOT

It's hard to prepare and eat elaborate holiday meals for the eight (in Israel) or nine (outside Israel for some branches of Judaism) days of Sukkot, but that doesn't stop us from trying. Actually, the elaborate meals are confined to the first and last days. The middle of the holiday is observed with a lesser degree of fervor; those days are called *chol hamoed*, or secular holidays. Even Orthodox Jews are permitted to work, though many schools and organizations stay closed.

But meals on those first and last days are lavish, filled with the bounty of the harvest that they celebrate. In Sephardic homes, they start with a dozen or so mezze, small plates of salads, dips, and pickled vegetables, followed by fish, soups, and stews that incorporate newly harvested produce. In Iran, an eggplant casserole was often served; in Turkey and Greece, moussaka was the casserole of choice. After all that, meat and poultry dishes are served, followed by sweet pastries and fruit compotes. Often the meals include dozens of dishes, prepared by groups of women who have learned to make them from their mothers. They gather in the largest kitchen to cooperate in creating the beautiful, many-flavored meals.

Ashkenazi meals are less elaborate, but also include fish, soup, vegetable, and meat courses. In Poland, *gebruteka uter*, made from cow's udder, is a much-loved delicacy. Stews, such as Romanian *guvetch*, a vegetable stew, and soups, such as

Russian cabbage and beef soup, were typical fare. Many of the foods cooked for Rosh Hashanah, like carrot *tsimmes* and honey cookies called lebkuchen, were brought out again.

STUFFED

Although no specific dishes are mandated on Sukkot, stuffed foods are often served. There are many theories on why this is so, and people make up new ones all the time. One theory says that stuffing food corresponds with stuffing your sukkah with guests. Another suggests that the part that is stuffed acts as a cornucopia, holding all the foods of the harvest. Perhaps the neat little packages were just an easy way to transport food to the sukkah.

In any case, all kinds of foods are stuffed into each other, providing many ways to create interesting and delicious food to enjoy with friends and family in the sukkah. In a recipe from the Balkan countries, ground lamb is mixed with rice, mint, and cumin, and stuffed into grape leaves (the leaves still hung on the vines around Sukkot time, and this was a good way to use them). Peppers, squash, and tomatoes—the last of the summer harvest—are hollowed out and stuffed with grains mixed with vegetables or meat. Artichokes are teased apart and stuffed with a mixture of breadcrumb and herbs. Even dates and olives are stuffed.

Kreplach (see page 66), which are often included in Shabbat and holiday meals, are popular on Sukkot and its companion holidays and especially on Hoshana Rabba. Other stuffed pasta, like ravioli and tortellini, were often included. Strudel (see pages 226–228), which consists of thin layers of pastry stuffed with sweet or savory fillings, were also served. In Hungary, a savory cabbage and apple strudel was a common main dish.

But the go-to vegetable for stuffing, the recipe that is entrenched in cuisines throughout eastern Europe and appropriated as a quintessential Jewish food, is stuffed cabbage. Cabbages are native to Europe and farmers learned to grow them as far back as 1000 BCE. By the Middle Ages, they were a staple throughout Europe, particularly in central and eastern Europe; they made their way to the Middle East as well. Cabbages are easy to grow and do not require the best soils, the warmest temperatures, or full sun. They grow quickly and are among the first vegetables to mature after winter; they also keep well and are still edible well into winter. It's no wonder that Jewish cooks accepted this as a main ingredient and used it often.

STUFFED CABBAGE: *HOLOPCHES*

Called cholopches, holishkes, and prakas in eastern Europe, and holubuky in Slovenia, balandeliai in Lithuania, sarma in Slovenia, and holubtsi in Ukraine, stuffed cabbage is a staple for both every day and holiday use throughout Europe and the rest of the world. They are particularly popular in Poland, where they are known as golapki, which means "little pigeons," and are made with rice or barley and beef or pork. Russians call them galooptsies, which also mean little pigeons, and mix sour cream in to the sauce. Hungarian töltött káposzta are wrapped in pickled cabbage leaves and, of course, include paprika. In France, chou farci contains pork, chicken livers, and breadcrumbs, simmered in white wine (French Jews left out the pork or substituted chicken, turkey, or beef).

In Sweden, they are called kaldolma; they were supposedly brought to Sweden by Swedish King Charles XII in the early seventeenth century. Charles had fled his country for the Ottoman Empire to ask the Emperor for help with defeating the Russians; when he returned, his creditors followed him and brought the dish with them.

The following version, which omits pork and dairy products, is typical of the stuffed cabbage dishes served in Ashkenazi homes. It appears on the table during all the fall holidays—Rosh Hashanah, pre-fast Yom Kippur, and Sukkot, but especially on Hoshana Rabba and Simchat Torah (its rolled form connects it to the Torah scrolls). Hasidic cooks, who love sweet things, often add honey, grated or powdered ginger, chopped apples, and/or raisins to the meat mixture.

• • • • •

6 to 8 servings

INGREDIENTS

1 large head green cabbage; savoy cabbage works well
1 cup rice
2 tablespoons plus 1 teaspoon vegetable oil
1 teaspoon margarine (or additional vegetable oil)
2 or more large cloves garlic, minced
1 large onion, minced
1 pound ground beef, chicken, or turkey
16 ounces tomato sauce, homemade or store-bought
2 sprigs parsley, minced
Salt and pepper to taste
½ teaspoon cumin, paprika, thyme, oregano, or any combination of your
    favorite herbs or spices

Prepare the cabbages leaves. Some cooks find that putting the whole cabbage into the freezer overnight makes the leaves pliable when it is removed and thawed. Others boil the whole cabbage in salted boiling water for one minute, then remove leaves and press them to remove as much water as possible, then freeze and thaw. Either way, separate the softened leaves, keeping them as whole as possible. Smaller or torn leaves can be used to line the baking pan.

Cook the rice in salted water with one teaspoon of vegetable oil until it is just done; do not overcook. Drain completely if all the water is not absorbed.

Preheat oven to 350°F. Grease a nine- by thirteen-inch baking pan with margarine or oil.

Heat the remaining oil in a large skillet. Add the garlic and onion, and sauté over medium heat until soft and fragrant, about two minutes. Add the ground meat; stir and toss until it is thoroughly cooked, about five minutes. Add the rice and stir to combine. Reserve about three-quarters of a cup of tomato sauce. Add the rest of the tomato sauce, parsley, salt, pepper, and cumin, and stir to combine. Reduce heat to low; simmer for about twenty minutes until all the sauce is absorbed and the mixture is fairly cohesive. Taste and adjust seasonings.

Spread your prepared cabbage leave on a table; you should have about twenty-four leaves. Use any extra leaves to line the casserole; pour a quarter cup of the reserved tomato sauce over the bottom. Place about a tablespoon of filling on the center of each leaf; roll into a log and tuck in the ends securely on both sides; each log should be about one and a half by three inches. Place the logs in the baking dish, packing them tightly so that the sides touch; you should have room for about twelve logs. When the first layer is complete, pour another quarter cup of tomato sauce over it and add the second layer, with the logs placed in the opposite direction, so that each log is not directly on top of another one. Pour the last quarter cup of tomato sauce over the top.

Bake in the preheated oven until the sauce is thick and bubbly, around twenty minutes. Cool slightly but serve hot; include some of the cabbage from the bottom of the baking dish on each plate.

• • • • •

Sephardic families also prepare stuffed foods for Sukkot, but—like most Sephardic dishes—their stuffed foods are more complex and contain more layers of flavor than Ashkenazi versions. Middle Eastern spices, such as mint, cumin, coriander, turmeric, cinnamon, nutmeg, and ginger, and grains, such as bulgur and couscous, replace the plain salt, pepper, and rice that are usually enough for eastern European cooks. Several spice mixes and sauces, such as za'atar, harissa, and matboucha (see pages 14–15) provide heat and exotic tastes. Both desserts and main dishes are flavored with sweetened fruit and honey.

One popular dish served throughout fall is *Tomat y Sevoya Reynadas*, a recipe that comes from the island of Rhodes and whose name translates to "tomatoes and onions that are transformed into queens." The vegetables are hollowed out and stuffed with a meat filling; they are then dipped in egg and flour, and fried in a skillet, top down, so that a fried crust forms. Finally, they are simmered in a rich vegetable stock. Kuba (see pages 44–46), dough made of buckwheat stuffed with meat, are also popular on Sukkot.

MEHSHI (STUFFED VEGETABLES)

Mehshi means stuffed vegetables in Arabic; many Middle Eastern countries have their own versions, flavored with local spice mixtures. Zucchini and tomatoes are not the only vegetables used for stuffing; baby eggplants, peppers, and onions are also stuffed. Quince and/or tamarind paste sometimes replaces the dried fruit in this recipe.

• • • • •

4 to 6 servings
INGREDIENTS

Your choice of vegetables for stuffing: zucchini, mushrooms, eggplants, peppers, onions

For the filling:
¼ cup sliced almond or pine nuts (optional)
1 tablespoon oil
2 cloves garlic, minced
1 small onion, minced
1½ pounds ground meat—turkey, beef, chicken, or lamb
½ teaspoon cinnamon
½ teaspoon cumin, more or less to taste
1 tablespoon chopped parsley or cilantro
½ teaspoon salt
¼ cup water
½ cup cooked white or brown rice
¼ cup dried fruit (raisins, prunes, apricots, dates)
½ cup tomato sauce

For the sauce:
3 tablespoons olive oil
3 cloves garlic, minced
1 medium onion, diced
2 tablespoons parsley

1 32-ounce can tomato sauce or puree

¼ cup dried fruit

½ teaspoon cumin

Prepare the vegetables for stuffing. Cut them into serving-size pieces—a large zucchini should be cut into three logs; baby eggplants should be cut in half; remove the stems from mushrooms; remove the top of the pepper and scoop out the seeds. Using a sharp paring knife, remove the center of each piece to create a hole for stuffing (mushrooms come with their own holes)—but make sure there is a strong wall left. Wash the vegetable chunks that are to be stuffed and let them drain in a colander. Chop the pulp that you've carved out into small pieces.

To make the sauce: Heat the oil in a saucepan. Add the garlic and onion, and sauté over medium heat until golden. Add the parsley and toss until wilted. Add the rest of the ingredients and toss to combine. Simmer over low heat while you prepare the rest of the recipe; don't allow it to come to a boil. It should be thick enough to coat a spoon, but not thick enough to eat with a fork. Add water, a tablespoon at a time, if necessary.

To make the filling: If you are using them, toast the nuts in the oven or in a small frying pan over low heat; watch them carefully so that they do not burn and remove them from the heat immediately when they begin to color.

Heat oil in a large skillet. Add the garlic and onion; sauté until they are soft. Add the rest of filling ingredients and the chopped-up vegetables pieces that you removed from the vegetables. Toss until the meat is completely browned and all the other ingredients are incorporated. Allow it to cool slightly.

Place the vegetables at the bottom of a large, shallow saucepan, cavity facing up. If they don't stand up steadily, remove a sliver from the bottom. Stuff each vegetable with the filling; if there is filling left over, roll it into meatballs and bake them in a separate pot or freeze them for another meal. Pour the hot sauce over the vegetables. Bring the sauce to a boil, and then cover the pot and reduce the heat to low. Cook over medium heat, checking frequently to make sure the sauce is not boiling or sticking to the bottom of the pot. Cook for about an hour or until the sauce has thickened but has not burned or become a solid paste.

• • • • •

SHEMINI ATZERET AND SIMCHAT TORAH: SWEET SORROW AND DEEP JOY

After Hoshana Rabba, when the seven days of Sukkot are seemingly over—we come back for another day. Most people, even Jews, don't know about this holiday; those not affiliated with Judaism usually don't know it's happening (except in

New York, where it is celebrated by the suspension of alternate side of the street parking). Rashi, an eleventh-century sage who lived in France and wrote one of the most respected, comprehensive, line-by-line commentaries on the Torah and Talmud, explains the core of the holiday with a parable: "God is like a king who invites all his children to a feast to last for just so many days; when the time comes for them to depart, He says to them: 'My children, I have a request to make of you. Stay yet another day; I hate to see you go'" (Rashi on *Leviticus*, 23:36). Leaving the holiday is sweet sorrow, but is also full of joy.

The holidays of Simchat Torah and Shemini Atzeret are co-joined twins; in Israel (and for some branches of Judaism), they are celebrated on the same day but in all other countries, they each have their own day. This is because rabbis were not sure how to time the holidays outside of Israel—should they observe on the days on which they fell in the Holy Land or on the days on which they fell in the diaspora. Not wanting to err, and with no one to ask who would give a concrete answer, they kept all holidays that required a cessation of work for two days. Orthodox and Conservative Jews have retained these two-day holidays for the first and last days of Sukkot and Passover and for Shavuot; Reform, and other branches of Judaism, have gone back to a single day.

A major component of Shemini Atzeret is the recitation of *Tefilat HaGeshem*, the prayer for rain, in which Jews beg God for rain, which they need for sustenance. The holiday occurs at the beginning of the rainy season, and rain was critical to the agrarian community in Israel. This prayer was not mentioned in the Torah when Shemini Atzeret was designated as holiday, *Tefilat HaGeshem* was written by Rabbi Eleazar Ha-Kallir, a poet who lived in Israel around the seventh century who wrote much of the liturgy that is read on Sukkot.

Although most people don't eat in the Sukkah on Shemini Atzeret, many do visit and have some meals there, just because they enjoy it. Most of the foods that are eaten on the High Holy Days and Sukkot are also eaten on Shemini Atzeret and Simchat Torah.

WATER RITUALS

At some point during the holiday of Sukkot, many families, congregations, schools, and organizations hold a boisterous party called *Simchat Beit HaShoeva*, literally the joy of the drawing of water. It's based on a ritual performed in the Temple during the time of the Talmud. During the holiday of Sukkot, sacrifices of oxen were burnt on the altar every day—a total of seventy oxen were brought—and wine was poured on the altar. But on one of the days, instead of wine, water was poured on the altar. This drawing of water was accompanied by huge feasts, singing, dancing, and jugglers, some of whom twirled lit torches. The event was so awesome that the sages say that "One who has never witnessed *Simchat Beit HaShoeva* has never known true joy."[3] Today, we follow safety regulations and leave out the fire as well as the oxen, but there's great merriment in the dancing, singing, and feasting. There's no specific food served—a look at recent parties shows that pizza, barbecue, and vegan food are all appropriate—as long as it is enjoyable. And it is understood that there's no point in holding the party just to fill our bellies; it's a tradition to invite the needy to partake and to discuss the true meaning of the holiday at this party. It's a perfect example of the all-inclusive nature of Sukkot.

THE JOY OF TORAH

Simchat Torah, the second feature in the double bill that ends Sukkot, is centered around the Torah, the guidebook to Judaism, handed to Moses on Mount Sinai. The word "Torah" means instruction and the books of the Torah contain both a history of the Jews' journey and a moral code. There's a legend that a man once asked Shammai and Hillel, two first-century sages, to teach him the whole Torah while he stood on one leg. Shammai chased him away, telling him that this complex document required a lifetime of study. But gentle, humble Hillel told him: "What you yourself hate, don't do to your neighbor. That is essence of the Torah. Everything else is just commentary. Now go and study it."

The Torah starts with the story about how God created the heavens and the Earth and continues through Abraham's recognition of the one true God and his founding of monotheism. The Jewish journey through slavery in Egypt, the Exodus, wandering in the desert, and preparation for entry into the Promised Land follow in the Five Books of Moses. Other parts of the Torah continue the history of the Jews, from the time of the Prophets and the Kings. But historical reference is only one part of the Torah; it is more valuable for its code of conduct, which, as Hillel pointed out, includes not only instruction on how humans are to approach God, but also how they are to interact with their fellow humans. Throughout the Torah and all its commentary, we learn to respect not only God, but people, animals, and the Earth.

TORAH PARTS

The basic Torah—the words that are inscribed on the scrolls that are paraded about on Simchat Torah—consists of the five books of Moses—*Genesis, Exodus, Leviticus, Numbers,* and *Deuteronomy.* But many include the other sacred books— The Prophets (*Joshua, the Judges, Samuel I and II, Kings I and II, Isiah, Jeremiah, Ezekiel,* and *twelve Minor Prophets*) and Writings (*Psalms, Proverbs, Job, the Megillot—Ruth, Lamentations, Song of Songs, Esther,* and *Ecclesiastes*)—and *Daniel, Ezra* and *Nehemiah,* and *Chronicles.* The Oral Torah, which was given to Moses on Mount Sinai and then memorized and handed down verbally from generation to generation, is also considered to be part of the Torah, along with the version that was finally written down (The Talmud and the *Mishnah*) and the myriad commentaries on all of them.

One of the central beliefs of Jews, particularly Orthodox Jews, is that the written part of the Torah was given to Moses on Mount Sinai. Many historians, however, posit that all of the Torah was transmitted orally to Moses, and then written versions were transcribed in the sixth to fourth centuries BCE, during the time of Babylonian captivity.

When we read from the Torah on Shabbat and holidays, we do it from a special scrolled edition. The words of the Torah are written on a long parchment that is then rolled up on poles; as each section is read, the Torah is unfurled to expose the next part. The Torah is written on the parchment by meticulous scribes called *soferim.* Each letter must be perfect and there are rigid rules for correcting mistakes—no liquid paper is allowed. To show respect for the Torah, it is kept in a special armoire-like cabinet called the *Aron Kodesh,* the holy closet. Usually, just one of the Torah scrolls are removed from the *Aron Kodesh* on a Shabbat or festival, but on Simchat Torah, they all come out and congregants parade around the synagogue or temple carrying them in a ceremony called *hakafot* (circling) that is repeated seven times so that everyone gets a chance.

Before, during, and after the *hakafot,* food was served—the stuffed pastas and vegetables that accompany all Sukkot meals, as well as desserts made with apples. Apples, the ubiquitous fall fruit, are an important part of the *hakafot.* Children who participate in the ceremony are often given Israeli flags to wave, and they are topped with shiny red apples.

To commemorate the Torah's rolled form, cooks looked for foods that furl and unfurl. An example is Rodancha, a coiled eggplant-filled pastry that originated in

Salonika and is now a favorite Syrian Sukkot dish. For Ashkenazi families, rolled sweets such as jelly rolls and rugelach fill the need for furled foods.

RUGELACH

Rugelach have crossed the Jewish food barrier; they can be found in supermarkets in South Dakota, where they're eaten by people who are not specifically looking for Jewish food. They are an American version of a central European pastry called kipfen. The name rugelach is probably connected to the Yiddish *rog* or corner.

Many rugelah (rugelach is plural) recipes use a cream cheese pastry, which is moister than the yeast-based pastry below, but doesn't hold its filling or unroll as well. Modern bakers have been creative with the filling, using all kinds of jams, nuts, spices, and chocolate.

• • • • •

INGREDIENTS

For the dough:
2 tablespoons hot water, just below the boiling point
¼ cup plus 1 teaspoon sugar
2½ teaspoons of dry yeast
4½ cups of flour, more for dusting
1 egg, beaten
¼ cup sugar
4 tablespoons (½ stick) butter or margarine, softened (vegetable oil can be substituted)
¼ cup of warm water, mixed with ¼ cup of milk or milk substitute
Oil, butter, or margarine for greasing the mixing bowl and the baking pan

For the filling and assembly:
¼ cup melted butter, margarine, or vegetable oil
½ cup white sugar
1 tablespoon cinnamon
¼ cup cocoa
2 tablespoons mini chocolate chips, optional

Put the hot water in a small bowl; it should be very hot, but not boiling—too hot will kill the yeast, too cold will prevent it from rising, so getting it right is a skill. Add the teaspoon of sugar and mix to dissolve. Add the yeast; mix well until it starts to bubble. Let it sit for five minutes until it becomes bubbly or foamy.

Put the flour in a large bowl and make a well in the center. Pour the beaten eggs into the well; add the sugar and butter. Add the water/milk, and mix it all together with a spoon. Add the yeast mixture and continue mixing until it forms a soft, shaggy dough. If it's too sticky, add flour, a tablespoon at a time; if it's too dry, add water, a tablespoon at a time. When the dough reaches the point where you can lift it out of the bowl and knead it, place it on a floured board. Knead the dough until it is smooth and shape it into a ball.

Wash, dry, and very lightly oil the mixing bowl. Put the dough into the mixing bowl and cover with a slightly damp cloth. Let it sit in a warm place for about an hour or until it has risen to about double its size. Punch it down, return to bowl, and let it rise again for about half an hour.

Mix the filling ingredients. Preheat the oven to 350°F. Grease two baking pans or cookie sheets.

Cut the dough into two even pieces and form into balls. Flatten one of the pieces and shape it into a disc then roll out to a sixteen-ince circle. Smear half the softened butter, margarine, or oil over the top, then sprinkle/spread about three-eighths of the filling over that. Repeat with the rest of the dough.

Cut each circle, pizza style, into sixteen triangles. Starting with the wide end, roll each triangle. Dip them into the rest of the filling mixture and shake off the excess. Place them on the greased cookie sheet, with space around them.

Bake in the pre-heated oven for about twenty minutes; after fifteen minutes, check frequently to make sure the bottoms are not browning. Take them out of the oven and remove them from the baking pan with a pancake turner immediately—otherwise the sugar will caramelize and they will burn.

When they are cool, store the ones you are not eating right away in zipper bags in the freezer—they have no shelf life.

• • • • •

SUKKOT TRADITIONS AROUND THE WORLD

Italy

In her book, *Classic Italian Jewish Cooking,* Eda Servi Machlin writes about the food and wine served on Sukkot in Pitigliano, the Tuscan village where she grew up. For breakfast, her family ate *ciambelle,* an Italian version of bagels, often smeared with ricotta cheese. When they made *Kiddush* in the sukkah, they drank a sweet wine that her father made from local grapes.

Ukraine

A special adaptation of the spiral Rosh Hashanah challah is made for Hoshana Rabba in the Ukrainian village of Volhynia. According to the Midrash, God hands down his final judgment on Hoshana Rabbah; one end of the spiral is flattened out and shaped into a hand to receive the verdict.

Bukharia
Bukharian Jews decorate their sukkahs with large, fragrant fruits (such as giant melons and grapes) and herbs such as mint and basil to display the season's bounty. A favorite Sukkot dish is *oshi toshi*, grape leaves stuffed with rice and ground meat.

Hungary
Cabbage is reputed to be an antidote to intoxication, so is appropriate for festivals that include a lot of drinking, such as Purim and Simchat Torah. Hungarian Jews serve cabbage dishes, such as cabbage strudel and stuffed cabbage on Simchat Torah.

India
Until the nineteenth century, Indian Jews celebrated a local harvest holiday called *Khiricha San*—the pudding holiday—during which people ate a corn and coconut pudding. Later, they began more traditional observances and built sukkahs with roofs of coconut palm branches.

Germany
In Germany, a dish of cabbage boiled in water is served on Hoshana Rabba. It's called *kohl mit vasser*, which means cabbage with water. The name is similar to *kol mevaser* (the voice of the herald) a prayer read on Hoshana Rabba to speed the coming of the Messiah. The term *Kol Mevaser* is used for many Yiddish and Hebrew periodicals and radio stations, all over the word, dating back to the early twentieth century.

France
One of the oddest decorations was hung on sukkah doors in the Alsace region of France: a red onion with rooster feathers inserted in it. It was supposed to have magical powers to ward off evil.

Syria
Sukkot was an important holiday for the Jews of Aleppo, Syria. Every family would build a sukkah and import *etrogs* from Tripoli and myrtle from Antioch. The whole family would eat in the sukkah, and sometimes even sleep there, leaving to visit other families. Sweet pastries, sherbet, coffee, and candies were always served. Muslim neighbors visited as well.

4

Hanukkah

The Festival of Lights—and Fried Foods

The events that are celebrated on Hanukkah took place around 160 BCE, about three hundred years after Esther starred in the Purim story and her own *Megillah*. But Esther's *Megillah* made it into the Torah and the story of Hanukkah didn't. Instead, it is part of the Apocrypha (an addendum to the holy books) in *The Book of Maccabees I and II*. Hanukkah is only briefly, tangentially mentioned in the *Mishnah*, which was written about 350 years after its events took place. One theory contends that the *Mishnah*'s main editor, Rabbi Yehudah Hanasi (his name means Judah the Prince, and he was a descendant of King David), omitted mentioning the Maccabees because they were not pious enough and because, as *kohanim*, they should not have accepted secular or military rulership. Others believe that after the destruction of the Second Temple, it seemed a bit pointless to dwell on how it was saved in the Hanukkah story. For several millennia, the Hanukkah celebration was barely observed.

There is a short piece about Hanukkah in the Talmud (which was compiled around 200 to 500 CE) focusing on the miracle of the oil rather than on the historical battle:

> Commencing with the [twenty-fifth] day of the month of Kislev there are eight days upon which there shall be neither mourning nor fasting. For when the Greeks entered the Temple, they defiled all the oil that was there. It was when the might of the Hasmonean dynasty overcame and vanquished them that, upon search, only a single cruse of undefiled oil, sealed by the High Priest, was found. In it was oil enough for the needs of a single day. A miracle was wrought and it burned eight days. The next year they ordained these days a holiday with songs and praises. (*Talmud Shabbat*, 21b)

REFLECTIONS

Not by might, nor by power, but by My Spirit.—*Zechariah*, 4:6

In North America, Hanukkah has become, and will likely continue to be, one of the most popular of Jewish holidays, if not the most popular. There are significant reasons for this, including the joyfulness centered on the lights, the exchanging of gifts, playing games, and tasty foods. The only required ritual is to light candles on each of the eight nights and recite blessings. With the addition of singing some Hanukkah songs, the entire ceremony is finished in a matter of minutes.

For more than twenty-one centuries, Jews have celebrated Hanukkah, essentially an oral holiday whereby each and every family is left to retell the story on its own. Unlike Passover, which has its book of rituals (the *Haggadah*) to help guide its story at the seder meal, Hanukkah has the candlelighting ceremony to fulfill its main religious obligation: the kindling of the candles on the *hanukkiah* (Hanukkah candelabrum). Increasing the lights each night serves as a physical reminder of the miracle of Hanukkah, the triumph of the few over the many, the fight for religious freedom in the face of the threat of forced assimilation. These lights also act as a symbol of Jewish resolve to publicize the miracle of Hanukkah to the community at large.

Interestingly, there are some that posit that the origin of the lights is probably not Jewish at all. According to several Bible scholars, in the back of Hanukkah there lies a pagan festival of either the autumn equinox or the winter solstice, both of which occasions were and still are marked in many parts of the world by the lighting of candles or fires.

Hanukkah, in addition to being known as the Festival of Dedication and the Festival of Fried Foods, is also known as *"Hag HaUrim"*—the Festival of Lights. According to a recent astrological theory, Halley's comet came very close to the Earth's atmosphere during the time of the Hanukkah story in 165 BCE. The comet's tail could be seen as a wondrous light in the sky and was likely seen by the Jews after the victory of the Maccabees. One theory has it that because of this great and amazing light in the sky, Hanukkah has come to be known as the Festival of Lights.[1]

Another interesting fact, as recorded in the *Book of Maccabees II* (written in Greek and designed to encourage Egyptian Jewry to adopt the observance of Hanukkah), is that during the rededication of the Temple ceremony after the Maccabean victory, the Jewish people chanted psalms of praise and celebrated by carrying and waving *lulavim* (palm branches) and *etrogim* (citron fruits), which are typically used during the fall festival of Sukkot. It is likely that the first Hanukkah celebration—that first rededication—functioned as a sort of "second Sukkot," a "make-up" Sukkot, since the festival of Sukkot could not be observed that year while the war was in progress.

Hanukkah has encouraged many a small group to fight against injustice and oppression. It has been a source of inspiration in the movement to liberate the Land of Israel and establish it as an independent state. It has stimulated the Jews to withstand assimilation and the temptation of false gods, and to champion the ideals of one's heritage in the midst of an overwhelming majority. And it has been a reminder that miracles are possible, as conveyed in the prophetic lesson recited on the Sabbath of Hanukkah, "Not by might, nor by power, but by My spirit, says the Lord of Hosts." The sages transformed the text into a divine warning: Groups aiming to "force the end" through military power should reconsider such plans of action.

The fundamental message of Hanukkah is very much a spiritual one. In a time of darkness, people had the courage to struggle for freedom. Theirs was a victory of the weak over the strong, the few over the many, and the righteous over the arrogant. It was a victory for all ages and all peoples.

THE HANUKKAH STORY

The story of Hanukkah is political and military, with a miracle tacked on to the end. The root cause of the main event was the defeat of King Ptolemy of Egypt by King Antiochus III the Great of Syria around 200 BCE, which put Judea under the rule of the Seleucid Empire of Syria. For many years, the Jews lived in peace under the empire. Religious Jews were allowed to follow their faith, while a growing sector of secular Jews accepted Hellenization. In doing so, they followed the ideas of Greek culture, which included polytheism and a passion for beauty, athleticism, and excellence. But when Antiochus III died, his son, Antiochus IV Epiphanes, sided with the Hellenizers; he invaded Judea and outlawed all practice of Judaism. Studying the Torah, circumcision, and kosher slaughter were banned; non-compliance was punishable by death. Secularization was not going quite fast enough, so Antiochus sent bands of soldiers to towns where the faithful still lived. They set up altars and prepared pork dishes, and offered the choice of betraying the faith or dying. Many accepted death.

When the band of soldiers reached a town called Modi'in in the hills of Jerusalem, they encountered Mattathias, a Jewish leader who chose neither betrayal nor death. Instead, he killed both a Jew who was prepared to break his faith and a soldier who was forcing him to do so. His five sons—Eliezer, Simon, Johanan, Jonathan, and Judah—rallied around him. In what had to be one of the most dramatic scenes ever, Mattathias raised his sword and called out to the townspeople: "Whoever is for God, come with me." And many did. They ran for the hills to hide and plan.

The faithful, especially the sons of Mattathias, acquired the name of Maccabees. Some say the word is an acronym for Mattathias' slogan: *Mi Kamocha Ba-elim Adonai* (Who compares among gods to God). Others say the name comes from the word *macav*, or hammer.

And hammer they did. The small band of amateur soldiers defeated every army that was sent to conquer them. At first, the king sent small cohorts; by the end, huge armies, with tens of thousands of trained soldiers facing the rebels. And the rebels won, over and over, until they chased the invaders from their land and recaptured the holy city of Jerusalem. They entered the Temple, ready to resume services and found a mess—desecrated by partying and debauchery, with only a single vial of oil left intact for lighting the menorah (the eight-light candelabra used in the Temple). The small vial contained only enough oil to keep the menorah lit for a single day. And it would take eight days to produce more.

Up until this point, all parts of the Hanukkah story fall in the realm of possibility. The leaders had to be extraordinarily skillful, dedicated, charismatic, and lucky, and the enemy had to make mistakes—but it could have happened, and it did. But when the menorah burned for a full eight days on a day's worth of oil, a miracle was declared. And that is the miracle of Hanukkah. The Temple was rededicated—the root of the word "Hanukkah" is renewal—on the twenty-fifth day of Kislev. Mattathias' sons and their descendants—the Hasmonean dynasty—went on to rule Israel for almost five hundred years, until the destruction of the Temple in 70 CE. And the holiday of Hanukkah was established to commemorate the events.

APOCRYPHA

The story of Hanukkah as told in *Books I and II of The Maccabees*, appears in an appendix to the Torah called the Apocrypha (from a Greek word meaning "hidden"), a collection of writings that are more commonly used in Christian, rather than Jewish, teachings. Many New Testament works, including *The Book of Common Prayer*, originated in the Apocrypha. Although the Apocrypha is not officially included in the Jewish version of the Old Testament, some parts are included in Jewish liturgy and relate historical Jewish events. Some of it was written in Hebrew in the time of the Second Temple, including the *Book of Judith*, which was later connected to Hanukkah even though Judith probably lived several hundreds of years before the Maccabees.

There was no mention of Hanukkah food in the Talmud, and very little elaboration on the military feats. When the *Shulchan Aruch* (The Code of Jewish Law) was written in the sixteenth century, food is mentioned only to say that "the large extravagant meals that we make on Hanukkah are considered a voluntary meal; for they did not establish (a decree) to eat a meal or to be festive." Eating on Hanukkah is considered "a small mitzvah" (*Shulchan Aruch, Orach Chayim* 670:1). Most of the Hanukkah rules in the *Shulchan Aruch* refer to how, when, and where to light the candles, not to foods that are to be eaten or the glory of the Maccabean victory.

No specific foods were connected to Hanukkah when the holiday was first decreed. But, though the Maccabees and the generations that followed had never heard of *latkes* and *sufganiyot*, they did know how to spread out a feast. Cooking was fairly sophisticated by their time. Oils, both olive and sesame, were used to season and cook. Meats—mostly goat and lamb—were cooked in a variety of ways, mostly roasted on spits. Vegetables, such as peas, mushrooms, radishes, leeks, and wild greens, were available and food was spiced with parsley, fenugreek, mint, thyme, and coriander. The process of fermentation had existed for about seven thousand years, so there was bread (though it was probably flat, like pita) and plenty of wine. Lentil stews were filling and nutritious; we know that lentils were popular from the story of Cain and Abel. And, in the land of milk and honey, dairy products and sweetness, sometimes combined, rounded out the meals (though the laws of *kashrut* meant that dairy was never combined with meat). There may have been a small, sweet deep-fried cake puff, similar to ancient Greek *loukomades*— one of the earliest sweets that people ate—which were precursors to *sufganiyot*. So even the understated celebration of Hanukkah probably led to some heavy-duty cooking, and we do know that beautiful menorahs were crafted and displayed in every Jewish community

HANUKKAH FOOD IN THE MIDDLE AGES

After the destruction of the Temple, the Jews scattered throughout the Middle East and small new Jewish communities were established in Europe. Although these communities were far from Israel, they continued to celebrate Hanukkah. Two documents—a poem called *Even Bohan*[2] by a French-Italian rabbi and a copy of the *Book of Judith* with annotations by an anonymous writer—give us evidence of the foods eaten on Hanukkah around the thirteenth through fifteenth centuries in Europe. In these writings, the authors list foods that were eaten on festivals and make recommendations that changed the menu for Hanukkah. In both documents, it is clear that fried foods; cheese and other dairy products; honey; breads; a porridge made of flour, honey, and oil; and cakes dipped in honey were usually part of holiday feasting. Frying pans have a central role in food preparation, and there were noodles and both boiled and fried dough. Something called *qreplin* are mentioned; they seem to be precursors of *kreplach* (the Jewish form of ravioli). Some of these foods appear in these Jewish texts before they were recorded in non-Jewish documents.

But even though a significant list of Jewish foods was compiled, and even though the beautiful elaborate menorahs that have survived indicate that Hanukkah was important, it didn't hold a candle to Rosh Hashanah, Purim, or Passover in significance to the Jewish calendar.

HANUKKAH FINDS ITS GROOVE

When and why, then, did Hanukkah become the vital holiday that we celebrate today?

Two elements came into play, in two different time periods. First, as Christmas celebrations became more elaborate and commercial in the last few hundred years, Jewish families looked for an alternative so they would not feel left out of the merriment. Hanukkah occurs around the same time of year and filled the bill. The tradition of giving gifts for Christmas—based on the myrrh and frankincense that the Wise Men gave to Mary and on pagan rituals—melded with the Jewish tradition of giving *gelt* (money) to the needy, and giving some to children, intending that they would pass it on and learn about giving charity. Some purists feel that foil-wrapped chocolate coins, menorah-shaped cookies, and daily gifts lead us away from Judaism and borrow from the Christian holidays. But Hanukkah gift-giving is justified by many who believe that making holidays nicer will bring people, especially children, closer to the religion; even ultra-orthodox Jews exchange gifts (or give them to children) on Hanukkah.

Hanukkah got another bump in popularity when Zionists began flocking to Israel. A small band of dedicated Jewish soldiers, operating with extraordinary military skill (and under the protection of God) had vanquished an army that was many times their size and won back control of their sacred places—how could that story not resonate with the early pioneers? Jewish leaders in the time of the Talmud looked down on the Maccabees; Zionist leaders revered them. Shaul Tchernichowski, a Russian-born poet and doctor who moved to Palestine in the 1930s, wrote a poem comparing the pioneers to them, declaring that each pioneer is a Maccabee.[3] Menashe Ravina worked them into *"Mi Yimalel"* (Who Can Recount?), a folk song that has become the anthem of Hanukkah, in which he says that there is a Macabbee, a hero, in every generation. Israel's favorite beer and soccer team are named Maccabee. It is no wonder that the holiday that celebrates them is celebrated with enthusiasm.

FOOD BECOMES A FACTOR

After several centuries of celebrating Hanukkah with songs and prayers, food became an integral part of the holiday following the publication of a poem by an influential rabbi named Kalonymus ben Kalonymus ben Meir who lived in western Europe from the late twelfth through the mid-thirteenth centuries. Kalonymus was a member of a rabbinical dynasty that led Jewish communities in Greece, Italy, France, and Germany starting in the ninth century and extending through the six- teenth. Members of Kalonymus families were *halachists*, philosophers and poets as well as spiritual leaders; they are responsible for a significant portion of the liturgy and for the development of Jewish communities in Germany.

Though he lived at the very start of the Renaissance, Kalonymus ben Kalonymus ben Meir was a full-blown Renaissance man. He was born in Arles and studied in Salonica, Greece. He studied medicine; translated treatises by Euclid, Galen, and Aristotle into Hebrew; and wrote original works on astronomy, arithmetic, geometry, and ethics, as well as a comic parody called *Masseket Purim*. He lived in Rome for many years, and while he was there, he wrote a book called *Even Bohen*, in which he included a poem that listed appropriate foods for Purim and Hanukkah. For Hanukkah, he recommended fried foods in honor of the miracle of the oil that lasted for eight days:

In honor of the Hasmonean, . . . the important women should gather
Knowledgeable about making food [*biryah*] and cooking *levivot*
Large and round, the whole size of the frying pan . . .
And above all they should take fine wheat flour
And make *sufganin* and *isqaritin* from it
And the drinking should be what is proper to festivals, with joy over every single cup.[4]

Many of the words that Kalonymus used in this poem don't have the same mean- ing as they do today. In his time, *levivot* referred to any food cooked in a frying pan; *sufganim* were cakes baked of soft risen dough; and *isquartin* were "dough products baked on a brazier, eaten hot and dipped in sweet or honeyed wine."[5] But the intent was clear—fried is right for Hanukkah.

The poem went viral, at least as viral as possible in his era. Over the next sev- eral decades, Jews designated a fried cheese pancake that was popular in Italy as a Hanukkah dish and it, along with other fried foods, appeared in many reports of Hanukkah celebrations.

THE EVOLUTION OF THE LATKE

The latke, and fried food in general, was not new in Kalonymus' time; it was a step in a long timeline of cooking history. About 1.9 million years ago—well before modern brains evolved—early humanoids realized that applying heat to food made it easier to chew. This was a life-changing development. It meant that the species could spend less time nourishing itself and more time honing other skills; they could also ingest more calories, which helped their brains grow larger. Cooking became an activity; groups set up places to control fires on which they could heat their food. The earliest campfire, found in a cave in South Africa, is about a million years old. Another very early site, Gesher Bnot Yaacov in Israel, holds the remnants of multiple hearths and dates back about eight hundred thousand years. Many millennia later, someone found that placing food on a heated rock was better than placing it directly on a flame—less food was lost and it tasted better. And after another several hundred thousand years, around 5000 BCE, the frying pan was invented in Mesopotamia (along with many other accouterments of modern life such as wheels, chariots, time, agriculture, and mathematics), which let people fry more efficiently.

At first, animal fats such as lard were used for frying, but by 3000 BCE, soybean oil was being pressed in China. Olive oil was mentioned in ancient Greek recipes around 1000 BCE. The Torah mentions bread cooked on a griddle, and by the Roman Age, around 100 CE, an inventive cook realized that unborn bird embryos could be used in a multitude of ways. Eggs had been eaten since the dinosaurs used them for nourishment, but it wasn't until much later that the many ways that eggs could enhance other foods, particularly grains, was discovered. The omelet and egg-based breads and cakes opened up new directions. Eggs also found their way into pancakes, lightening them up.

The potato pancakes that are ubiquitous on Hanukkah today are relatively recent, but the pancake itself—ground or grated grains or vegetables, combined with liquid to make a batter, which is then heated on a flat surface until it becomes a solid, flat cake—has been around since the Stone Age. Primitive humanoids began making tools from stone around three million years ago, when their diet consisted of mostly meat. But by thirty thousand years ago, they were grinding grains—residue of flours on grinding stones dating back that far have been found in Italy, Russia, and other European and Near East sites. By that time, humans were consuming plants as well as meat, giving themselves a more sustainable, nutritious diet than protein alone could provide. Eating plant material was not a new concept—herbivorous dinosaurs grew to mammoth size on plants alone—but until the Neanderthal Age, precursors to humans ate mostly protein. Somewhere around that time, give or take a few dozen millennia, they learned to cultivate the grains they needed, to mix them with water or other liquids, and to bake them or fry them on heated, greased rocks.

Scientists learned a lot from the mummified remains of Otzi the Iceman, a 5,300-year-old frozen Neanderthal skeleton that was found in a glacier in the Oztal Alps in 1991. Otzi's stomach contained the remains of ibex and deer meat, but he had also eaten ground einkorn wheat bran. Bits of char on the bran showed that the wheat had come in contact with fire. Though Otzi had no pancake turner at his disposal, he knew how to create some kind of bread or pancake.

By the Golden Age of Greece, pancakes had become more palatable; they were sweetened with honey and fried in olive oil. By then, griddles were available and frying was popular. The sweet cakes, called *kreion*, were combined with cakes of sweet cheese. Still, nothing was added to leaven them and they remained flat and hard. During the Roman Age, eggs were added to the recipe—as seen in Apicus' fourth-century cookbook—and fluffiness ensued. But these pancakes disappeared from menus after the Fall of Rome and for the next several centuries, pancakes reverted to their chewy, heavy form. Ground grains such as rye and barley were often included in the pancake batter.

During the Crusades, cooking techniques and cookware (such as terracotta griddles) that had long been popular in the Middle East and north Africa were brought to Europe. In the late Middle Ages, Italian cooks again began to add milk, cheese, and butter to their batters. Pancakes became a delicacy that spread throughout Europe. It was around that time that Rabbi Kalonymus suggested that fried foods be served on Hanukkah in honor of the miracle of the oil that lasted for eight days. The obvious candidate was a luscious ricotta cheese pancake (ricotta is a fresh, whole-milk cheese made with whey that was left over from making harder cheeses; it dates back to the Bronze Age, about 2000 BCE, when ceramic vessels used to boil milk began to appear). These ricotta pancakes were served on Hanukkah tables throughout the Middle Ages and well up into the nineteenth century; they are still a well-known dish in Italy today.

ITALIAN RICOTTA PANCAKES

When potato pancakes took over as the prime Hanukkah food, these lovely, light pancakes lost favor; it's time to bring them back. They are faster and easier to make than potato pancakes and are much lower on the glycemic scale. They fry up beautifully in just a minute or two and need only a fraction of the oil that potato pancakes require.

Though whole-milk ricotta yields the best results, part-skim ricotta and even cottage cheese are acceptable substitutes. If you prefer to use whole-wheat flour, substitute half the white flour with whole wheat—but you'll lose some of the lightness. If you have an oil mister, you can use it to grease the pan—you don't need a heavy coating of oil.

You'll probably need to make them in two batches unless you have a double-size griddle. But they cook so quickly that the first batch will still be hot when the second batch is done. In Italy today, these pancakes are served year-round and on Hanukkah. Rice pancakes (*fritelli di risi por Chanuka*—rice, mixed with raisins, pine nuts, eggs, and lemon juice) are sometimes substituted, or served with them. Hungarian Jews in America eat cheese pancakes as well.

• • • • •

12 pancakes, 4 servings

INGREDIENTS

1 egg, beaten
¼ cup ricotta cheese, preferably whole-milk
¼ cup all-purpose flour
½ teaspoon salt
¼ teaspoon freshly ground black or white pepper
¼ teaspoon baking powder
1 teaspoon vegetable oil
1 tablespoon of honey, optional
½ teaspoon cinnamon, optional

Combine the egg, ricotta, flour, salt, pepper, and baking powder in a bowl just until the flour is absorbed; do not overmix. Heat a griddle and spread or spray the oil over it until it forms a light coat. Drop the batter onto the griddle by the tablespoonful. Let them cook for about a minute, then flip one with a pancake turner to test; if it's not lightly browned, leave it for another thirty seconds—these cook quickly, don't let them get too brown. When they're all flipped, the second side will cook in less than a minute. If desired, drizzle honey over them and sprinkle with cinnamon. Serve immediately.

• • • • •

Cheese pancakes were the fried food of choice on the Hanukkah table for several hundred years; they traveled with Jewish communities up through Spain and Italy to central Europe when Jews were invited to live there. Other ingredients were added, including turnips, cabbage, and radishes. Sometimes, latkes were made with flour, barley, or lentils. In Russia, blini, silver-dollar-sized buckwheat pancakes, took the place of vegetable latkes on Hanukkah and year-round. Because of prohibition of mixing meat with dairy, vegetable pancakes—fried in schmaltz (animal fat)—were served with meat meals and they became more common because butter was scarce and expensive. There were no potatoes in sight.

That's because there were no potatoes in Europe at all. Hard to believe that this staple vegetable, which we think of as old-fashioned and traditional, did not appear in Europe until the end of the sixteenth century. For a few hundred years, they received a mixed reception. Though scientists recognized their nutritional value (an acre of potato plants yields double the calories of an acre of grains) and the enthusiasm of some farmers, there was no wide-scale production of potatoes. They were grown mostly in home plots and used for animal feed.

Then, in the 1830s, grain and many vegetable crops failed across Europe. Suddenly, the potato was the best game in town and it took only about a decade for it to become the major source of nutrition throughout Europe. From Ireland to Russia, fields were converted from grains to potatoes and both peasants and landowners learned to love them. Somewhere around that time, someone tried them out for latkes, and they quickly surpassed cheese, turnips, and everything else as the go-to latke variety.

Jews were not the only ones eating potato pancakes in the nineteenth century. They were called *kartoffelpuffer* in Austria, *reibekuchen* in Germany, and *placki ziemniaczane* in Poland. There are versions outside Europe as well, such as the Iranian *kotlet*. The British called them tattie fish because they looked like fried fish; Ireland's boxty is similar. The term "latke" first appeared in 1927, in an article in *American Mercury Magazine*. It may be derived from the Greek word *eladion* (oil cake) or the Russian word *oladya*, a wheat pancake.

Immigrants brought latkes to America in the late nineteenth century; recipes for potato pancakes appear in cookbooks written by German-Jewish authors: *Aunt Babette's* (1899) and *The Settlement House Cookbook* (1901). Latkes—and Jewish culture in general—reached prime-time popularity when they were discussed on the radio and television show "Meet the Goldbergs" which started in 1931 and lasted for twenty years. According to one Goldberg character, "Vhen de latkes get cold, dey ain't got no taste."[6]

LATKE AND VARIATIONS

There are many ways to make latkes; in some families, there are strong opinions on which way is best. One main area of contention is the leavening agent; some latketeers find that a pinch of baking powder works best; others add an egg. In a recent very unscientific taste test, it was determined that the leavening agent makes very little difference—except to the most strongly opinionated—and does not affect crispiness, greasiness, lightness, or taste. What does make a difference: Using fresh, high-quality starchy potatoes (such as russet, Idaho, or Yukon Gold, but not waxy ones such as fingerlings) and a light, neutral oil; making sure the oil is very hot (but not smoking) before the batter is added; and giving the latkes time to cook.

The basic recipe below is for purists: potatoes, oil, a leavening, salt, and pepper. Many people grate some onion in with the potatoes and still consider themselves purists.

• • • • •

2 servings for each pound of potatoes or other vegetables

INGREDIENTS

3 pounds of potatoes
1 large egg or ¼ teaspoon baking soda
1 teaspoon salt
¼ teaspoon pepper
About 3 tablespoons vegetable oil

Grate the potatoes in a food processor or by hand on the small holes of a box grater. (Some people think that knuckle blood is part of the mix, but that's probably just a tradition; if you're busy or don't want the pain, the food processor is just fine.) When the potatoes are all grated, let them sit for about ten minutes and then pour off the water; if you leave them longer than that, they turn brown. While the potatoes are sitting, add the leavening (egg or baking soda), salt, and pepper, and mix well. Heat your largest frying pan for about thirty seconds, then add vegetable oil, just a solid coating on the bottom—these are not deep fried. When the oil is very hot but not smoking, drop one to two tablespoons of batter for each latke. About eight will fit on an eleven-inch pan; don't crowd them or it will be too hard to turn them. When the edges are brown—don't be impatient, these are raw potatoes and need a few minutes—flip them and fry the other side. Flip again if the first side is not crispy and brown. When both sides are nice and brown, turn them onto a plate lined with paper towels to drain and serve hot.

Variations: You can grate other vegetables with the potatoes. Sweet potatoes, beets, parsnips, carrots, winter squash, zucchini, greens, and kohlrabi can all be mixed with the potatoes. Seasonings, including garlic, ginger, curry powder, or any of your favorite herbs and spices, can be added as well.

A few combinations—for all, grate the vegetables, add egg or baking soda (one egg or a pinch of baking soda for about three pounds of vegetables), salt, and pepper:

1 pound cubed winter squash; 1 pound chopped kale; ½ pound carrots; 1 small onion; season with thyme and oregano

1 pound sweet potatoes; 1 pound potatoes; 2 small apples; 1 shallot; 1 teaspoon grated ginger; ½ teaspoon brown sugar

1 pound cubed pumpkin or butternut squash; 2 tablespoons orange zest; 2 tablespoons brown sugar; 1 cup of flour; ½ teaspoon cinnamon; ¼ cup raisins; ¼ cup almonds or pine nuts (this dish is called *zucca baruca* (holy pumpkin) in Italy

Toppings

Dollops of sour cream or applesauce are traditional toppings, and there's absolutely nothing wrong with them. But if you want to be creative, top with guacamole, tahini paste, any of the myriad salsa recipes, horseradish sauce, salmon roe (on top of sour cream), shaved gravlax, or a sprinkling of chopped mixed herbs.

• • • • •

OLIVES AND OIL

People grew olives before they could speak—the olive tree, *Olea europaea*, was the first tree ever cultivated by humans. Wild olive trees date back about twelve thousand years; they originated somewhere along the Mediterranean coast, either in Greece or in what is now the Middle East. By eight thousand years ago, primitive humans were gathering wild olives and by six thousand years ago they were planting trees. Olive trees were considered so important in Israel that cutting them down was forbidden.

Olives were first eaten as fruit, even though the fruits were bitter. By 4000 BCE, humans figured out how to press them for oil—small bottles used for olive oil, called amphora, date back to that time. The first pressings were done by hand, but cultivation and trading of trees and oil became big business. Crete, Syria, and pre-Israel Canaan became centers for olive oil production and trade. Olive oil is mentioned in *Exodus*, which is usually dated around 1100 BCE: "And thou shalt command the children of Israel, that they bring unto thee pure olive oil beaten for the light, to cause a lamp to burn continually" (*Exodus*, 27:20). The most primitive olive oil presses date back four thousand years ago; by 100 CE, the presses were everywhere and producing millions of gallons of oil. Archaeologists have found sites filled with olive pits near Mount Carmel.

Besides its use for eating and frying, olive oil was a part of many religious ceremonies. People purified themselves by anointing themselves with olive oil. Pure olive oil was used to light the menorah in the temple—a key element in the Hanukkah story.

The olive tree is also the longest-lived tree in existence. Short, gnarled olive trees dot modern landscapes, living relics of ancient times. The olive groves in the hills of Jerusalem are about two thousand years old. Although olive oil production flagged in Israel for several millennia, it is being revived today. About fifteen thousand tons of extra-virgin olive oil are sold in or exported from Israel every year.[7]

BEYOND LATKES

Latkes were not the only traditional Hanukkah food in Ashkenazi homes in the nineteenth and twentieth centuries. Geese were popular main dishes for Hanukkah at meat meals for the same reason that they were often part of the Christmas meal: After growing fat over the summer and fall, early winter was the best time to slaughter them. In addition to the centerpiece roast goose, *gribenes* (also called *grieven*) were a holiday delicacy. In the spirit of never throwing anything away, Jewish cooks fried bits of goose skin in rendered goose fat; though quite unhealthy, the result is delicious (and similar to pork cracklings). Geese are hard to find these days, but chicken fat and skin provide great *gribenes*.

There are two ways to obtain free chicken fat—or schmaltz, which means fat but has acquired a host of other meanings. If you make chicken soup, simply let it rest in the refrigerator for a few hours. The schmaltz will rise to the top and can be skimmed off in a clump. Or, cut away all visible fat from a chicken (or goose or duck). Melt the fat in a pan and then pick out any gristle or meat. To make the *gribenes*, cut the skin into bits (about two inches by two inches, but make no effort to keep them uniform). Heat the fat in a frying pan until it's melted and bubbling; add chopped onions, the bits of skin, salt, and pepper, and stir fry until they are crispy. *Gribenes* can be eaten as a side dish or added to soups and stews when you're not counting calories, fat, or cholesterol.

Gribenes were sometimes used as a special Hanukkah filling for *varenicki*, a filled pastry that was popular in central Europe, particularly Ukraine and western Russia. They are called *pierogi* in Poland and were filled with meat or potatoes, then were boiled or fried. They are relatives to *kreplach* (see pages 66–71) and all the other filled dough recipes such as ravioli, empanadas, and Chinese dumplings. On Hanukkah, a fried dairy version was also served.

The menu in Sephardic homes was and is somewhat different. Fried fish is more likely to be the main dish, accompanied by vegetable side dishes such as leek fritters (see page 61) and cauliflower salad. Cheese, including Kasser (an aged hard cheese from Turkey or Greece), nuts, citrus fruits, and dried fruit round out the meal, which is finished with the local form of sweet fried dough or doughnut— *sfenj* in Morocco, *bumuelos* in Turkey, *zangoola* in Iraq, and *zvingous* in Greece. Sesame seed candy (*sukariyot soomsoom*) are popular all year in Sephardic homes, but especially on Hanukkah.

THE HEROINES OF HANUKKAH, AND CHEESECAKE

Hanukkah is known as a woman-centric holiday. Unlike many other Jewish laws that don't obligate women, women are required to be part of the lighting of Hanukkah candles and to avoid work while they are lit. (Nothing stops them from standing over a hot stove and frying latkes for everyone, though.) Some say that this inclusion of women, even in the most Orthodox circles, is to commemorate the roles of two heroic women whose names are associated with Hanukkah. The stories of both are told in the Apocrypha.

The first is Judith, a beautiful widow from an important family. She lived during the sixth century BCE, when Nebuchadnezzar, a Babylonian tyrant, reigned over Israel. Holofernes, one of Nebuchadnezzar's generals, was terrorizing Jewish communities and Judith decided to put a stop to it. She used her beauty and Holofernes' attraction to her to gain entrance to his tent; she brought a basket filled with wine, salty cheese, and warm milk with her. Holofernes enjoyed the food and drink, then, as expected, became drowsy. At that point, Judith pulled a knife from her basket, chopped off his head, and carried the severed head back to show her neighbors. The story has been depicted in several deliciously gory artworks, including a sculpture by Donatello and paintings by Cranach, Titian, Caravaggio, Orazio Gentileschi, and his daughter Artemisa Gentileschi, who devoted a whole series to the subject. Gustav Klimt created a modern version.

Judith lived around four hundred years before the Maccabees, but her story somehow became enfolded in the story of Hanukkah (possibly because both appear in the Apocrypha). It is in Judith's honor that dairy foods—cheese latkes, cheesecakes, that dollop of sour cream—are included in Hanukkah feasts, although beheadings are no longer part of the tradition.

The story of Hannah (sometimes called Miriam) is related in the *Book of Maccabees II*. When Antiochus was forcing Jews to betray their faith by eating pork and worshipping idols, he arrested Hannah's seven sons, who ranged in age from young adulthood to just seven years old. One by one, he offered them bribes to follow his orders, then tortured them. One by one, they refused and died, right down to the seven-year-old. Their mother watched and supported their decisions and has been lauded as a heroine for her unflinching faith.

SWEETS AND SPONGES

Dessert is an important part of the Hanukkah meal in both Ashkenazi and Sephardic homes and followed the dairy-and-fried regimen. Cheesecake, best known for its Shavuot appearance (see pages 210–211), is also a Hanukkah treat. But more common are the many kinds of fried doughnuts that appeared in dozens of variations throughout the Jewish world, culminating in the *sufganiyot* that take over every bakery in Israel for the eight days of Hanukkah.

The term *sufganiya*—most sources say the root of the word is related to the word "sponge"—was coined in modern Israel, but the jelly doughnuts that fall under this term have been known in many parts of the world for centuries. And the tradition of sweetening and frying dough is even older and more widespread.

One strand of the story involves churros, long chunks of dough fried in oil, then coated with sugar and cinnamon. Competing legends tell of churros being invented by Spanish nomads who had no access to bread-making equipment or being brought to Spain from China by Portuguese explorers. In the Chinese version of the story, churros are based on *youtiao*, a fried breadstick that is served for breakfast throughout southeast Asia. In any case, the recipe became more sophisticated as the sweetened dough was extruded through a star-shaped die. Churros became a beloved delicacy throughout Spain and remain a staple in Spain, South America, and the southwestern United States.

Jews played a role in spreading this dish to other parts of Europe. When they were expelled from Spain in 1492, Jews brought their favorite foods with them to Italy, including churros. Italian chefs adopted and adapted the tasty tidbit. Its reach went even further when Pantarelli, one of Catherine de Medici's chefs, picked it up and began experimenting with it. When Catherine went to Paris to marry Henry II, she took that chef with her, and he took his churros; there, he added eggs to the recipe to invent a precursor to *pate de choux*, the basis for many French dessert recipes right up to modern times. (French food historians disagree with this story, rejecting the idea that Italian chefs influenced French cuisine.)

Meanwhile, in eastern Europe, deep-fried dough was taking shape as a jelly-filled doughnut. In the first cookbook printed, a German book called *Kuchenmeisteri*, there was a recipe for *gefullte krapfen*, a stuffed doughnut. As time went by, the price of sugar decreased and the doughnuts became sweeter and more popular (it probably didn't hurt that they were no longer called *krapfen*). By the beginning of the twentieth century, fried doughnuts filled with jelly and called Berliners were a popular New Year's Eve dessert. A similar confection called *ponchki* were popular in Poland. When Zionists from eastern Europe began to flow into what was then Palestine in the 1920s, they brought these pastries with them—where they were adopted as the official dessert of Israel's Hanukkah, in large part because of a campaign by the Histadrut.

The Histadrut, Israel's national labor union, was founded in 1920, well before the State of Israel was established in 1948. Its mission was to promote the welfare of the immigrant workers who were beginning new lives under the British mandate. The Histadrut became one of the driving forces of Israeli nationalism and remains so today (about one-third of Israel's population are members of the Histadrut). The union, led by David Ben-Gurion who would become Israel's first prime minister, actively sought work for its members, including the bakers who had come from Europe. They saw an opportunity in the *sufganiya*. Unlike latkes, which could be easily fried at home, *sufganiyot* required some equipment—deep fryers, syringes. The Histadrut began to advertise *sufganiyot* as the perfect food for Hanukkah. And it worked. Today, about fifteen million *sufganiyot* are sold in Israel during each Hanukkah season, about three for every resident. Other than to those with American or European backgrounds, latkes are little known in Israel—it's the *sufganiya* that heralds the holiday. And although many Sephardic communities retain their own doughnut traditions, they eat *sufganiyot* as well.

SUFGANIYOT

• • • • •

Makes 12 to 16 sufganiyot

INGREDIENTS

4½ teaspoons (2 packets) yeast
¼ cup warm milk or water
¾ cup milk (very hot, but not boiling; whole or 2 percent)
1 cup + 2 tablespoons flour, divided
3 egg yolks
½ teaspoon vanilla or almond extract
1 teaspoon grated lemon or orange rind (optional)
⅓ cup sugar
4 tablespoons butter, softened
Vegetable oil for frying
½ cup jam
Confectioners' sugar for dusting

In a small bowl, mix the yeast and the warm milk or water until the yeast is dissolved. Leave it in a warm place until it is foamy or bubbly.

Meanwhile, combine the hot milk and a half cup of flour in a large bowl and beat until smooth; allow it to cool. Add the yeast mixture to the flour mixture, stir to combine, and set aside in a warm place for thirty minutes.

When the dough is ready, add the egg yolks, vanilla or almond extract, lemon or orange rind, and sugar and stir to combine. Then add another half cup of flour and the butter, and mix to combine. Transfer the dough onto a floured board and knead for about five to ten minutes until it is smooth and elastic (you can also make the dough in a food processor with a dough hook). Add the remaining two tablespoons flour if needed, or even a bit more. Wash, dry, and oil the bowl, then return the dough to the bowl and cover with a damp cloth or plastic wrap. Leave the bowl in a warm place for about forty-five minutes or until doubled in bulk.

Form the dough into balls about one inch in diameter and let them rise for about thirty minutes. Add vegetable oil to a large pot until it comes about three inches up the sides. Heat to 300°F and then lower the heat so that oil stays at just under boiling. Prepare a plate lined with paper towels. Drop the dough balls into the oil; they can be close but not touching and remember that they will puff up as they cook. You may have to fry them in batches. Fry until they are light golden brown on all sides; they should turn on their own, but if they don't, help them along with a wooden spoon. Remove them with a slotted spoon and let them drain on paper towels.

When the *sufganiyot* are cool enough to handle, insert about a teaspoon of jam into each by injecting with a syringe or icing tube. If you don't have one, cut a small hole into each *sufganiya* with a small knife and push the filling in with a spoon. Sprinkle with or roll in confectioners' sugar and serve immediately.

• • • • •

MORE FRIED DESSERTS

There are many local versions of sweet fried dough in Sephardic communities; most start with a yeast dough. The ones called *bumuelos*—they were brought from Spain to the Ottoman Empire and spread throughout north Africa and the Middle East—use dough that is highly flavored; liqueurs such as ouzo, arac, anisette or Pernod, or fennel or sesame seeds are incorporated into the dough before it is deep-fried. *Zelebi* (also called *Zlabia*) are based on a north African pastry that is so ancient that it appears on murals in the tombs of the pharaohs. *Zelebi* batter is squeezed into hot oil and, if the cook is adept, it forms a rosette; they're a Hanukkah treat all over the Middle East, though in Iraq, they're called *zangoola*. In Moroccan Jewish neighborhoods, *sfenj* are eaten in just about every home on Hanukkah. They're different from many of the other fried dough recipes in that there is no sugar in the batter; the sweetening is done to the already-fried pastry. Often, the dough is flavored with orange juice and/or rind, particularly with Jaffa oranges that are abundant around Hanukkah time.

HANUKKAH TRADITIONS AROUND THE WORLD

India
In the Jewish communities of India, both the lighting ceremonies and the food conform to Indian norms. Menorahs are made of bronze, which is more common and cheaper in India than silver. Instead of candles or olive oil, wicks are dipped in coconut oil—there are no olive groves in India. Indian Jews eat fried foods and dairy on Hanukkah, but *latkes* and *sufganiyot* are replaced with *burfi* (a sweet dish made with condensed milk that is often served on Diwali, the Hindi Festival of Light), samosas (fried dough with savory fillings), and modak (deep-fried stuffed sweet dumplings). Halavaa, drizzled in honey, is also served.

North Africa
In the Jewish communities of Yemen and north Africa, the sixth night of Hanukkah—which is also the first day of the month of Tevet—was celebrated as *Chag HaBanot*, the holiday of the daughters. This holiday commemorates the importance of Judith and Hannah, two women connected to Hanukkah. The synagogue would be opened specifically for women on this night; they would dance, touch the Torahs, and bless their daughters and other women. Cheese was a big part of the feast that was eaten on *Chag HaBanot*, in honor of the cheese that Judith fed to Holofernes before she killed him. *Chag HaBanot* is not well-known today—many modern Sephardic families have never heard of it—but some feminist Jews are working to revive it.

Italy
Precipizi is Italy's version of sweet fried dough. To make them, mix equal amounts of flour, confectioner's sugar, olive oil, and whatever flavor liqueur you like (start with about a tablespoon of each). Form them into small balls, fry them in more olive oil, and then toss them, still hot, into a bowl of honey. Remove them quickly, cut them into smaller sticks or leave them as balls; place on a clean, oiled surface so that they won't stick. *Frittelle di Hanukkah* are also made: Diamond-shaped pieces of bread are stuffed with raisins and anise seeds, then fried and coated with honey. These sweet treats top off elaborate meals that include eggplant fried in olive oil and *pollo frito per Hanukkah*, fried chicken that is marinated in lemon, olive oil, nutmeg, and garlic before it is dredged in egg and flour and fried.

Iraq
Potatoes are not common in Iraq, so Iraqi Jews served a *latke*-like pancake made from carrots on Hanukkah. Dessert was fried funnel cakes called *zengoula*, which

are very much like southeast Asian *jalebi*. They're made from a yeast dough mixed with cornstarch to make them wonderfully crisp and extruded in coils from a pastry tube before they're deep-fried. Then they're dusted with sugar and soaked in a sugar-lemon syrup.

Atlanta, Georgia, United States of America
Every Tuesday, all year round except for the weeks preceding Passover, the sisterhood of Congregation Ohr Veshalom gets together and fries and then freezes borekas—by the time Hanukkah comes, they have thousands of them, filled with spinach, mushrooms, eggplant, and potatoes. For the past fifty years, the congregation has held a bazaar a few weeks before Hanukkah, where they sell every last one in a few hours. Most members of the congregation are descendants of immigrants from the Island of Rhodes, where the Jewish community dated back to the time of the Maccabees. Jews thrived there until the fifteenth century when the Ottoman Empire took over and expelled most of them.

Morocco
A special dessert of sweetened couscous is served in Morocco on the sixth night of Hanukkah, which is also the first day of Tevet. Dried fruit, cinnamon, sugar, blanched almonds and pistachios, and orange juice and zest are mixed into cooked couscous. It's then mounded on a plate and decorated with more cinnamon.

Turkey
On the eighth day of Hanukkah, Jews in Turkey celebrate *Merenda*, which means "snack" or "potluck meal." They gather in each others' homes, bringing food to share, including *bumuelos* and *pastelikos*, honey and almond-filled fritters. Children run from home to home, singing and chanting. Among their songs were *"Merenda de Chanuka,"* in which children asked for flour—"Give us flour, so that God will give you life"—and garlic to distribute to the poor so that all could enjoy Hanukkah food.[8]

5

❖ ❖

Tu B'Shevat

Happy Birthday to Trees

Tu B'Shevat was established as an economic practicality rather than a spiritual celebration. Its closest counterpart in Western civilizations is the day taxes are due, which in the United States also falls on the fifteenth day of a month in spring. According to Jewish law, fruit from new trees could not be harvested until the trees were five years old, and tithes (contributions to the Temple) were not required until the tree's third birthday. It was therefore necessary to establish a day from which to count the age of every tree, and the fifteenth day of Shevat, the fifth month (or the eleventh, depending on which calendar is used), was designated as that day. It does not appear in the Torah and it is mentioned only once in the *Mishnah*—in the tractate about Rosh Hashanah, which simply states that it was the New Year's Day for trees (*Rosh Hashanah L'Ilanot*). There were no other rules, customs, prayers, or observances noted.

The name Tu B'Shevat means the fifteenth of the month of Shevat. The word "Tu" is made up of the letters Tet, the ninth letter of the Hebrew alphabet, and Vav, the sixth Hebrew letter, totaling fifteen. Normally, when numbers are used in such dates, Yud, the tenth letter, would be added to Hey, the fifth letter, for a simpler total. But the Yud and the Hey also make up one of most sacred names of God, and it was decided that they should not be used for this purpose. The "Tu" formation is also used in "Tu B'Av," the fifteenth day of month of Av, the fourth or tenth month. Tu B'Av is a variation of Valentine's Day, mentioned in the Talmud as being a day to find a spouse. Women wear white dresses and walk or dance in vineyards, looking for available grooms.

REFLECTIONS

If you are planting a tree and see the Messiah coming, finish planting the tree and then go and greet the Messiah.—Avot de Rabbi Natan, 31b

Believe it or not, in Judaism, New Year's Day comes four times a year. The New Year for Kings and Festivals is the first of the Hebrew month called Nisan (in the spring). The first of the Hebrew month called Elul (in the summer) is the New Year for the tithe of cattle. The first of the Hebrew month of Tishrei is the New Year for years (*Rosh Hashanah*), for planting, and for the tithing of vegetables. The fifteenth of Shevat, marking the first day of spring in the Land of Israel, occurs six weeks after Hanukkah. The Talmud refers to it as *Rosh Hashanah L'Ilanot*, the New Year for trees, also known as Tu B'Shevat. Today, it generally falls between mid-January and mid-February.

In the Land of Israel, always largely waterless, trees were regarded as special gifts of God. There are many symbolic allusions to trees in the Torah, especially the olive tree which sends up new shoots to continue the life of the old tree that dies. Trees are represented as symbols of goodness and nobility. The upright person is compared to a tree planted near a stream that bears fruit in due season, with leaves that never fade (*Psalms*, 1:3).

Throughout the world, religious Jews strive to eat foods on Tu B'Shevat that are characteristic of the land of Israel, specifically the seven types of fruits and grains mentioned in *Deuteronomy* (8:8). Israeli-grown carob, a fruit with the decidedly un-Jewish name of St. John's Bread, is a popular choice.

In Israel, it was customary to plant a tree when a child was born: a cedar for a boy and a cypress for a girl, who cared for their own trees as they were growing up. Branches from their own trees were used for the poles of the wedding canopy (*huppah*) on the day of their respective marriage ceremony.

Environmentally aware Jews often choose Tu B'Shevat as a day to increase awareness and care for the environment. Families create ecology pacts that include recycling agreements, other ecological matters, and the preservation of the Earth, which they read and sign on Tu B'Shevat. In places where there are forests with maple trees, Jewish communities have sponsored maple tree sapping opportunities led by local forest rangers.

The commemoration of Tu B'Shevat offers a stepping stone to spring. As the sap begins to flow again and brings the trees to life, people feel renewed by the promise of spring. The awakening of a tree's life is observed, representing rebirth and hope for the future. In a very special way, Tu B'Shevat celebrates both the Creator and the creation. Psalm 104, often recited on Tu B'Shevat expresses this sentiment:

The trees of God have their fill
The cedars of Lebanon which You planted,
Where the birds make their nests,
As for the stork, the fir trees are her house.

Despite the fiscal basis of Tu B'Shevat's origin, even the most pragmatic agent of the Internal Tithing Service could not have failed to notice the miracles that erupted around the date that was chosen for this economic obligation. In the days before and after Tu B'Shevat—the last days of winter, before the spring rains— there is an extraordinary change in the landscape. First, the almond tree opens its exquisite blossoms; in Hebrew, the almond tree is called "*shah-kayd*," which means awake, alert, watchful. A harbinger, the almond is followed by pink and white rockrose and the purple Judas tree (known as redbud or cercis in the United States). At the same times, the fields come alive with the vibrant colors of wild- flowers—*kalanit* (anemone), *rakefet* (cyclamen), *narkis* (narcissus), *irus* (iris), and *tourmus* (lupine). Then, after the spring rains, the citrus trees blossom and bear fruit and intoxicating fragrances.

It took about fifteen hundred years for the glory that surrounds Tu B'Shevat to be translated into a celebration. For many of those years, the day was largely ignored. Once the Temple was destroyed, there was no need for tithing. When Jews scat- tered throughout Europe, they were far from the trees of Israel and therefore did not need to pay attention to the five-years-before-harvest rules that were the basis of the holiday of Tu B'Shevat. Although there is some evidence that Jews made it a practice to eat fruit on Tu B'Shevat through the early Middle Ages, especially in cold climates far from Israel, Tu B'Shevat was simply not a big deal. And then Kabbalists of Safed embraced it and made it one of the most important days of their year, sanctified with prayers, reflection, joy, and a Tu B'Shevat Seder that rivals the Passover ritual for complexity and symbolism.

THE KABALLAH AND THE KABBALISTS OF SAFED

Mainstream Judaism is a practical religion. Its laws and customs make life more structured and easy, providing support and advice on how to eat, marry, raise children, and even plow fields and build houses. Of course, there's a spiritual aspect and a connection to God—it's a religion, not a user's manual—but the day-to-day aspects of Judaism can be observed without a great amount of soul-searching. There's another aspect to the Jewish religion, one that deals with deeper relationships between humans and God, the universe, and their own souls. Writings about that aspect of Judaism are called Kabbalah. The exact meaning of the word "kabbalah" is debatable, but its root is in a Hebrew word that means "to accept" or "receive." The Kabbalah is based on a group of ancient writings that go back thousands of years. Some Kabbalists say that it originated in oral traditions passed down from Adam and find hints of it in throughout the Torah. The writings of Rabbi Shimon Bar Yochai, a brilliant scholar who lived during the time of the *Mishnah*, explained some of the esoteric teachings in a tome called the *Zohar* (the Light), though they are nearly impossible to comprehend. Rabbi Bar Yochai (see page 194) was a student of the famed Rabbi Akiva, who was tortured and killed by the Romans. Rabbi Bar Yochai spoke out against the oppressors and faced a similar punishment. He fled to the caves of Meron, where he buried himself in the ground and took sustenance from a single carob tree and a spring of water while compiling the book that later generations of Kabbalists used as a starting point for their philosophy.

Kabbalah was severely restricted by the Talmudic leaders; it was just too dangerous. A legend tells of four rabbinic leaders who delved into the Kabbalistic garden: One went crazy, one died, one destroyed the garden, and only Rabbi Akiva was able to handle it. There were only a few adherents who kept its flame alive through the early centuries of the common era, but Kabbalah gained traction again in Spain and southern France during the Golden Age of Judaism in the twelfth and thirteenth centuries. Respected rabbis, including Isaac the Blind (1160–1235) and the Ramban (1194–1270), integrated Kabbalah teachings in their commentaries on the Torah. Groups of Kabbalists, with names such as "The Unique Cherub Circle," met in secret to discuss their philosophies. When the Jews were expelled from Spain and ended up in different places all over the world, some took the Kabbalah with them. Although it never went mainstream—it was just too complicated for the masses—it has always had its devotees, both Christian and Jewish, serious and superficial, ranging from dedicated scholars to Madonna and Paris Hilton.

What, exactly, is Kabbalah? Since people have gone mad studying it, it's probably not a good idea to delve too deeply here. The official Kabbalah Centre explains it:

"Kabbalah is an ancient paradigm for living. It teaches that all of the branches of our lives—health, relationships, careers—emanate from the same trunk and the same root. It's the technology of how the universe works at the core level. It's a way of looking at the world that can connect you to the kind of permanent fulfillment you seek."[1] Kabbalah is divided into two main components (and many smaller ones). Contemplative Kabbalah examines the character of God and uses techniques, such as meditations on specific symbols and letters, to understand and bring ourselves closer to Him. Practical Kabbalah—which is recommended only for those who have reached a high degree of saintliness (in other words: don't try this at home)—employs incantations to alter reality. For example, many believed that they could create a golem (an early version of the zombie) from earth or other inanimate objects. Practical Kabbalah encompasses magic and supernatural elements—visitations from prophets and dead people, talking animals, dybbuks (extra souls, usually malicious, that enter and possess humans), and demons such as the temptress Lilith. Both branches of Kabbalah have the same goal: to help us understand the mysteries of the universe. The passion and mysticism embedded in Kabbalah found a new outlet in the Hasidic movement of the eighteenth century (see pages 8–9).

After the expulsion from Spain, many prominent scholars, including Kabbalists, ended up in a small but beautiful town called Safed (*Tzfat* in Hebrew) perched in the hills of Galilee. Safed's name is derived from the word for "overlook" (*tzofeh*)—it is the highest city in Israel, affording breathtaking views from the Mediterranean Sea to the Sea of Galilee. The Crusaders took advantage of its strategic value and built citadels there. It is one of the four holy cities of Israel—the others are Jerusalem, Hebron, and Tiberias—famous for its natural beauty and clear air. It is also very close to the caves of Meron where Rabbi Shimon Bar Yochai wrote the Zohar while hiding from the Romans. It's no wonder that some of the best Jewish minds of the fifteenth century ended up there.

Among the rabbis who settled in Safed was Rabbi Joseph Karo, who was born in Toledo, Spain, and emigrated to Safed in 1537. Already known for scholarly writings at that time, he established a major yeshiva there and wrote one of the most important volumes of Jewish Law, the *Shulchan Aruch* (translation: Set Table), which organized laws in an easy-to-follow order. Rabbi Karo joined several other major figures, including Rabbi Moshe Cordovero, a native Safedian who heard voices telling him to study the Kabbalah when he was twenty years old. He wrote two early books on Kabbalah: *Ohr Yakor* (Precious Light), a commentary on the Zohar, and *Pardes Rimonin* (Orchard of Pomegranates), in which he organized and analyzed all Kabbalah writings up to his time. The arrival in Safed of Rabbi Isaac Luria in 1569 cemented the city as the center for Kabbalah study, and it remains so to this day.

RABBI ISAAC LURIA OF SAFED

One of the most influential thinkers of the Kabbalist movement—and of all Judaism—was a young rabbi named Rabbi Isaac Luria. Rabbi Luria was born in Jerusalem in 1534 to a father who had emigrated from Romania and a mother who came from Spain after the expulsion. Legend has it that the prophet Elijah appeared to Rabbi Luria's father before he was born; Elijah prophesied that the child would deliver the Jews from evil and although many of his teachings would not be accepted, he would reveal many of the mysteries of the universe. Rabbi Luria was orphaned at a young age, but a wealthy uncle made sure he was educated in both religious and secular subjects; at one point, he seemed to be turning to a career in business.

But in his early twenties, he became obsessed with the study of the Zohar. He secluded himself from his family for seven years, barely uttering a word, even to his wife—though some believe he had frequent conversations with Elijah. When he returned to Jerusalem, his Kabbalistic teachings were not widely accepted, until he moved to Safed. There, he became a disciple of Rabbi Moses Cordovero—but Rabbi Cordovero died several months after Rabbi Luria arrived and Rabbi Luria became the key figure in Safed. Under the name of Arizel or Ari (the Lion), he wrote several books that revolutionized Kabbalah teachings, making them just a bit more understandable. He taught that doing good works was an antidote to evil, which was a comfort during the upheavals of the medieval era. Modern Kabbalism is based on his teachings. Rabbi Luria died at age thirty-eight during an epidemic in 1572.

The Kabbalists in Safed continued the Kabbalist tradition of exploring the spiritual connections between humans, God, and the essence of the universe. Nature, which includes trees and their fruit, fit cleanly into their quest, and taking on Tu B'Shevat as their holiday was a natural progression. Food in general was an important subject for Kabbalists. As Jonathan Brumberg-Kraus writes, "Kabbalistic meal rituals evoke . . . metaphors to heighten the intensity of the experience of the physical activity of eating."[2] God, using Earth as a conduit, provides food for all creatures. When we ingest this food, we are recycling bits of God's creation for our own growth and energy. So a day that marked the birthday of trees, a day on which people thought about distributing it to their leaders as part of their communal responsibility, had to be important for the Kabbalists. And Safed, surrounded by views of the tree-studded landscape (though not as tree-studded as it would become a few centuries later), is where the Kabbalists claimed Tu B'Shevat as a major holiday.

Toward the end of the sixteenth century, they formalized a process to transform eating and drinking into an examination of the nature of our souls and the mysteries of the planet. The crux of this examination was the Tu B'Shevat Seder. Like the Passover Seder, it created a specific order (the meaning of the word Seder is "order"). But the Passover Seder was organized to relate a historical event; the Tu B'Shevat Seder arranged philosophy, personality, and spirituality by stylizing the symbolism of specific foods and connecting them to spiritual concepts and human traits. Human characteristics were linked to foods—nuts with hard shells were associated with stubborn humans, pomegranates with peace and humility. Chewing food completely was said to spark inspiration and understanding.

The students of Rabbi Luria prepared a fifty-page pamphlet called *Pri Etz Hadar* (The Fruit of the Glorious Tree) that included psalms, passages from the Torah, and other writings. The introduction to the pamphlet expressed its underlying theme:

> You have made trees and grasses grow from the earth according to the supernal patterns and designs, so that human beings can gain *chochma* [wisdom] and *bina* [understanding] through them, and thus to grasp the hidden. . . . From every living soul is enlivened from the spiritual power that resides in the fruit, from the fruit of the mouth of Your holy angels who guard its fruit.

The Tu B'Shevat Seder is organized around four cups of wine, similar to the four cups drunk at the Passover Seder. A different type of fruit is eaten with each cup of wine and psalms, poems, and other writings are read and discussed; the readings scrutinize the wonders of nature, examine its mysteries, and praise its magnificence and creator. At the same time, they link the physical manifestations of nature—the fruit of its trees—to human characteristics and activity and to the seasons of the year.

The first cup drunk is the clearest of white wines, symbolizing the paleness of winter. It is accompanied by fruit with hard, inedible shells—nuts, oranges, avocados, melons, bananas, mangoes, coconuts, and pomegranates are offered. This first phase is connected—for those willing to see the link—to the physical world and to physical labor, and to people who are guarded and hard to know.

Next, a cup of white wine is mixed with a bit of red wine, blending into a pale rose (a golden sauterne is sometimes substituted); the stirring of new life, new hope that occurs in spring is invoked. Fruit with inedible pits—peaches, cherries, plums, dates—are served with the second cup. It's a more emotional and creative aspect of humanity, flickering with the promise of new growth.

The third cup of wine is darker; the mix moves to more red wine, less white. The fruit served with this course is almost entirely edible—berries, apples, pears, grapes, figs. This wholeness connects to openness and fullness, to the lushness and abundance of summer and to intellectual achievements.

Finally, the fourth cup of wine is served, either totally red or with a single drop of white. The Kabbalists were a bit vague on the fruit to be served with this course, extolling the future and spirituality without suggesting specific foods that were to be eaten. Later generations filled in the blanks, recommending seeds, such as sunflower seeds or pumpkin seeds, as the accompaniment. This is the most spiritual and mysterious course.

It's hard to consider the stylized progression of the Tu B'Shevat Seder without noticing that it's a wee bit contrived, or possibly even thinking that it's a little silly. But at its core is a conscious effort to recognize and appreciate the connections of ourselves to our food and to our surroundings. The Kabbalists believed that focusing on the symbolism and facets of the Tu B'Shevat foods would lead to constructive discussions that would in turn inspire deeper understanding and spiritual awakenings. And who can argue with that? Today, we use the words "mindfulness" or "conscious consumption," but we're really following through on the Kabbalistic concept of thinking before we eat. As current generations grapple with the necessity and benefits of eating sustainable foods, we go through the same stages of thought, considering how and where it comes from and how using it affects our environment.

ASHURE

There are not many recipes specific to Tu B'Shevat; most families create their own favorites that use fresh and dried fruit and products from Israel, celebrating both trees and Israeli agriculture. But one ancient dish is used in many Sephardic homes to close the Tu B'Shevat Seder. This dish, called Ashure or Assure (the word means "ten" in Arabic, similar to the Hebrew "*esser*"), is made throughout the Middle East and other Mediterranean countries and is tied to many legends, traditions, and religions. In Turkish and Armenian culture, it is called "Kofyas" or "Noah's Pudding." According to folk tales, Noah's wife whipped it up when the ark landed on Mount Ararat after the great flood receded, using up all the leftovers in her kitchen (she must have brought a lot of pots with her). In Muslim countries, it is made to honor the martyrdom of one of Mohammed's grandsons and to celebrate the survival of another. In Greece, it's a funeral food. In Syria and north Africa, a similar wheatberry and barley is called belila; pine nuts, almonds, pistachios, and rose water are included.

It was incorporated into the Tu B'Shevat tradition because it uses so many of the fruits, grains, and other products for which Israel is famous—five of the seven varieties (*sheva minim*) on which Israeli agriculture is based are used in the recipe. The Kabbalists assigned their own symbolism to the recipe: for them, the word ten refers to the Ten Commandments and the original recipe included ten ingredients, one for each commandment.

No one ever said it was an easy dish to prepare—but it's a good group project and several people can take turns on the extreme stirring required. You'll need to use just about every pot in the house to cook four separate grains and legumes, as well as a sauce that needs to be stirred and watched carefully. Wheatberries, a key ingredient, were hard to find at one time, but they have become trendy and are now available in most stores.

This is a variable and forgiving recipe; though the wheatberries are an integral part of it, everything else can be adjusted according to taste and availability. In a pinch, substitute couscous for the wheatberries.

• • • • •

10 to 12 servings

INGREDIENTS

½ cup dried chickpeas
½ cup dried pinto or navy beans
1½ cups chopped dried fruits—raisins, dates, apricots, prunes
1 cup brandy
Salt, for boiling grains and legumes, about 1 teaspoon
1½ cups wheatberries
1 cup long grain brown rice
¼ cup honey
2 cups whole milk or light cream; coconut or almond milk may be substituted
    for a vegan or pareve version
½ cup nuts: slivered almonds (toasted), pistachios, pecans, peanuts, plus extra
    for garnish
1 teaspoon cinnamon
½ teaspoon grated orange zest
Pomegranate seeds, for garnish, optional
Candied fruit, for garnish, optional
Confectioners' sugar for dusting, optional

The night before, place the chickpeas and beans in separate bowls; cover with water and soak overnight.

Early on the day on which you'll be serving the dish, soak the dried fruit in brandy for several hours.

Cook the grains and legumes.

Put the wheatberries in a large pot with about two quarts of salted water. Bring to a boil, then reduce heat and simmer for about two hours until soft. Drain (not all the water will be absorbed; reserve about one cup of the water) and set aside.

Cook the rice in two and a half cups of salted water until soft; drain and set aside.

Drain the chickpeas and beans, cover with salted water in separate large pots and boil until soft, about forty-five minutes to one hour.

In a very large saucepan, place the reserved wheatberry water and the honey. Over low heat, stir until a thick syrup forms—it will take about fifteen to twenty minutes and will burn if you leave it. Add the milk or cream, reduce heat to very low and stir constantly for about thirty minutes until the syrup becomes creamy.

Add the fruit and brandy to the syrup and continue stirring until incorporated.

Add the reserved wheatberries, rice, chickpeas, and beans to the saucepan, about a cup at a time. Stir gently and keep stirring until the syrup has been absorbed by the grains and legumes. Add the nuts, cinnamon, and orange zest, and stir to distribute evenly.

Allow to cool slightly, then arrange on a large serving platter or in individual bowls. Garnish with additional nuts, pomegranate seeds, and candied fruit as desired. Dust with confectioners' sugar.

This dish is usually chilled for several hours and served cold, but is also good warm or at room temperature.

• • • • •

THE SPREAD OF TU B'SHEVAT

After the Kabbalists, Tu B'Shevat seeped into the culture of Jews all over the world. *Pri Etz Hadar*, the pamphlet that described the seder, was printed in 1728, as part of a Venetian anthology of spiritual essays. It was not accepted by the Ashkenazic community—some even forbade it—but was embraced by Sephardim. It's more popular than ever today. Several progressive Jewish organizations, including Hazon,[3] have created haggadot for the Tu B'Shevat Seder (see endnote for more information about Hazon and the Tu B'Shevat Seder); families and congregations in Israel and throughout the world hold these gatherings every year. They maintain the Kabbalists' original goals by discussing and considering the source of their food; today, many Jews have updated the Seder by adding the topic of sustainability (which is an easy fit).

In Europe (and later in America), where the fifteenth day of Shevat fell in the dead of winter, people used the holiday as a day to remember their homeland, to yearn for and celebrate the fruit of Israel. In Ashkenazic homes, it was a minor holiday; people made an effort to display and eat fruit and other produce from

Israel on that day. Because it was hard to find fresh produce in the middle of winter, dried fruit was usually substituted; dried fruit strudels were served for dessert and dried apricots, prunes, and almonds were included in meals and snacks. In Hasidic homes, the *etrog* (citron) from Sukkot was often made into a jam or pickle and served on Tu B'Shevat. In Germany, the recipe selected for Tu B'Shevat was often *schnitzelkloese*, fried dumplings with fruit. In Hungary, it was *borleves*, wine soup with fruit.

Sephardic families, many of whom lived in the warmer climates of north Africa, celebrated the holiday more intensely. It was called *Las Frutas*, the holiday of the fruit. Children were given a day off from school, elaborate meals were prepared, and there was singing and dancing. The Kabbalists' Seder was sometimes followed, if not religiously then as a social occasion. Tu B'Shevat became a day to gather with friends and neighbors and to find as much fruit—fresh, dried, candied—as possible. In many homes, the goal was to eat fifteen different kinds of produce, in deference to the "tu" in Tu B'Shevat. Other cultures, including India and Iraq, sought to gather fifty or even one hundred varieties.

Recipes that used fruit and nuts became Tu B'Shevat classics. In north African countries, including Morocco, *Salata latsheen*, an orange salad with a sesame dressing, was often served. Bukharan households included *dimlama* (a stew that included meats, potatoes, vegetables, and fruit) and *sava* (a baked rice and fruit dish) in Tu B'Shevat feasts.

The land of Israel produces an amazing array of produce and other foods. Of these, seven varieties (*sheva* means seven; *minim* are varieties) have been designated as special: wheat, barley, grapes, figs, pomegranates, olives, and dates/honey (see pages 56–75 for more about the *sheva minim* and the date/honey dilemma). All are native to Israel and define its landscape; all have been cultivated and eaten since ancient times and are present in many traditional recipes. For Tu B'Shevat, when we celebrate the fruits of the trees and the fruits of the Earth, we can combine all the *sheva minim* in a single salad—wheat-based couscous and chewy barley, with raisins (made from grapes), chopped figs and dates, and a dressing made from pomegranate molasses and olive oil covers every base.

A TIME TO PLANT

Towards the end of the twentieth century, as pioneers began to flock to Israel, Tu B'Shevat acquired a new meaning and purpose. In 1890, Rabbi Ze'ev Yafetz organized a Tu B'Shevat trip to an experimental agricultural settlement called Zichron Yaakov to plant trees. The settlement eventually became the home of Carmel wines, the first vineyard of modern Israel. And the practice of planting trees on Tu

B'Shevat became popular, especially among schoolchildren. By 1908, the Jewish Teachers Association and later the Jewish National Fund were promoting the custom. Today, about half a million people in Israel participate in tree planting every year on Tu B'Shevat.[4]

TREES AND ISRAEL

When the Jews first entered Canaan, it was full of trees; virgin forests covered the plains and the mountains. With its new inhabitants, the need for arable land increased. The tribe of Menashe complained to Joshua, their leader, that they had no food and no land to farm. In a decision that would be hotly contested today, Joshua told them: "Go up into the forests and clear them of trees; then you will have good farmland" (*Joshua*, 27:18). This may have worked for a time—just as clearing rainforests to produce grain to feed cattle worked for a time—but it led to serious deforestation in the region. Without trees, the topsoil eroded and over centuries, the fertility of the land decreased.

But, despite Joshua's instructions, trees have always been revered by Jews and in Jewish teaching. The Torah itself is called "The Tree of Life" (*Etz Chaim*): "She is a tree of life to those who lay hold of her; those who hold her fast are called blessed" (*Proverbs*, 3:18). Trees are central to the Torah, with starring roles in the Garden of Eden and God's appearance to Moses (okay, it was a bush that was burning). *Isaiah* (41:19) lists the trees of Israel:

> I will plant in the wilderness the cedar, the acacia-tree, and the myrtle, and the olive-tree; I will set in the desert the cypress, the plane-tree, and the larch together; That they may see, and know, and consider, and understand together, that the hand of the Lord hath done this, and the Holy One of Israel hath created it.

Though it took several centuries, trees became a focus for Jews in Israel once again by the late nineteenth century, both for their fruit and for their contribution to the fertility of the soil. Tu B'Shevat became the day to celebrate this reverence.

The movement to increase the number of trees in Palestine was spearheaded by the Jewish National Fund, an offshoot of *Keren Kayemet L'Yisroel*, which was established at the Fifth Zionist Congress in 1903. As the members of the Congress looked for ways to improve the quality of life in the region, they focused on food and how to make it grow. They came up with a plan to raise funds to fuel these improvements: They convinced Jews all over the world to keep little blue boxes in their homes and to fill them with small coins; within ten years, more than a million Jewish homes had one of these boxes, and placing coins in the boxes became a cherished connection to the land of Israel.[5] One of their first projects to be funded with the blue-box coins was a group of olive groves in the town of Hulda. The fund also supported research and development of modern agricultural techniques and the establishment of agricultural kibbutzim throughout the country (see pages 174–176 for more about the kibbutz movement). The Jewish National Fund was also one of the main forces in creating Tel Aviv, the first modern Jewish city in Israel, in the early 1900s.

On January 26, 1926, the Jewish National Fund was incorporated in the United States, with six action areas: ecology and afforestation, water, community development, research and development, tourism and recreation, and education. But perhaps the most prominent and valuable of Jewish National Fund's goals was to plant trees throughout Israel. They purchased land across the country and developed efficient fundraising methods that allowed Americans to participate in the building of a Jewish State.

And it worked. The very first pioneers in Israel knew that planting trees was critical to their success; in the nineteenth century, they increased the number of trees in Palestine from about fifteen thousand to two million.[6] After the Jewish National Fund came into the picture, the number of trees increased to seven million. By the end of the twentieth century, the Jewish National Fund had planted over two hundred million trees in Israel; Israel is one of only two countries that has increased the number of trees in their land in the twentieth and twenty-first centuries.

Finding the right stock to create lush, stable forests was not easy. For several years, the Jewish National Fund tried to cultivate stone pines (also known as umbrella pines), which grow to eighty-five feet tall; have wide, flat canopies; and produce edible nuts. But the trees did not survive in all habitats; after three years, few of them were still alive. But their next candidate, the smaller Aleppo pine, was a winner. Also native to the region, it had remained in small patches in the Galilee since biblical times. Now known as the Jerusalem pine, these trees provide the country with shade, reduce soil erosion, and produce oxygen through photosynthesis.

When the State of Israel was established in 1948, its leaders knew that, despite other pressing problems—such as coining money, defending the country, creating jobs, and welcoming Jews from every part of the diaspora—planting trees was a priority. In the second session of the Knesset, Israel's first prime minister, David Ben-Gurion, said,

> We must plant hundreds of thousands of trees. We must cover the mountains and the uncultivatable lands, the hills and the sand dunes and the barren plains. . . .We would be unfaithful to one of the two main tasks of the state—the revival of the desert—if we were to carry out only plans which satisfy our immediate needs. We are an entirely new State, which has to make up for the neglect of generations, for sins that have been perpetuated against our land as well as for sins committed against our people.[7]

Tu B'Shevat became a day set aside not only to wish every tree a happy birthday, but also to promote rebirth, renewal, and progression. For many years, Tu B'Shevat was a school holiday, marked by parades and tree-planting events. Kids go to school on Tu B'Shevat today, but most homes celebrate in some way and stores display special fruits for the holiday. The government and other institutions use this day for special events. The cornerstone for the main building of Jerusalem's Hebrew University was laid on Tu B'Shevat in 1918; the one for Haifa's Technion was set on that day in 1925. On Tu B'Shevat in 1949, two major events took place: the cornerstone ceremony for the Knesset and the dedication of the Forest of the Defenders (*Yaar HaMeginim*), honoring those who fought in the War of Independence.

CAROB TREES

Along with almonds, figs, and date palms, a tree that is closely associated with Tu B'Shevat is the carob, a legume that is native to the region and dates back to the Neolithic period; ten thousand-year-old carob seeds have been found in Jericho and Haifa. It was the fresh fruit most often eaten outside of Israel on Tu B'Shevat—dried fruit was the norm—because its long pods didn't spoil in transit. They did however become hard, dry, and almost painful to chew; Israelis are surprised to hear that non-Israeli Jews don't like carob because the version they eat in Israel has a delicious pulp. Carob has a second connection to Tu B'Shevat—it was the tree that Rabbi Shimon Bar Yochai, a founder of the Kabbalist movement, used for sustenance while in hiding. A honeylike syrup made from the pulp is a popular sweetener is Israel, and the seeds are ground into flour that some people use as a substitute for chocolate, though it requires a lot of imagination to equate the bland taste of carob with the deliciousness of chocolate.

The tree grows to fifty feet tall and has a broad spreading canopy. Its Hebrew name is *charoov*, possibly because of its sword-shaped pods (*cherev* means sword) or because it becomes dry (*charov*). It's also known as the life-saving tree because it grows in many places where other foods don't thrive—for example, near Rabbi Bar Yochai's cave. In Yiddish, it's called *bokser*, or buck's horn, again after the shape of its pods. In English, it's St. John's Bread—the ascetic St. John subsisted on them (or maybe on locusts; the words are similar and scholars aren't sure which one is referred to by Mark and Matthew in the New Testament).

ORANGE GROVES

The crop that defines Israel's agricultural identity today is not one of the seven varieties that were cultivated in biblical times—it's not even native to the region. The first citrus plants, which were the size of berries, probably originated in Southeast Asia or Australia. Even the *etrog* (citron) that is mentioned in *Leviticus* and used on Sukkot was brought to Israel from India.

Orange trees were planted in the Middle Eastern region to satisfy a need for vitamin C among the mariners on the trade routes. During the Middle Ages, ship owners found that their sailors were unable to function because they were developing scurvy on long ocean voyages. Palestine was a midpoint stop between the Far East ports where silk and spices were bought for exporting to the European markets that were so greedy for them. Farmers in Palestine realized that they could profit from supplying healthy fruit to the sailors and that oranges, lemons, and grapefruit thrived in their climate. From the twelfth to the eighteenth centuries, growing citrus fruits was a small but steady industry.

In the nineteenth century, importing food to Europe become more profitable as the middle class expanded and a larger number of people were able to afford more than just the basics. At the same time, newer, faster steamships made exporting food more feasible; food could travel from Middle Eastern farms to European tables in just a few days rather than the weeks that were previously required. Farmers looked for tastier and more durable citrus products and found the Shamouti orange. It was big and sweet, with very few seeds and a thick peel that made it last longer than other varieties. Palestinian farmers began to plant it near Jaffa around 1850 and renamed it the Jaffa orange. By the 1870s, they were exporting thirty-eight million of them annually.[8]

In the nineteenth century, most orange groves were owned by wealthy Palestinian businessmen. Although they were profitable, they were not very efficient and were affected by disease and the normal vagaries of agriculture. When the Jewish settlers began coming to Palestine at the end of the nineteenth century, they joined with the Palestinians to install new technology that improved the quality and quantity of the fruits and introduced new varieties. It was a successful collaboration for both.

The citrus industry has continued to grow. In the 1920s and 1930s, American, European, and Canadian entrepreneurs began to invest in Palestine. They purchased land and brought in the most modern equipment, technology, and farm plans. The agricultural innovations, such as drip irrigation (see page 178) that helped the young state make the desert bloom, improved the quality and quantity of the citrus crops as well. Today, almost two hundred thousand tons of citrus products are shipped worldwide annually and more than twice that number are used in Israel.[9] Several new varieties of pink grapefruits, clementines, and mandarins were developed by Israeli scientists; they provide an almost year-round growing season and some of the sweetest fruit in the world. Their delicate fragrance perfumes the air, their blossoms enhance the view, and their deliciousness permeates every kind of food served in Israel.

ISRAELI CHICKEN IN CITRUS SAUCE

What better way to celebrate trees and their fruits—with a focus on Israel's miraculous citrus crops—than with a dish prepared with oranges, lemons, and other citrus fruits?

Fresh squeezed juices taste best, but frozen concentrates are easier. Avoid bottled lemon juice—it often adds a chemical flavor.

If you can find imported Jaffa oranges, they are especially flavorful and appropriate.

• • • • •

4 to 6 servings

INGREDIENTS

1 large orange, preferably organic
¾ cup orange juice, or ¼ cup frozen concentrate
2 tablespoons lemon juice
¼ cup grapefruit, tangerine, clementine, Meyer lemon, or mandarin juice (optional)
4 tablespoons honey, more or less to taste
1 teaspoon chopped garlic
6 chicken thighs, about 2½ pounds
1 teaspoon salt
¼ teaspoon cayenne pepper
¼ cup flour
2 tablespoons olive oil
1 teaspoon sesame oil
Golden raisins, toasted almonds (optional)

Using a vegetable peeler, peel thin strips of zest from the orange (if you're not using an organic orange, skip this step and increase the amount of orange juice to one cup), removing as much of the white pith as possible. Add the strips to a large bowl.

Peel and section the orange, removing pith and membrane as much as possible. Add the sections to the bowl. Add all the juices to the bowl; stir in the honey and garlic.

Add the chicken pieces to the bowl; turn to coat and leave in the refrigerator for several hours.

Preheat oven to 375°F.

Combine the salt, pepper, and flour. Remove the chicken from the marinade and pat dry. Dredge the chicken pieces in the flour, on both sides. Heat the olive and sesame oils in a large frying pan and sauté the chicken, turning frequently until just browned on all sides; you're not cooking them now. If you don't have a large enough pan to turn the pieces easily, do it in two batches—it won't come out right if you crowd them.

Remove the chicken pieces from the pan and place them in a roasting pan. Pour the marinade into a small pot, bring to a boil, and boil for two minutes to get rid of any possible bacteria. Then pour the marinade into the frying pan with the juices from the chicken and cook over low heat, stirring constantly for about ten minutes until thickened. You should have at least a cup of this sauce. Add raisins if you are using them. Pour the sauce over the chicken parts in the roasting pan and toss to coat. Place the roasting pan in the preheated oven and cook for about thirty-five minutes, basting frequently; check for doneness by inserting a meat thermometer in the thickest part (it should read 170°F). Remove from oven and spoon any extra sauce over the chicken. Serve over rice or couscous; garnish with toasted almonds if desired.

• • • • •

TU B'SHEVAT AND VALUES

Many people call Tu B'Shevat a minor holiday, and in many ways, it is: there's no group of laws surrounding it and for most of Jewish history it was barely celebrated. But it touches on deep-rooted Jewish values. Tu B'Shevat's first purpose—as a way to schedule tithing—aligns with the idea of communal responsibility: Every person must contribute a share. It's a holiday that focuses on protecting nature both because the natural world is a reflection of God and because it is a practical way of ensuring our own survival. The concept of *Shmirat Ha'teva* (protecting nature) appears throughout Jewish writings; the Talmud includes myriad ways to keep soil alive through crop rotation and companion plantings, and exhorts against cutting down trees in time of war. The mass tree planting that accompanied Tu B'Shevat is a prime example of *Tikkun Olam*—fixing the world. Though none of us can, by ourselves, solve the world's problems, we can make a dent with an act like planting a tree. And the millions of trees, planted one by one, paid for by coins collected all over the world, have made the air cleaner, the soil more healthy, and life more livable. A minor holiday? Perhaps that's true—but Tu B'Shevat is also joyous, valuable, and profound.

TU B'SHEVAT TRADITIONS AROUND THE WORLD

Italy

Edda Servi Machlin, author of *The Classic Cuisine of the Italian Jews*, remembers Tu B'Shevat in her small Italian town. Children saved coins in small blue tin boxes, called Bossolo, all year long to buy trees in Palestine. On Tu B'Shevat, there was much singing and dancing in circles, imitating the way children danced in Israel after planting trees. There were no sweets or candies distributed, but children received small bags of dried fruits.

Uzbekistan, Kurdistan, and Bukhara

Tu B'Shevat is referred to "the Day of Eating the Seven Species." A big festive meal that includes all of the *sheva minim* is eaten.

Morocco

The wealthiest community members invite all their neighbors to a Tu B'Shevat meal. Before the guests leave, their hosts fill their hats with all kinds of fruit to take home.

Greece

Greek Jewish women who want to become pregnant plant raisins and candy near trees on Tu B'Shevat evening. A Greek legend says that on the night of Tu B'Shevat, angels tap the head of every plant and command it to grow. Children were allowed to stay up late to try to see the angel. Seeds for planting the following season were often blessed on Tu B'Shevat.

Turkey

Each member of a Jewish family was given a special food on Tu B'Shevat and recited an appropriate blessing. Fathers received wheat and asked for the ability to earn his food easily; mothers received fruit and prayed to have many children. Boys got olives, girls got pomegranates, and babies were given honey and apples (though hopefully these babies were over one year old, past the age when babies could be killed by a botulism found in honey). Halvah was given to visitors as gifts.

6

Purim

Until You Don't Know the Difference

Anyone who thinks that Jewish holidays are somber and sober has never celebrated Purim. Rosh Hashanah, the Jewish New Year, in contrast, is a serious time during which we reflect on our sins and pray for forgiveness—with none of the revelry attached to secular New Year's celebrations. We save that revelry for Purim, the holiday that has everything—not only the uninhibited drinking of New Year's Eve, but the masquerading of Halloween, the feasting of Thanksgiving, the cookie baking of Christmas, and the decorated eggs of Easter.

Purim is based on a highly dramatic story (told in a section of the Old Testament called a *megillah*) replete with a silly king, an arch villain, an uncompromising hero, a courageous heroine, and a beauty pageant that is a forerunner of *The Bachelor*. The story is filled with palace intrigue, murderous plots, secrets that have never been revealed, and last-minute escapes. Though the name of God appears nowhere within the story, it is understood that one side has heavenly protection and the good guys get a happy ending.

Purim is a holiday that fits the borscht belt view of Jewish history (They tried to kill us. We survived. Let's eat.) perfectly. It's one of the few places in the Torah where we are directed to go out and have fun—where we are "obligated" to indulge in "feasting and rejoicing" (*Esther*, 9:22)—forever after; we're told to keep drinking until we don't know the difference between the hero and the villain. As the *Megillah* states, "And these days are commemorated and celebrated in every generation, by every family, in every province and every city. And these days of Purim will never pass from among the Jews nor shall their memory depart from their descendants" (*Esther*, 9:28).

REFLECTIONS

When Adar comes, rejoicing increases.—*Talmud Taanit*, 29a

The festival of Purim is observed just a month and a day before Passover. "On Purim," says a Jewish proverb, "everything is permissible." Purim is the one time of year when the normal rules of behavior are suspended somewhat, when even the most devout Jews dare to make a mockery of things that are normally considered sacred. But Jewish piety is a balance, a mixture of the spiritual and the physical. It is out of this context that the Purim celebration is born.

Purim celebrates the successful overthrow of a plot to destroy the Jews of ancient Persia. While there is some scholarly debate about the historical veracity of what is accounted in the *Book of Esther*, the essential message of survival rings true for Jews in all generations, including our own.

On the evening of Purim (and again in the morning in traditional settings), the *Megillah* (a small scroll on which the *Book of Esther* is hand inscribed) is read aloud with special cantillations. The scroll is spread out and read like a letter. To blot out the memory of Amalek (following the instruction of *Deuteronomy*, 25:19), thunderous noises are made with noisemakers whenever the villain Haman's name is mentioned. Very often during services, a Purim skit is staged, which adds to the frivolity. Those in attendance are encouraged to dress in costume, which adds to the fun.

Following the pattern of the Purim in the Torah, there are also local Purim celebrations in some communities on other dates. These commemorate occasions when these communities, like the Jewry of Persia, were rescued from destruction and annihilation. For example, in the 1970s, Rabbi Norman Frimer, director of Hillel, was among those kidnapped and held hostage by Muslim terrorists in Washington, DC. All of the hostages survived, and ever since the rabbi conduced (he died in 1993; his family continues the tradition) an annual special Purim celebration with his family on the Hebrew date on which he was released.

There are some interesting curiosities related to Purim. One of them occurs in the *Book of Esther*, where Queen Esther is also known by her alternate name Hadassah, the same name as the Zionist Women's Organization, one of the largest Jewish organizations in the world. Here, the story is told that after a visit to Palestine, the great Jewish leader Henrietta Szold decided to form a Zionist organization for women. She envisioned this group working for the health of women and children in what was later to become the modern State of Israel. The founding meeting was held at Congregation Emanu-El in New York City, and the date of the meeting was Purim in 1912. The women constituted themselves as the Hadassah chapter of the Daughters of Zion. Eventually, the name would become simply Hadassah.

THE STORY OF PURIM

The story of Purim, as related in the *Megillah* of Esther, begins with a humongous party. Achashverosh, the King of Persia (historians tentatively identify him as Xerxes I of Persia, who ruled from 486 to 435 BCE and was famous for an invasion of Greece that ultimately failed), the king of 127 lands from India to Africa, invited all his ministers to a six-month-long celebration. During the all-male party, he decided to show off his wife Vashti and commanded her to appear. Vashti, in a show of independence that marks her as one of the earliest feminists, refused. (She would probably be an honored heroine, but the Midrash, possibly for male chauvinist reasons, tells us that she was a thoroughly nasty person in other respects.) The ministers, fearing that their wives would decide that they, too, could ignore them, urged the king to get rid of Vashti and find a more suitable queen. All agreed: Vashti vanished and letters were sent throughout the kingdom declaring that men would not be challenged in their own homes. Everyone was satisfied, until the king awoke the next morning and realized that he was short a queen. His solution predated a modern phenomenon: He would hold a contest to find a new wife. Virgins from all over his kingdom would come for nightly auditions so he could make his choice.

One of the women who joined the pageant was the beautiful, orphaned Jewess Esther. She went at the suggestion of her uncle Mordecai, who had been exiled from Jerusalem by King Nebuchadnezzar, along with most of the Jewish population. The king immediately loved and chose her. Esther kept her faith secret. Mordecai visited the king's court often, to make sure Esther was okay.

At around the same time, the king promoted his deputy, a man named Haman—the villain of the piece—to a position above all the other ministers. Haman demanded that everyone in the kingdom, except the king, bow down to him; Mordecai refused, saying that he worshipped only one God and it surely was not Haman. So Haman hatched a plot to kill not only Mordecai, but all the Jews in the kingdom. He decided on a date for the big slaughter by writing dates on small "lots"—bits of paper or stone which are called Purim in Persian—and staging a lottery. The date that won was the thirteenth day of the month of Adar. He presented his plan to the king, explaining that there was a group of people within his kingdom that would not obey his laws—and offering to pay ten thousand talents for the privilege of killing them all. The king told Haman to do as he pleased and sent letters throughout the kingdom telling them to kill all Jews, and take all their possessions, on the thirteenth of Adar.

Mordecai and the rest of the Jews learned of the plot and were terrified. But Mordecai knew he had an ally in the king's court in his niece Esther and that it was time for Esther to take advantage of her undercover status. The problem was that the king had a habit of killing women who were not properly subservient, so approaching him without an invitation was tricky. Esther prayed and fasted—and all the Jews of Persia fasted along with her. Fortunately, the king liked her and approved her request for a feast with the king and his deputy Haman. Haman was delighted to be singled out by the queen but was still seething at Mordecai. Pumped, he decided to erect a gallows so that he could hang Mordecai personally.

During dinner, Esther turned to the king and asked how he would react if someone killed not only her, but all her people. Esther had impressed Achashverosh enough that the thought infuriated him—and then Esther revealed that she was Jewish and that Haman was planning to kill everyone she knew the next day. That made the king furious and he quickly ordered that Haman be killed instead of Mordecai and that Haman's murderous plan be canceled. Mordecai was appointed second in command and the Jews of Persia were able to live in peace from then on.

The holiday of Purim was established and the story of Esther was recorded and inserted into the Old Testament. It was decreed that a celebration would take place forevermore on the fourteenth and fifteenth of Adar, with feasting and giving gifts from house to house and especially to the poor. And then the *Megillah* ends, with everyone living happily ever after.

WHAT IS A *MEGILLAH*?

The word "*megillah*" has entered the English language—the "whole *megillah*" usually refers to a complicated tale, often one that is told at greater length than the listener would like. In Hebrew, it means a scroll and a *megillah* is usually read from a handwritten scroll that is unfurled during the recitation.

The *Book of Esther* is one of five *Megillot* (plural for *Megillah*) that appear in the Torah. Two of them—Ruth and Esther—are the kind of complicated story that give the word *megillah* its slang meaning. The others—*Shir Hashirim* (*Song of Songs*), *Aichah* (*Lamentations*), and *Koheleth* (*Ecclesiastes*)—are poetic and philosophical treatises.

The Torah is divided into three main parts. The first is the Five Books of Moses, sometime called Torah: *Beraishit* (which translates to "In the Beginning"—*Genesis* in English); *Shemot* (literally Names, *Exodus* in English); *Vayikra* (And He Called/ *Leviticus*); BaMidbar (In the Desert/*Numbers*); and *Devarim* (Things/*Deuteronomy*). The second main section is *Neviim*, or *Prophets*, which include *Joshua, The Judges, Samuel I* and *II, Kings I* and *II, Isaiah, Jeremiah*, and *Ezekiel*, plus twelve minor prophets. The last main section is *Ketuvim* (writings), which is where the *Megillot* fit. In addition to the *Megillot, Ketuvim* include the books of *Job, Proverbs, Psalms, Daniel, Ezra, Nehemiah* (or *Ezra-Nehemiah*), and *Chronicles I* and *II*.

PURIM FOOD

Purim celebrations are wrapped around two huge food events: *Mishloach Manot* (the "giving of portions") that according to both customs and laws laid down in the *Shulchan Aruch* should include at least two types of food and should preferably be homemade; and the lavish meal that takes place at the end of the holiday, a no-holds-barred extravaganza that can take hours and is made more festive by liberal drinking. In fact, the Talmud states, and the *Shulchan Aruch* repeats, that it is important to drink "until you don't know the difference between blessing Mordecai and cursing Haman" (*Talmud Megillah* 7b; *Code of Jewish Law*, 695:2). Add costumes, singing, and bawdy skits to the mix, and the result is a holiday that very few people don't cherish. On Purim, anything goes. Many rabbis approved of mixed dancing and cross-dressing on that day only; yeshiva students, dressed as women, could flirt with the rabbi's wife and generally make drunken fools of themselves. Purim plays—called *Purimspiels*—made little sense but everyone had fun performing them during the Middle Ages, when fun was often hard to come by. Today, since we know that alcohol intoxication can be deadly, few people consider getting drunk to be a good deed. But banquets held on Purim are still often called "Ad Lo Yada" (until you don't know) dinners. And children dress up in costumes—they used to be Queen Esther and King Achashverosh, now they are more often Spiderman and Elsa from *Frozen*—as they deliver *Mishloach Manot* to friends and neighbors.

The origin of *Mishloach Manot* is right in the *Megillah*; when the fighting is over and the holiday begins, Mordecai directs people to enjoy "a day of feasting, rejoicing and sending portions of food one to another" (*Esther*, 9:19). Dozens of rabbis weighed in on how this should be done. Most said that at least two items should be sent to at least one person. A few threw in more rules, such as that the quality of the gift should reflect the status of either the giver or the recipient, or both; and the *Shulchan Aruch* said when it comes to *Mishloach Manot*, more is better.

But far from esoteric *Halachic* teachings, enchanting traditions took root throughout the Jewish world, dusted with flour, sprinkled with sugar, stuffed with nuts and raisins and jam. Purim became an opportunity for talented bakers to show off as they assembled exquisite platters, laid with carefully decorated pastries, the finest fruits they could find and the best chocolate that money could buy. Even in the Middle Ages, people gained status by sending the most elaborate and delicious plates for *Mishloach Manot*. Planning and baking for Purim became a family affair, with children stirring the batter and licking the spoons for weeks in advance. Then, on Purim morning, platters would be packed and wrapped and messengers—usually children—would race through the streets making their deliveries and being rewarded with small sums of money (Purim *gelt*). Today, many families take advantage of services that deliver professional *Mishloach Manot*. The services make money and often organizations sponsor the deliveries as fundraisers. But where's the joy in that? Will anyone cherish memories of online ordering?

There was no detail given in the *Megillah* for what the portions should contain. In Talmudic times, people thought a hunk or two of meat was the right way to go. By the end of the Middle Ages, when sugar became affordable in eastern Europe—because of newly discovered ways to grow, extract, and refine it and because New World sources that were closer became available—most people included sweet confections in their *Mishloach Manot*. Muslims in the Middle East called Purim "id al sukar"—the sugar festival.[1]

The traditions continue; many communities and families have their own specialties, borrowed from the country in which they live. In many cases, pastries are shaped like some part of Haman's supposed attire or anatomy—his hats, ears, eyes, and pockets were represented. In Sephardic communities, sweet cakes, filled with nuts, and marzipan are made for Purim; in Iraq, zingula, a sweet fried pancake (also a Hanukkah favorite) often has a spot on *Mishloach Manot* plates. Less exotic—to us—local fare such as Rice Krispie Treats and brownies are prepared by American families. In Rhodes and other Sephardic communities, a unique pastry called "folares" is often made for Purim. They seem to borrow from the Easter tradition of decorated eggs. Or maybe the Easter tradition borrowed from

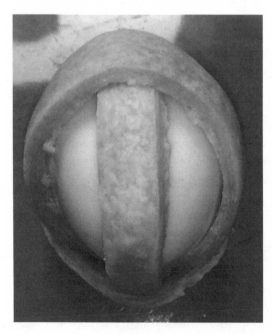

Folares.

folares, though the first decorated Easter eggs were made by early Christians in Mesopotamia, who used red dye to symbolize Jesus's blood. To make folares, prepare a boreka dough (see page 141) and hardboiled eggs; the eggs are sometimes decorated with dyes. Wrap the dough around the bottom of the eggs, leaving the top exposed. Cut two strips of dough and attach them, wrapping around the bottoms of the dough-covered eggs and extending over the top; this is supposed to look like a cage surrounding Haman's head. Bake at 350°F until dough is slightly browned.

HAMAN'S HATS—NOT

Though there are many entries in the Purim cookbook, one pastry is synonymous with the holiday. Hamentaschen have gone mainstream—you'll find them year-round in bakeries, even in areas where no one has ever heard of Purim or met a Jew—but they still have a tight connection with Haman. Children are often taught that the word hamantaschen means "Haman's hat" and that Haman wore a hat that had three corners. There's even a song about it, complete with hand motions. Actually, there's no evidence that Haman wore such a hat, or any hat. The man with the three-cornered hat was Napoleon, who lived more than two thousand years later. Hamantaschen are based on an eastern European pastry called "mohntaschen" or poppy seed (*mohn*) pockets (*taschen*). Somewhere along the way, someone realized that adding a "ha" to the beginning of the word "mohntascen" would make these pastries appropriate for Purim, and so the hamentaschen came to be. The partially hidden filling is another connection; a reference to the secrets of the festival. Originally, they were called *Oznei Haman*, or Haman's ears, which were probably not triangular (there's no evidence that he came from the planet Vulcan). But the Midrash does tell us that Haman's ears were very furled and crinkled, and a somewhat different pastry by the same name is shaped with folds and furls that might resemble an ear (they're similar to French palmieres and are popular among French Jews on Purim).

There is also a theory (not based on concrete fact) that Mordecai, afraid to communicate openly with Jews about the coming catastrophe, wrote letters and hid them in pastries,[2] which is a very nice story that doesn't hold up well to logical scrutiny—although it works for fortune cookies, most people would not put critical information in a jam-filled cookie.

Originally, in Europe, hamentaschen were filled with a paste made with poppy seeds—the seeds of the beautiful poppy flower that is the source of morphine and heroin. Growing poppies was, and still is, banned in some places to deter the trade in opium. Poppy seeds have no opiate effect on people unless they are processed specifically for that purpose—rigorous scientific research has proven that—but they will identify as opiates in a drug test, a fairly common plot point in television shows.

Hamentaschen began to show up in Jewish literature in the Middle Ages. Ben Yehuda, who wrote the first modern Jewish dictionary, cites a reference to a food that sounds like hamentaschen in the writings of Abarbanel (1437–1508). Another early mention is in a Purim skit by Yehuda Somno (1527–1592),[3] an Italian Jew, who theorized that eating Haman would be a good way to destroy him, so why not snack on a cookie that looks like one of his ears? The pastry was mentioned in skits and parodies over the next several hundred years in many parts of Europe. Lady

Judith Cohen Montefiore included a recipe for Haman fritters in *The Jewish Manual*[4] in 1846. And memoirs of Jewish life in the nineteenth and twentieth centuries in eastern and western Europe include them consistently. By the nineteenth century, fruit jams (especially a dense prune jam called *lekvar* and apricot jam) were often substituted for poppy seeds, and by the twentieth century, inventive chefs came up with new fillings and doughs to make dozens of different hamentaschen.

HAMENTASCHEN

• • • • •

Makes 24
INGREDIENTS

For the dough:
2 to 2½ cups flour
1 tablespoon baking powder
½ teaspoon baking soda
½ teaspoon salt
½ cup sugar
¾ cup oil
2 eggs
¼ cup coffee or juice (apple or orange)
2 cups filling (see below)
1 egg for brushing

For the filling:
Poppy seed filling: A traditional, but not always crowd-pleasing, filling especially if there are children in the crowd.

Jam: Plum, apricot, and raspberry are seen most often, but cherry, blueberry, orange, fig, and peach are just as good. If you're not a traditionalist and are looking for a way to shake up your *Mishloach Manot* plate, the tiny triangle inside the hamentash is a place to start; experiment with spiced jams and combinations— sweet hot pepper jelly? Banana-peanut butter? Papaya-ginger?—for something sophisticated and unique.

Chocolate is never a mistake. Make chocolate meringue by beating two egg whites until frothy, then adding half a teaspoon of cream of tartar and half cup of confectioner's sugar—a tablespoon or two at a time—beating after each addition. Add one teaspoon of vanilla or chocolate liqueur and three tablespoons of cocoa and continue beating until mixture is thick and shiny.

Combine the flour, baking powder, baking soda, and salt in a small bowl. Place the sugar, oil, eggs, and coffee/juice in a large bowl. Beat with an electric mixer or by hand until the mixture is smooth and the sugar is dissolved. Add the flour mixture, half a cup at a time, beating between additions until you have a soft dough; it should not be very sticky. If it is, add more flour, a tablespoon at a time.

Form the dough into a large ball and divide the ball into two pieces. Flatten each piece, wrap in wax paper or plastic wrap, and refrigerate for an hour (if you're in a hurry, freeze for ten minutes).

Place one of the discs on a floured board and roll to a thickness of about an eighth of an inch. Using a round cookie cutter or the rim of a glass, cut two-inch rounds and place them on a greased cookie sheet, spaced so that they are not touching. Repeat with the second disc on a second cookie sheet.

Preheat oven to 375°F.

Place about a teaspoon of filling on each circle. Lift both sides of the dough over the filling and pinch the dough together to form the top of a triangle. Then lift the bottom of the circle to meet the two sides, and pinch to create a triangle. The dough should not completely cover the filling.

Mix the last egg with one tablespoon of water. Brush the top and sides of the triangle and pinch again to seal tightly.

Bake for fifteen to twenty minutes until the hamentashen are a light gold color; don't wait until they are completely brown. Cool completely before eating.

Variation: The cookie-type dough in this recipe is a recent modification that makes the recipe easier and faster to prepare. Until the twentieth century, most hamentaschen were made with a yeast dough, and some people prefer it. You can use the dough that is in the rugelah recipe (see page 148) with your favorite filling.

∎ ∎ ∎ ∎ ∎

SEPHARDIC *MISHLOACH MANOT*

Although hamentaschen have been adopted by most Jewish communities as the Purim standard, Sephardic families still include other favorite sweets in their *Mishloach Manot*. Moroccan cooking is famous for its sweet desserts. They often include savory baked goods made with nuts or semolina flour and coated with honey or sugar syrup, including boulukouniu, a candy made with sesame seeds and honey and biskochos, a biscuit that looks like a lobed pretzel, sprinkled with cinnamon and sugar or sesame seeds, and ghourebi, a sugar cookie. Some cookies have hidden fillings, such as date-nut cookies that hide a filling of chopped walnuts and dates flavored with whiskey. In Iraq, *Mishloach Manot* platters are often shaped like fish and include hadgi badah, a not-very-sweet round cookie made from ground almonds and spiced with cardamom.

HADGI BADAH

Rosewater is a traditional ingredient in hadgi badah; sometimes the cook uses it to wet his or her hands when shaping the cookies rather than mixing it into the batter. Orange juice and cinnamon are not traditional in this recipe, but they are easier to find.

• • • • •

24 cookies

INGREDIENTS

1 teaspoon oil for greasing cookie sheet
1½ cups all-purpose flour
1 cup almond flour or ground almonds or walnuts (or a combination)
½ teaspoon ground cardamom
½ teaspoon cinnamon, optional
¼ teaspoon salt
½ teaspoon baking powder
1 cup sugar
3 egg whites plus 1 egg yolk
1 tablespoon orange juice or rosewater
24 whole almonds and/or raisins or pistachios

Preheat oven to 375°F. Prepare a cookie sheet lined with foil or parchment; grease it lightly with oil.

Put the flour, ground almonds, cardamom, salt, baking powder, and sugar in a food processor. Pulse a few times to mix.

Combine the oil, eggs, and juice/rosewater in a small bowl. Beat to combine. Turn the processor to low speed and slowly add this mixture to the dry ingredients through the tube. Stop when the ingredients are combined and a soft dough is formed.

Shape the dough into walnut-sized balls. Place them on the cookie sheet about two inches apart. Flatten them gently to about a half-inch thick. Place a raisin or nut (or both) in the center of each cookie.

Bake in the pre-heated oven for ten to fifteen minutes. After ten minutes, check every minute or so to make sure they are not burning. Allow to cool completely before serving.

• • • • •

GIFTS TO THE POOR

The directive to send portions to people you know on Purim results in people sending them to you as well as you sending to them—so in addition to all the leftovers from their own platters, families who participate in the tradition are usually able to snack on multiple portions that arrive from friends, neighbors, and relatives, which results in sugar overload. Purim is not a holiday of total self-indulgence though. Right after the instruction to send out portions, there is an instruction to send "*matanot l'evyonim,*" gifts to the poor. And the Talmud tells us that if a person does not have the means to take care of both non-needy and needy people, one should give to the needy only.

Taking care of the less fortunate is a core value of Judaism, and the fact that it's written into the celebration—and into most holiday traditions—is evidence of its importance. Judaism is certainly not unique in this practice. Most religions advocate charity, and most houses of worship are involved in taking care of those in need. But Jewish organizations are particularly adept at it.

The practice of charity falls under the heading of "*chesed,*" which translates roughly to goodness or kindness, with some love thrown in. *Chesed* is one concept that every Jewish community, from Ultra-Orthodox and Modern Orthodox to Conservative and Reform and Reconstructionist, agree upon.

And Jewish practicality has caused Jews to organize these kindnesses into very effective measures, called "*Gemilut Chasidim*" (sometimes abbreviated as g'mach), which means the transfer of kindness. There are g'machs that loan money for business or personal use at low interest, groups that visit the sick and bring food to those who don't have any, and groups that invite strangers in need to meals, especially on Shabbat. Emergency medical aid—called Hatzolah—is available to all. A particularly intelligent practice that developed in many congregations is gathering supplies for items that are not needed everyday—extra baby cribs or wheelchairs, dinnerware for large groups, garden or construction tools—and making them available for those who can't afford to buy them, or who don't want to waste the resources that go into producing them when they are not used most of the time (a Jewish version of the sharing economy). All of these fit into the ethic of *Tikkun Olam*, repairing the world. And even as we eat the last boreka and hamentash, drink one more glass of wine, and laugh at the last Purimspiel, that ideal remains in our minds.

THE FEAST OF PURIM

In memory of the feast that Esther prepared for Haman and Achashverosh, the holiday of Purim ends with a feast that starts in mid-afternoon and ends in a song that must be sung before the sun sets. Called a *"Seudah"* (a meal or feast), it's a time for people to get together with friends and relatives, to lay out their finest dinnerware and cook their best food, and to just enjoy. Purim is a holiday for children; sated and excited from all the sugary snacks they've grabbed from *Mishloach Manot* platters and dressed up in costumes, they are the stars of the show, but their elders revert to a childlike state as well.

The feast usually begins with a challah. Moroccan Jews bake a special challah for Purim called *boyoja ungola di Purim*, wrapped around hard-boiled eggs that symbolize Haman's eyes. In Russia, Jews borrowed a sweet Easter bread called kulich for their Purim meal. Easter kulich had a dough similar to Italian panettone and was baked in a columnar pan that resembled a coffee can; in later times, coffee cans were used. The top was glazed with a confectioners' sugar frosting. Purim kulich is braided into a six-strand bread that is supposed to resemble the rope that was used to hang Haman. The braiding sounds much more complicated than it is. Once the first ropes are in place, the others follow easily.

There's usually a fish course served first. Fish is a symbol of Purim and of the month of Adar in which it falls. That's partly because fish is a universal symbol of fertility, abundance, and happiness, and partly because fish is the zodiac sign for the month of Adar. Banners for Purim festivities often include images of fish, and fish are sometimes engraved or painted on *Mishloach Manot* plates. Usually, whatever fish is popular on Shabbat is also served on Purim—gefilte fish in eastern European countries, baked cod in Italy, spiced white fish in North Africa.

Vegetarian courses are also popular and some people keep their Purim *seudot* totally vegetarian or even vegan. According to Midrash, when Esther lived in Achashverosh's house, she stuck to a vegan diet, eating nuts, legumes, seeds, grains, and vegetables because she did not want to eat non-kosher meat. In her honor, several bean and chickpea salads appear on the Purim table.

Another Purim favorite—also served on most other holidays—is borekas. The fact that they are usually vegetarian gives them a connection to Purim, as does the fact that they are delicious.

BOREKAS

Borekas is probably the most common of the Sephardi stuffed savory dough recipes. Bulemas (spiral puff pastry rolls), sambusek (half-moons or triangles with a buttery pastry), and kuba/kibbe (the wrapper is made with pressed bulgar, see page 45) are similar. They are part of the tradition that includes empanadas, ravioli, tortellini, and many Asian dumplings. Borekas probably originated in Turkey as an adaptation of filled pastries from Asia.

An easier way to make borekas is to use packaged puff pastry, rolled thin; there's nothing wrong with taking a shortcut every once in a while.

• • • • •

Serves 12
INGREDIENTS

For the dough:
3 cups flour (more if needed)
1 teaspoon salt
1 cup very hot water (heat in microwave)
1 cup vegetable oil

For assembly:
1 egg, beaten
2 tablespoons sesame seeds
Vegetable oil, for greasing pan

Mix the flour and salt in a bowl. Add the water and oil, and mix quickly with a fork until a soft dough forms. Turn the dough onto a floured board and knead just until smooth. If it too sticky to handle, add more flour, a tablespoon at a time. If it is too stiff to knead easily, add hot water, a tablespoon at a time. Shape the dough into balls, about a generous tablespoon of dough in each. Leave the balls on the board to rest, covering them with a slightly damp cloth. Meanwhile, make the filling.

Preheat the oven to 400°F. Generously grease a baking sheet with vegetable oil.

After the dough has rested for about twenty minutes, use a rolling pin to flatten each ball into a round or oval shape; it should be about three inches in diameter or on the long side of the oval and about a quarter-inch thick. Place a teaspoon of filling in the center of each. Fold in half, and crimp the edge with tines of a fork. Brush the tops with the egg, sealing the edges with egg or water. Place the borekas, close but not touching, on the baking sheet. Bake for twenty-five to thirty minutes until they are golden brown.

Fillings:
For vegetarian borekas, mix all the ingredients and adjust seasonings.

VEGETARIAN FILLINGS
Potato
3 cups mashed potatoes
3 tablespoons sautéed onions
1 teaspoon salt

2 tablespoons butter
2 tablespoons milk or cream
Salt and pepper to taste

Spinach-Cheese-Cream
1 10-ounce package frozen spinach or 1 pound fresh spinach, cooked and
   squeezed dry
1 cup grated cheese—parmesan, mozzarella, feta, or your favorite
½ cup sour cream
2 tablespoons fine breadcrumbs
Salt and pepper to taste

Eggplant and Rice
1 cup cooked rice
2 cups cubed eggplant, sautéed or broiled until soft
2 cups grated or crumbled cheese, mozzarella, parmesan, feta
1 teaspoon salt

Broccoli and Mushrooms
2 cups broccoli, broken into small pieces and cooked until tender crisp
1 cup sliced mushrooms, sautéed in butter until soft
2 cups grated or crumbled cheese (mozzarella, parmesan, feta)
2 tablespoons fine breadcrumbs
Salt and pepper to taste

MEAT FILLINGS
Ground Meat and Vegetables
2 tablespoons oil
1 medium onion, diced
1 small zucchini, diced
½ cup mushrooms, sliced
8 ounces ground beef, chicken, turkey, or lamb
¼ cup tomato sauce
2 tablespoons matzah meal or bread crumbs
Salt and pepper to taste

Heat the oil in a skillet over medium heat. Add the vegetables and sauté until
soft. Crumble in the ground beef and toss until fully browned. Add the tomato

sauce and cook, stirring, until it is all absorbed. Add the matzah meal/bread crumbs and stir until the mixture is fully combined. Add salt and pepper to taste.

Barbecue Shredded Meat
8 ounces grilled or roasted lamb or beef, shredded
¼ cup barbecue sauce
Toss the meat with the barbecue sauce.

• • • • •

Although many Purim *Seudot* are dairy or vegetarian affairs, meat is by no means rare. Turkey dishes are popular, since Achashverosh ruled from India to Ethiopia; in Hebrew, the word "Hodoo" is used for both the country (India) and the bird (turkey). Turkey bean soup has become a Purim staple because it includes both turkey and the beans that Esther ate. Borekas are often served with a meat filling, made with sautéed onion and ground beef or lamb, spiced with cumin or cinnamon. In some homes, breast of veal with a pocket for a filling is the main dish.

There's another reason why borekas, as well as hamentaschen, *kreplach*, stuffed cabbage, and pocketed breast of veal are Purim-appropriate. They represent secrecy and hidden meanings in the way one part of the dish conceals another part.

And Purim is all about secrecy: Esther hiding her religion, Mordecai sending hidden messages to his compatriots. Moreover, the Kabbalists believe that there are layers of the Purim story that have not yet been revealed to us. Contrary to its apparent frivolity, they consider it one of the holiest days in the Jewish calendar—Yom Kippur, also called Yom Kippurim, which most people consider super-holy, is just a shadow of Purim; the "ki" in Kippur is a contraction for "kimo" which means "similar to, but lesser than." We won't find out what that significance is until the Messiah comes, but let's hope, whatever it is, that it doesn't distract from the fun of Purim.

The meal ends with more sweets, just in case we haven't been eating them all day. And in Jerusalem, it starts all over the next day when Shushan Purim is celebrated. Purim is celebrated not on the thirteenth of Adar when the battles against Haman's forces took place, but on the fourteenth of Adar, when there was peace. In Shushan, the capital city of Persia, and in Jerusalem, the battles were fiercer and lasted another day, so the celebration takes place on the fifteenth of Adar. The day is called Shushan Purim and allows people to have not one day of this joyous holiday, but two.

PURIM CUSTOMS AROUND THE WORLD

Iraq

Purim was celebrated for two days in Baghdad; a total of six lavish feasts were served on these days. Schools were closed, and children participated fully in every meal. One popular dish at these meals was *Sambusak El Tawa*, a turnover filled with spiced chickpeas and vegetables in remembrance of Esther's vegetarian diet. Eating foods stuffed with hidden fillings is a symbol of the secret plots and palace intrigue that swirled during the events that Purim commemorates.

Uzbekistan

Bukharan Jews have a cool and somewhat smelly custom: They build a huge snowman to represent Haman and attach all kinds of trash to it—eggshells, orange peels, moldy bread—to show their disrespect. At the end of the day, they build a huge bonfire and kill the villain by melting him.

Bulgaria

The Purim *Seudah* often included a dish called *"Caveos di Aman"* or Haman's hair. It consisted of thin spaghetti or vermicelli, served with hard-boiled eggs and black olives, and dressed with lemon juice, olive oil, salt, and pepper.

Iran

In Iran, formerly known as Persia, where the story of Esther originally took place, *Mishloach Manot* plates are especially elaborate and include sweet as well as savory items, including sambusek, pastries filled with meat or cheese, and masafan (almond paste baked in the shape of a star).

Ukraine

Before World War II, well-to-do Jewish families in Ukraine would enjoy elaborate meat meals on Purim afternoon, including pot roast or turkey, latkes, and a honey-apple-nut strudel called fluden (and, of course, hamentaschen).

Greece and Turkey

The Jews in both of these countries bake Haman's fingers—phyllo dough brushed with butter, oil, or margarine and filled with a mixture of sugar, chopped pistachios or almonds, chopped orange rind, and cinnamon—on Purim. The recipe may have been brought from Salonika to Turkey in the 1420s, when Jews were forced to migrate by Ottoman rulers.

Fossano, Italy

The Jews in this northern Italian town celebrate their own Purim right after Passover. During the Napoleonic Wars at the end of the eighteenth century, during Passover, resentful Christians attacked the Jewish community in their synagogue and were ready to commit mayhem. Suddenly a bomb from the invading French troops fell on the attackers and frightened them away. The day is celebrated as a miracle and the hole where the bomb hit the building has been turned into a window.

Libya

Libyans eat a dessert called "The Rose." To make it, thin strips of sweet dough are wrapped around a fork to form a rose, then deep-fried. It is often eaten on Purim, probably connected to the Purim song *"Shoshanat Yakov"*—the rose of Jacob—which celebrates Jewish victories and is sung on Purim after the reading of the *Megillah*.

Fifteenth-Century Spain

The ninth to twelfth century was a Golden Age for the Jews of Spain. Jewish poets, scholars, and scientists were revered, and Jews were free to practice their religion and celebrate their holidays. By the fifteenth century, things changed. Jews were persecuted, killed, and finally banished. A few, called Marranos or Anusim, remained in Spain, keeping their religion secret and performing their rituals only in hiding. When Purim came, they wanted to celebrate, but the rowdy, lavish rites of Purim would have gotten them killed. Instead, they commemorated Purim by fasting, as Queen Esther did, allowing themselves a less entertaining but still significant connection to the holiday.

7

❖ ❖

Passover

The Slaves Rise Up, the Dough Stays Flat

The Exodus from Egypt, following centuries of slavery, is the most significant event in the formation of the Jewish nation. Many of the characteristics associated with Jews—both positive and negative—are in full view during these events. We start with a very unsavory incident—brothers plotting against another brother—and later see hesitance in the face of danger and a lot of whining. But we also see how Joseph's intelligence and advance planning saved both his own people and the people of Egypt; how a mother saved her infant son from death; and how, when push came to shove, six hundred thousand people took a risky plunge to escape slaughter.

Later—after more whining—the Jews formed one of the most representative governments imaginable. All citizens (actually, all male citizens, but that was standard at the time) formed groups of ten; each group of ten elected a leader who joined the leaders of other groups of ten. Those groups of ten represented one hundred people and elected a leader who joined other leaders of a hundred—and so on, from ten to one hundred to one thousand to ten thousand to one hundred thousand, at which point six leaders reported directly to Moses. No one was ever more than seven steps removed from the high command.

At this time, the Jewish nation was united and went on to conquer the Holy Land. Success lasted for several hundred years before we were dispersed, again and again. But memories of how we left Egypt are recalled every year at Passover, showing us where our strength and character come from. When we sit down to the Seder, in countries all over the globe, many of us far from the Promised Land, we talk about our beginning and remember what we have in common.

REFLECTIONS

In each generation, every person should feel personally redeemed from Egypt.—Passover Haggadah

One of the oldest, most widely observed and colorful and dramatic of all the Jewish festivals is Passover (*Pesach*), also known in rabbinic literature as *Zeman Heiruteinu*—the season of liberation—celebrating the liberation of the Israelites from Egyptian slavery and the beginning of Jewish nationhood. It is the national birthday of the Jewish people, and its many laws and regulations have been observed in many different ways for centuries. Another name for Passover is *Hag Ha-Aviv*—the holiday of spring. The Jewish calendar is set so that certain holidays always occur in a particular season of the year. Thus, the holiday of liberation is also the holiday of spring, not by coincidence but by design. Following the darkness of winter when many plants lie dormant, spring marks the rebirth of the Earth with the bursting forth of budding trees. Similarly, the Israelite people, oppressed as slaves, burst forth out of Egypt into a new life's journey filled with many challenges but the gift of freedom.

The English name "Passover" is a literal translation of one of the two biblical names for the festival of *Pesach*. The Hebrew term *pesach*, which means "to pass over," is a reminder of the special divine protection that the Israelites enjoyed in Egypt during the tenth plague, when the angel of God passed over their houses while slaying every Egyptian firstborn male. The other biblical name for the holiday, *Hag HaMatzot* (Festival of Unleavened Bread), serves as a reminder of the unleavened bread that the Israelites hastily made when they hurriedly left Egypt and had no time to let their dough rise.

The observance of the very first Passover in Palestine is mentioned in the *Book of Joshua* (5:10–11). Here it is said that the Israelites, led by Joshua, successor to Moses, kept the feast at Gilgal. For about the next three centuries after his death, Passover played little or no role in the national life of the Jewish people, due to constant harassment by hostile neighbors. Samuel the Prophet revived Passover in the eleventh century BCE, and its celebration reached its zenith under King Solomon with the construction of the Temple in Jerusalem. In the *Second Book of Chronicles*, the Jewish priests are described as tossing the blood of the paschal lamb on the altar while the Levites sang psalms of praise.

The special home ceremony on the night of Passover, called the *Seder* (order), is based on the biblical injunction to parents to inform their children of the deliverance from Egypt: "And you shall tell your son in that day, saying: It is because of that which God did for me when I came out of Egypt" (*Exodus*, 13:8). By the beginning of the second century, we begin to find Talmudic references to various phases of the Seder ceremony as we know it today.

The questions asked by the youngest child (in the reading known as *Ma Nishtanah*) during the course of the Seder meal have changed over the centuries. The earliest version of these questions, preserved in the Jerusalem Talmud, contains only three questions, beginning with the Hebrew phrase *mah nishtanah* (why is it different?) which is used in present times as well. The Babylonian Talmud quotes four questions: why matzah is eaten, why bitter herbs are eaten, why meat is eaten exclusively roasted, and why food is dipped twice. The question about roasted meat has been eliminated due to the fact that there is no longer a Temple in Jerusalem, and the newest question (the fourth) is now "why on this night do we eat while reclining?" To recline is a sign of being free.

Passover has meant many things to the Jewish people throughout the ages. From their very beginning, they saw God's outstretched arm in history and owed their very existence as a people to their faith in divine intervention. The home observance of the Seder meal has strengthened family ties. As the springtide of nature fills each creature with joy and hope, so Israel's feast of redemption promises the great day of liberty to those who still chafe under the yoke of oppression.

THE STORY OF PASSOVER

The Passover story happened because of two common human feelings: jealousy, in the form of sibling rivalry, and hunger.

The sibling rivalry occurred in the family of the patriarch Jacob, son of Isaac and grandson of Abraham. Jacob had twelve sons from four different wives, but he didn't hide the fact that he loved the offspring of Rachel, his favorite wife, the most. He made a beautiful multi-colored coat for Joseph, Rachel's oldest son, and that was the straw that broke the camel's back for the rest of the kids. They went a little further than most brothers do to punish Joseph. They considered killing him, but ended up selling him to some passing traders, who took the boy from his home in Canaan to Egypt, where he was put to work in the home of a nobleman. But Joseph was a clever young man and his talents made the nobleman, and eventually the king, known as Pharaoh, take notice. Joseph predicted that there would be a famine in the region and suggested that Pharaoh store enough food to last for seven years. When the prophesy came true, Joseph became second-in-command to Pharaoh.

Meanwhile, back in Canaan, the famine was in full force and the family of Jacob was hungry. On a trip to Egypt, they learned that Joseph was still alive and in a position of authority; after toying with them a little (they certainly deserved it), Joseph invited the family to come to Egypt, where there was enough food. So seventy members of Jacob's family moved to Egypt and they prospered for many years.

But when Pharaoh died, after a generation that swelled the ranks of the Hebrews (as they were called), the new Pharaoh became nervous of the growing clan in his kingdom and decided to enslave them. And for the next few centuries, the Hebrews put in backbreaking labor building the cities and pyramids that the pharaohs ordered. Though they lived in poverty, they had many children and subsequent pharaohs still worried that they would try to take over—and ordered that every baby boy born to Hebrew parents be killed.

But a woman named Yocheved, also known as Shifra, gave birth prematurely and was able to hide her son until he was three months old. Then she put him in a small boat made of reeds and placed him in the Nile River, where Pharaoh's daughter used to go with her maids. Pharaoh's daughter took pity on the baby and pulled him from the water. (In the movie *The Ten Commandments*, Yvonne De Carlo, who plays the princess, says, "I will name you Moses because I pulled you from the water." She doesn't explain that the word "moshe" [the Hebrew form of Moses] means "pulled" in Hebrew—one of the great non sequiturs in cinema.) She takes little Moses home and raises him as a prince.

But when Moses becomes a man, he is infuriated when he sees overseers torturing the Hebrew slaves, and he kills an overseer. He has to run away to a distant town, where God appears to him in the guise of a burning bush and tells him to free his people. Moses goes to the Pharaoh and asks him to "let my people go." Pharaoh refuses, so God sends a plague—all the rivers in Egypt turn to blood. Pharaoh relents, the Hebrews get ready to go, and Pharaoh changes his mind. God sends another plague—frogs, this time, and the sequence is repeated: relent, ready, change of mind. This happens ten times in all—lice, wild animals, diseased livestock, boils, hail, locusts, darkness, and finally the slaughter of all Egyptian firstborn sons—because obviously, Pharaoh had some control issues. But the last one did the trick. God told the Jews to sacrifice lambs and to mark their doorposts with the blood (which became major elements of the holiday of Passover, see page 158). When the angel of God went on his killing spree, he passed over the residences with blood on their doorposts—hence the name Passover. With Egyptians families in despair over their dead sons, Pharaoh finally bowed to God's will and let the Hebrews leave.

The Hebrews were not going to take any chances. As they were preparing the meal that God had requested—laying out dough for flatbread, sacrificing the lamb—they realized that the Egyptian forces were in chaos. They grabbed their neighbors' jewelry and livestock—a reasonable recompense for hundreds of years of hard labor—and loaded the flatbread on their backs, not even waiting for it to rise. And they headed for the banks of the Red Sea.

Moses told them to jump right in to the heavily flowing waters, but it seemed like a good way to drown. They hesitated and noticed that Pharaoh had finally rallied his forces; they were right behind the Hebrews, rolling on chariots, girded with all the kingdom's weapons. With catastrophe in front of and behind them, they took the plunge. By this time, their population had increased to six hundred thousand souls, so it must have made quite a splash.

But they did not sink. Instead, God parted the waters and they walked on the dry land of the riverbed, singing halleluiahs all the way. (Some archaeologists believe that it was not unusual for the water to recede completely, as it was part of the ebb and flow of sea—but it was quite a miracle that it occurred exactly when they needed it.) Just as they reached the other side of the sea, with all that wet matzah on their backs, the Egyptian army reached the first side of the sea. They saw dry land and immediately entered to pursue the Hebrews. But God was still watching (or the tides were still working)—the river went back to its original position, drowning all the Egyptians and their horses. And the Jews were on their way to the Promised Land, with all their families, belongings, livestock, and wet matzah intact.

DID THE PASSOVER STORY ACTUALLY HAPPEN?

Some respected scholars insist that there is no evidence for the events related in *Exodus*, and that if it happened about thirty-five hundred years ago, as most historians believe (the accepted dates for the Exodus fall between 1570 and 1290 BCE), some remnants would remain behind. There should, they say, be a rusty chariot or two at the bottom of the Red Sea (after all, we have dinosaur bones from three hundred million years ago) or at least some mention of them in texts from the period. The experts on that side of the debate insist that the customs of Passover were derived from common events around springtime, such as eating unleavened bread (because farmers busy planting fields ate what was on hand) and marking doorposts with blood (because it was the time for slaughtering lambs, and the mark meant that the work was done).

Other scientists, just as qualified, find that there are shreds of evidence, all that would be expected from so ancient an event. The Ipuwer papyrus, written around 1650 BCE and found in the early nineteenth century,[1] mentions plagues that are similar to ones God brought down upon the Egyptians—bloody rivers, pestilence, darkness, deaths of the sons. Though the dates seem to contradict a connection, the text in the papyrus is surprisingly close to that of the Torah, and dates that far back are always approximate. Experts on this side of the debate also point out that some ancient Egyptian maps mark sites that are mentioned in the Passover story and that another papyrus mentions a slave named Shifra, an alternate for Moses' mother. There are bits of archaeological fact to counter the claim that there is not a shred of physical evidence—for example, digs in the land that was Canaan show that around the time that the Jews invaded it, pig bones disappeared from garbage pits[2]—making the issue one that is unlikely to ever be definitively decided.

THE FIRST PASSOVER

Right before He began killing Egypt's firstborn sons, the catastrophe that convinced Pharaoh to let the slaves leave, God gave Moses a set of instructions for how they were to prepare; these instructions became part of the holiday of Passover that was to be celebrated forever. First, find a lamb or goat that's the right size for the family; on the fourteenth of the month of Nisan, the lamb is to be slaughtered and its blood smeared on the doorframe. At night, roast the lamb and eat it with matzah and maror (bitter herbs). Eat it quickly, God said, with belts fastened, shoes on, staffs in hand. Other than the belts, the shoes, the staffs, and the hurry—this is a short version of the Seder we still hold on the night of the fourteenth of Nisan.

God continues, "This will be a day for you to remember and celebrate . . . from generation to generation . . . a perpetual regulation." And then, He (through Moses) lays down another law that makes the days of Passover different from all over days: "For seven days you are to eat matzah—on the first day remove the leaven from your houses. For whoever eats *chametz* [leavened bread] from the first to the seventh day is to be cut off from Israel." Many of the foods we eat on Jewish holidays are customs or symbols, but eating matzah on Passover is straight from the mouth of God. Not only is the food choice strictly regulated, but the punishment for disobedience is clear and dire—the punishment known as *"karet,"* or cutting off, is essentially death.

Just as it happened for the rules of kashrut, subsequent generations of Jews made the rules for removing *chametz* more stringent. This strengthening of the commandment happened faster than it did for kashrut, possibly because of the clearly stated punishment. By the time of the Talmud, Jews were feverishly cleaning their houses to make sure that not a speck of leaven remained. The Talmud instituted a method of making sure the house was clean: "On the evening of the [fourteenth], we search for *chametz* by the light of a candle." In many homes, this search (called *bedikat chametz*, the search for *chametz*) is still done, and it's fun for all—sort of a scavenger hunt, done with a candle, a feather to sweep out any bits of bread that are found, and a cup to keep them together. There was some worry that by the time of the search, the house would be so clean that no leaven would be found. So someone always placed bits of bread around the house (and then remembers where they are hidden, hopefully). The next morning, the last bits of leaven are burned; in religious neighborhoods in Brooklyn and elsewhere, boys tend fires in big cans so that all their neighbors can declare their homes *chametz*-free.

In many homes, the weeks before Passover are a frenzy of cleaning; every closet and cabinet is scoured, the cracks between tiles are scrubbed with toothbrushes, pockets are emptied of lint, and books are dusted to make sure there are no crumbs between the pages. Dishwashers, ovens, and refrigerators are taken apart so that the parts one never sees can be cleaned. In homes where the rules are followed strictly, any surface that will come into contact with food during the week of Passover is covered or "koshered" (entire books have been written on how to kosher a surface for Passover). Actual bread or flour is removed from the house, and any ingredients that are to be saved for after the holiday are put away in cabinets that will be closed for the duration of the holiday. There is a custom, still practiced by some, of selling all *chametz* that remains anywhere in the home to a non-Jew; there is an actual contract signed by both parties that states where the *chametz* is located and the price. A second contract sells the *chametz* back to the original owner.

Why is there so much attention paid to eradicating *chametz*? In rabbinic tradition, *chametz* symbolizes arrogance because bread raises itself above the level of the matzah, even though it is only filled with pockets of air. On Passover, we want to try to remove the *chametz* (representing our ego and excessive pride) from our hearts and homes.[3]

Passover cleaning, though labor-intensive and time-consuming, is a very beneficial tradition, like spring cleaning, but with excommunication and possibly death as a punishment for doing it wrong. There's a nice feeling when it's done and the whole house is certifiably clean at the same time. Homes that follow the Passover tradition never exceed a certain level of griminess because they must be cleaned thoroughly at least once a year.

When the cleaning is done, everything that touches food is put away and the Passover dishes come out, along with silverware, glasses, pots, pans, small appliances, and all the objects used for the ceremonies. Even people who are not strictly observant sometimes follow this custom to some degree, just for the pleasure of enjoying family heirlooms for one week of the year. Unlike the non-Passover dishes, these are not subject to everyday wear and breakage. It's not unusual for a family to have the Passover dishes that their great-grandparents used.

Another element of the Passover tradition that extended further than was stipulated in the Bible was the type of food that was considered *chametz*. Observant Jews avoid anything that is not certified "kosher for Passover"—foods manufactured on machinery that has touched *chametz* is forbidden, as well as anything that might, to someone, look like *chametz*. Rice, beans, and seeds all fall under this category, and Ashkenazi Jews don't use them on Passover. Sephardic Jews do eat these foods, so if you're looking for a varied Passover meal, you're better off in a Sephardi home.

All the focus on adherence to the eradication of chametz may lead one to wonder whether the holiday, for observant Jews, is mired in so much minutiae that it ignores other Jewish values. Rabbi Israel Salanter, an Orthodox rabbi in Lithuania in the mid-nineteenth century, was known as a strict follower of Passover rules. But he showed that he didn't forget the human element when one of his students asked him to point out the most important thing to watch for when baking matzahs. He told the student to make sure the old woman who kneaded the dough was not mistreated.[4]

SEVEN DAYS OF MATZAH

Matzah is an icon of the Jewish religion, not only as a food but as part of our shared identity. Larry Rivers (the grandfather of pop art, who was born Yitzchock Loiza Grossberg in 1922 in the Bronx) drove this point home when he created a huge triptych depicting the history of the Jews superimposed on three gigantic images of matzah.

The word "matzah" comes from a root that means pressed or squeezed. The matzah dough that the Hebrews took with them as they left slavery was pretty much the same as most of the bread that was baked in their time. They didn't add a dash of starter from a previous batch as they otherwise did, and they didn't give it time to form its own leaven, so it stayed flatter than usual. Although five different grains are permissible for Passover matzah (wheat, spelt, barley, rye, and oats, with oats as a last resort for people who can't eat the others), wheat flour is by far the most common. The only other ingredient is water. The process is simple: mix the ingredients, knead briefly, roll them out in big circles, score them, and bake them in a hot oven. Rabbis have determined that the process, from the moment the flour touches water to taking the baked matzah out of the oven, must not take more than eighteen minutes. Otherwise the forbidden leavening may start.

"YOU SHALL GUARD THE MATZAH"

The line above, from *Exodus* (12:17), requires that matzah eaten on Passover must be guarded to avoid any chance that it will rise. Most Jews, even those who are serious about observing the commandments, are willing to accept matzah that is made from wheat that is carefully watched from the time it is ground until it is baked. But for those looking for extra credit, there is *shmurah* (guarded) matzah— matzah that is guarded even before it is harvested. To make *shmurah* matzah— which sells for up to sixty dollars per pound—rabbis carefully inspect the field where the wheat is growing to determine when the stalks have reached the ideal level of moisture. They choose a clear, dry day for harvesting and then keep an eye on the wheat at every stage of transportation, grinding, and baking.

The *shmurah* matzah process eliminates the possibility that the wheat will rise, but there is also an unintended advantage: it's delicious. In *1,000 Foods to Eat Before You Die: A Food Lover's Life List,*[5] *New York Times* food critic Mimi Sheraton assures us that machine-made matzah doesn't hold a candle to the ones made in the small religious bakeries. And Dan Barber, chef at the famed Blue Hill Restaurant in New York, after watching a rabbi inspect a field of wheat and then tasting the resulting matzah, reported that, "the matzah I'd tasted must be proof not just of a higher understanding of agriculture but also of a higher understanding of deliciousness." He then asked the rabbi if this was intentional. "No. Absolutely not," he said. "It's just kosher law." Barber concluded that the work that goes into making the matzah as kosher as humanly possible also makes the farm better in other ways. As Klaas Martens, the farmer who worked with the rabbi, told him, "Mindfulness is a part of all my work now, and it benefits just about everything I grow."[6]

FROM HAND TO MACHINE

Until the middle of the nineteenth century in America, all matzah was made by hand, pretty much the same way as it was made by the Hebrew slaves as they were leaving Egypt. Most matzahs were made by synagogues, which distributed them to their congregants, and they often had special kitchens for this task. The matzahs were round or oval, irregular in shape and in doneness, and almost impossible to pack and transport without breakage.

By the middle of the nineteenth century, as more Jews moved to the New World, synagogues became less central to their lives, and commercial bakeries began to spring up to satisfy their matzah needs. Some of these were run by less-than-stringent owners, and were not patronized by more religious Jews. Then several matzah bakeries that were owned by trusted rabbis began to appear.

Matzah joined the Industrial Revolution in 1838 when Isaac Singer, an Alsatian Jew, invented a machine that could roll out the dough so that the laborious process of kneading it could be eliminated. It didn't take long before the machines were in use throughout Europe, and by 1850, there was even one in the United States. But not everyone liked it. It took jobs away from workers, mostly poor women, who depended on this seasonal work. Some rabbis felt it didn't guarantee kashrut, though others believed that by removing the human factor, it was more likely to produce an unleavened finished product. And many people disliked it on philosophical grounds, the same way many people today will pay more for a handmade product because they understand exactly how it's made and what goes into it. That argument can be pooh-poohed—until you compare the quality of those handmade artisanal products with the mass-produced versions that follow. Matzah is certainly no exception; the square matzahs that fit so nicely into boxes are not nearly as tasty as the irregular, round, handmade ones that cost many times the price.

In 1888, a Russian rabbi named Behr Manischewitz moved to Cincinnati and changed the shape of matzah and matzah-making forever, converting it from round and handmade to square and mass-produced. Rabbi Manischewitz possessed a rare combination of genuine piety and altruism with business skills. After starting a matzah factory, he embraced the new machinery and expanded it so that an assembly line of machinery mixed the ingredients, kneaded, rolled, scored, moved into a baking oven, and then packaged the matzahs. To make the matzahs acceptable to everyone, he called upon the most respected rabbis in Jerusalem to endorse his products. He provided financial support to the Israeli yeshivas and even sent his sons to study there. With the recommendations of the Jerusalem rabbinate, and a canny ad campaign, the Manischewitz matzah factory grew quickly, making more than a million matzahs a day.[7] By 1915, other entrepreneurs had set up matzah factories; Manischewitz either bought them (like New York's Horowitz-Margareten) or co-existed with them (like Streit's Matzoh factory, the last privately owned matzah bakery, which closed in 2015 when real estate on the Lower East Side of Manhattan made it too expensive to stay there—they recently moved to New Jersey).

Matzah's main role is its part in the Passover tradition, but it appears in other recipes and forms. Ground matzah, called matzah meal, is used to make the dumplings (matzah balls or *knaydlech*) that grace chicken soup and is an excellent breading ingredient. Matzah is used as a cracker for dips and spreads. But its most beloved form might be the matzah brei.

MATZAH BREI

Matzah brei originated in North America. Although people had already figured out that soaking matzah in water and then frying it in butter made a tasty dish (there's a recipe in *The Jewish Manual* [London, 1846]), it took American ingenuity to add the eggs. "Matzahs Dipped in Eggs" appeared in Aunt Babette's cookbook (Cincinnati, 1889) and the term matzah brei (brei means mash or porridge) came into use by the beginning of the twentieth century. America's square machine-made matzahs were easier to turn into matzah brei, and the fact that they were much cheaper than handmade matzahs made this a cheap dish (and a way to use up broken or extra matzahs). The classic version uses only matzah, water, eggs, salt, and pepper, plus oil or butter for frying—and it's scrumptious—but there's no reason not to add herbs, spices, other vegetables, or anything else. There's also no reason that it can't be topped with sauces and salsa; there's just no reason why it needs them.

One great controversy among matzah brei devotees is whether to fry the mixture as a cohesive pancake or scramble it. Another is whether it is permissible to eat matzah brei before or after Passover. There's no pressing reason not to enjoy it for the other fifty-one weeks of the year, except that saving it for Passover makes both it and Passover a little more special.

• • • • •

1 serving

INGREDIENTS

2 square matzahs
1 cup boiling water
1 beaten egg
Salt and pepper to taste
Butter or oil for frying

Place the matzahs in a bowl and pour the water over them. Let them sit for a minute, then drain, squeeze out the water, and crumble the matzahs into pieces; the matzah will be wet and will crumble easily.

Season the beaten egg with salt and pepper, and pour it over the matzah. Toss to coat the matzah pieces with egg.

If you're making a pancakelike matzah brei, heat the butter or oil in a seven- or eight-inch frying pan. Ladle the matzah mixture into the pan, press it down, and let it cook for about two minutes. Then run a pancake turner or spatula around the sides and under it. Turn it onto a plate, and then return to the pan with the cooked side down. Let the other side cook for another few minutes until it is brown and crispy all over, then slide onto a plate.

To scramble, add the matzah mixture to the buttered or oiled pan; use a bigger pan. Toss until the matzah is cooked to your liking.

Like omelets and scrambled eggs, both forms are best eaten immediately.

• • • • •

THE SEDER

The Passover Seder is one of the best-known events of the holiday and of all of Judaism; in a Pew Research study in 2014, 70 percent of all Jews questioned had attended a Seder that year (as opposed to 54 percent who had fasted for all or part of Yom Kippur).[8] The Seder is a festive event that integrates several of the most prominent aspects of Judaism's long history: our diversity; our propensity to remember our past and study it deeply; our love of getting together with our relatives; and, of course, food. At the Seder, food is both a joy and a symbol of past suffering. It is through a specific set of foods that we remember one of the seminal Jewish experiences and make sure that our children remember it, too.

As we sit at a table laden with symbolic foods, we ask, why is this night different from all others? We answer, for the next generation to hear, that it's because we were slaves to the pharaohs in Egypt, and everything we're about to do on this night is so that we will never forget how God freed us. We use all our senses to integrate these memories into our brains and our collective memories; we taste the matzah, we feel the cementlike texture of the *haroset*, we smell the sharpness of the bitter herbs, we watch as the leader points to each item on the Seder plate, we listen to the songs and the readings. There are fifteen steps in the "order" (the meaning of the word Seder is order) and each connects us in some way to the freedom that we achieved when we left Egypt.

The Passover Seder started out as the meal that God commanded the Jews to eat right before He drew them out of slavery. That first Seder consisted of only three items: pesach (the sacrificial lamb, roasted and eaten), matzah (the unleavened bread), and *maror* (bitter herbs). It stayed that way until the wars in the Promised Land subsided, at which point the writers of the *Mishnah* and Talmud added many elements, including the four cups of wine, the dippings of bitter herbs, the four questions, the reclining, and some of the readings. Sages in the tenth century organized these into the *haggadah*, the guide book to the Seder. The first *haggadah* still in existence dates back to around the eleventh century; it was found in Cairo in the twentieth century and is now held in the Center for Advanced Jewish Studies at the University of Pennsylvania.[9] That *haggadah* shows that most of the elements in the Seder were already in place, except for Elijah's cup and some of the later songs. But the Seder is not static and there is no halachah stating that it cannot be expanded. Today, some people add oranges to the Seder plate to celebrate women and sexual diversity, or add stories to remember fallen or imprisoned soldiers. Adding explanations and family remembrances makes the Seder more personal and more profound.

The first of the fifteen steps of the Seder is *Kadesh*, making the blessing over wine. The blessing is similar to the one made on Shabbat. This is the first of the four cups of wine that are drunk at the Seder. Drinking these four cups of wine, in addition to making everyone pleasantly tipsy, is a part of the telling of the story at the Seder meal. One explanation connects the four cups with the four expressions of redemption found in *Exodus* (6:6–7): "I am God, I will *free* you from the burdens of the Egyptians and *deliver* you from their bondage. I will *redeem* you with an outstretched arm and I will *take* you to be My people." When we sing the song "*Vehi She-Amdah*" (For this that has stood—for our forefathers and for us) at the beginning of the Seder, some people say that "this" is the wine itself—the fact that we make *Kiddush* every Shabbat, and don't drink wine with gentiles, is the reason that Judaism has stood for generations.

The next two steps are *U-Rechatz*—washing hands (because it's better to be clean and a sign of purity when starting a meal)—and *Karpas*. *Karpas*—a Greek word for fresh vegetable—is the first of the dipping steps and involves a vegetable (usually celery, parsley, or potato) dipped in salt water that symbolizes the tears that our ancestors shed during their period of slavery. There are several explanations given for the seeming obsession with dipping on Passover (such as that it recalls how Joseph's brothers dipped his coat in blood so his father would think he had been killed by wild animals), but the most reasonable is that it's done to make the children ask questions and become more involved.

Then we move to the first of the matzah steps. In step four, *Yachatz*, the middle of three matzahs on the Seder plate is split in two and one half is wrapped and put away—the *afikomen*. Children try to steal this wrapped matzah; it's needed at the end of the Seder and if the kids gain possession, they can get presents for its return. It's probably the only time that stealing is encouraged; it's a way to teach children their first lesson in extortion, and also to keep them involved in the proceeding.

And now it's time for *Magid* (step five), an extended session of reading and singing the story of Passover—the four questions asked by children, the answer that tells of how we were slaves and freed by God. The song *Dayenu*—literally, "Enough for Us"—praises God for all the steps he took in bringing us out of Egypt, giving us manna in the wilderness, bringing us to the Promised Land—is followed by several songs of praise, called Hallel.

And then we wash our hands again (*Rachtza*, step six) and get down to the symbolic foods. Matzah again—two pieces this time, for two blessings, Motzi and Matzah, steps seven and eight.

There's a bit of confusion about these next two elements in the Seder: *Maror* (bitter herbs) and *Koreich* (sandwich), steps nine and ten, both of which involve dipping. One would think that the bitter herb would be a vegetable with a decidedly bitter taste, but it's actually the lettuce that is used to wrap the tasty, sweet *haroset*. These are mentioned in the *Mishnah*, in a description of the Passover table: "unleavened bread and lettuce and *haroset*, even though the *haroset* is not a commandment." Romaine lettuce, supposedly, has a bitter taste after a while and is supposed to remind us of the bitterness of the slaves' lives. Some people use sharper greens, such as chicory or stinging nettle, and in Sephardic homes, parsley or scallions.

Haroset is reminiscent of the mortar that the Hebrews used in their forced building activities; the Hebrew word for clay is *charsis*, and Rabbi Moses ben Maimon (a twelfth-century Spanish sage and physician, known as Rambam or Maimonides) wrote that *haroset* was supposed to look like clay mixed with straw. He even provided a recipe: Crush "dates, dried figs, or raisins and the like . . . add vinegar, and mix them with spices." The sweetness of the *haroset* is meant to reduce the sting of the not-so-bitter herb

Over the years, *haroset* lost all but a passing resemblance to cement; instead, cooks from every country created signature versions that—rather than reminding us of misery—are quite delicious. The Persian version, called haleg, uses dates, pears, and oranges, plus a bit of cider vinegar. Yemenites use figs, dates, and nuts, spiced with cumin, cinnamon, ginger, and cardamom. Syrians add matzah meal in place of the straw used to make bricks. There's an Afghani version that includes bananas and a French style that's full of chestnuts. So there's no reason not to use whatever ingredients you like, as long as they remind you of cement.

ASHKENAZI *HAROSET*

There's a good reason why apples are used in the *haroset* that was used in eastern Europe—apples were about the only fruit that made it through winter. The apples also bring to mind the apple orchards where Jewish midwives tried to hide Jewish babies to avoid killing them during the years of slavery in Egypt.

●　●　●　●　●

Makes 2 cups

INGREDIENTS

2 to 3 apples (about 1 pound); use a mixture of tart and sweet varieties
½ cup chopped nuts (walnuts, pecans, filberts, almonds, brazil nuts)
¼ cup sweet red wine

½ teaspoon cinnamon
¼ teaspoon ground ginger

Place all the ingredients into the bowl of a food processor; pulse a few times until finely chopped. If you prefer a more cementlike *haroset*, continue processing until smooth.

•   •   •   •   •

MOROCCAN *HAROSET* BALLS

Moroccan Jews roll their *haroset* into balls; they eat them throughout Passover, sometimes squished between two pieces of matzah.

•   •   •   •   •

Makes 2 cups

INGREDIENTS

½ cup dried fruit—apricots, prunes, raisins
½ cup dried dates
2 or 3 figs
¼ cup almonds, shelled
¼ cup pistachios, shelled
¼ cup sweet red wine
½ teaspoon cinnamon
½ teaspoon ground ginger
½ cup ground nuts

Place all the ingredients except the ground nuts into a food processor; process until smooth. If the mixture is too chunky, add a bit more wine. Place the mixture into a bowl and refrigerate for about thirty minutes until it is a bit firmer. Then roll into walnut-size balls. Refrigerate for several hours until very firm, then roll each ball in the ground nuts.

•   •   •   •   •

THE SEDER CONTINUES

The second coming of bitter herbs involves grated horseradish served between two pieces of matzah. Here, too, the sharp sting of the herb is softened by the conciliatory matzah. Horseradish is a perennial root vegetable that is native to Europe and western Asia, but it was already used as a condiment in Egypt in 1500 BCE. Its painful burn is caused by a compound called *allyl isothiocyanate*, which is only released when the root is grated; the compound protects the plant from most animals who don't like it any more than the children who are convinced to taste it as part of the Seder.

Horseradish is not specified as part of the Seder in the Torah; in fact, historians believe that the bitter herb mentioned in the phrase "unleavened bread and bitter herbs" (*Exodus*, 12:8) is either hemlock or wormwood, both of which are deadly. The writers of the *Mishnah* clarified by listing vegetables that were acceptable as bitter herbs: "And these are the vegetables that a person may meet his requirements with on Passover: Lettuce, endive, cardoon, eryngo, and sea sow-thistle" (*Pesachim*, 2:6)—and still, no horseradish. Horseradish finally came up in the twelfth century, mentioned by Rabbi Eliezer ben Nathan as an ingredient in *haroset*. Horseradish came into use as the bitter herb later in the Middle Ages when Jews who had by then moved farther north in Europe found it hard to obtain lettuce in the colder regions at the start of the harvest season. A fourteenth-century Talmudic scholar, Rabbi Alexander Suslin, approved horseradish as a substitute for lettuce if lettuce could not be found.[10] Over time, it became the accepted and preferred bitter herb, and when Jews moved back to Palestine, they took it with them and grew it there. And they called it *hazeret*, which was on the original list of bitter herbs in the *Mishnah*, even though *hazeret* was probably some form of lettuce. Sephardic Jews, however, stuck with the original and use some kind of lettuce, usually chicory.

We eat the horseradish between two pieces of matzah, a practice instituted by Hillel; actually, Hillel combined all the elements of the original Seder (bit of roast meat from sacrificial lamb, the bitter herb, and the matzah) into his creation, which he called a "koreich." Despite claims by a British earl who lived about fifteen hundred years later, Hillel had actually invented the sandwich; we should be eating peanut butter and jelly hillels and pastrami hillels today. Hillel, a towering figure in Jewish history, was born in Babylon around 10 BCE and had a pivotal role in the writing of the *Mishnah*. He is also the writer of the searing call to action: "If I am not for myself, then who will be for me? But when I am only for myself, then what am I? And if not now, when?"

And finally, step eleven has arrived, and it's time to eat. The table is cleared and re-set for *Shulchan Aruch* (which means set table and is also the term used for a volume written by Rabbi Joseph Caro that is one of the most influential compilations of Jewish Law). There are no specific foods, though there are usually fish, soup, and meat courses; Ashkenazi families lean towards brisket. Spring vegetables, such as beets and rhubarb, often are served as side dishes, and potatoes and eggs are everywhere.

The Seder meal for Sephardim might start with *huevos haminados*, literally brown eggs, which are slow-cooked and served warm, sometimes over vegetables. The soup course is more likely to be leek than chicken, and the main course will probably be lamb, maybe in a stew. As always, Sephardi food is spiced more than Ashkenazi, with cumin, coriander, turmeric, ginger, and cinnamon, among others. Side dishes might include stuffed vegetables, artichokes (sometimes made with peas and/or mint), and frittatas.

Then, for dessert, we eat the hidden matzah after the kids who have stolen it get *afikomen* presents; this step, the twelfth, is called *Tzafun*, which means hidden. And the last three steps, *Barech*, *Hallel*, and *Nirtza*, bring another round of songs and praises. The finish is anticlimactic—*Chad Gadya*, meaning one goat. This incomprehensible song follows a goat that Father has bought for two *zuzim* as it and the creatures that follow it are devoured by ever-bigger beings, until God himself eats the last devourer. Philosophers have tried to explain why this song is a fitting end to the Seder ever since it was included in a Haggadah in Prague in 1590. It's vaguely allegorical, it has a catchy tune, and by this time we're all too drunk from the four cups of wine to worry why we're singing a song that is about as rational and profound as "I Know an Old Woman Who Swallowed a Fly." Next year in Jerusalem!

THE REST OF PASSOVER

When the Seder is over (for some Jews outside Israel, there is a second Seder on the second night of Passover) and the leftovers are all eaten, there's still nearly a week of no-bread, no-pasta, no-dough eating to live through. For Ashkenazi Jews, that prohibition includes all kinds of grains, even rice and beans, though Sephardim have never accepted those restrictions. Jews who observe the no-bread rules have assembled a collection of recipes that allow them to eat remarkably well through Passover. There's no reason why Passover recipes can't be eaten all year round, they're just not.

For Ashkenazim, until recently, Passover food was simple and relied on unprocessed ingredients—fresh fruits and vegetables; lots of fish, meat, and poultry; eggs; fresh cheeses; and cream. Matzah was used for dishes like matzah brei (see page 157) and matzah lasagna, a dish that substituted matzah for the lasagna sheets. Matzah meal was used for breading chicken cutlets and making dumplings. Today, special Passover stores are stocked with every kind of processed foods; you can buy canned vegetables, sugared breakfast cereal, and even imitation bread— certainly not an improvement over the simple fresh foods we used to rely on. Many families have their own Passover specialty, such as the potato fritters below.

CHREMSLACH

Chremslach are fritters, fried pancakes, and can be made with a variety of ingredients mixed with egg; different communities had their favorites and would insist that theirs were the only *chremslach* that counted. Fruit, matzah meal, ground meat, and potatoes have all been *"chremsled."* The word was unknown to most people until 2016, when it was the final word spelled correctly by the winner of the Scripps spelling bee.

The *chremslach* below are made from cooked potatoes that are forced through a ricer, a clever device that purees soft foods without electricity; it also makes the fluffiest mashed potatoes available. The riced potatoes are mixed with egg whites that have been beaten. One could also make *chremslach* with plain mashed potatoes and unbeaten eggs, but that would just show a lack of caring.

• • • • •

4 to 6 servings

INGREDIENTS

3 pounds of potatoes
4 quarts of water
1 teaspoon salt
4 eggs
Additional salt and pepper to taste
Oil for frying

Peel the potatoes and cut them into chunks. Place them in a large pot with the water and salt; boil until very soft. Remove from heat, drain completely, let them cool just until they can be handled (but not so much that they are hard to rice). Place them in a potato ricer, in batches, and rice them into a bowl.

Separate the eggs; put the whites into a large bowl. Try to remove any bits of yolk—the whites won't whip up well if there's yolk in them. Using an electric or manual mixer (or a whisk, if you have a strong hand), beat the egg whites until stiff peaks form—it will take a few minutes with an electric mixer, more if you're doing it by hand. Gently fold the yolks into the whites and stir to combine. Then fold in the riced potatoes, a cup at a time, and mix as gently as you can to avoid breaking down the beaten whites. Add salt and pepper to taste.

Prepare a large plate, lined with paper towels, for the finished *chremslach*. Heat oil in a large frying pan; the bottom of the pan should be thickly coated, but these are not deep-fried. The oil is hot enough when a bit of the batter sizzles immediately when dropped into the oil. Then drop the batter by tablespoons or larger if you wish (the larger they are, the harder they are to flip) into the hot oil. Leave them for about a minute until the edges start to brown, then flip them and fry the other side. You can keep flipping and frying them just until they are done—yellow mottled with brown—or if you like them crisper, until they are mostly browned on both sides. Remove to the paper towels to drain some of the oil, and fry the next batch.

They are best eaten immediately, but can be kept hot in a warm (not hot) oven for about an hour. Some people like them cold.

• • • • •

One might think that desserts—which are often flour-based cakes, cookies, and pies—would get short shrift on Passover, but there are many incredible sweet endings for Passover meals. Macaroons—little baked cookies usually made with egg whites, sugar, and ground nuts—are ubiquitous on Passover, whether bought in boxes or baked at home. Cooked fruit, flavored with cinnamon or lemon and sometimes with chocolate, is also popular. People have learned to use substitutes for flour—potato starch, ground nuts, matzah cake meal—for delicious cakes, sometimes topped with egg white meringues. The piece de resistance is often a flourless chocolate cake. These rich cakes are not specifically Jewish—chefs like Jean-George Vongerichten serve a flourless molten chocolate cake that has nothing to do with freed slaves, and there's an Italian version called Torte Caprese from the isle of Capri—but they do make a Passover dessert that makes living without leaven heavenly.

Sephardic Jews have their own repertoire of Passover specialties. Because they consider rice, beans, and other legumes—collectively called *kitniyot*, or small things—permissible, they have a much wider choice, so they are not tied to potatoes. (The Conservative Movement's Law Committee recently allowed *kitniyot* for Ashkenazic people as well.)

Sephardim use a lot of olive oil on Passover, and often use matzah farfel—matzahs crumbled into small bits—instead of matzah meal. Lamb appears frequently, including stuffed into lamb intestines. *Keftes* (patties) are made with meat, vegetables, and fish. Meat and chicken are often cooked using the sofrito technique, simmered in stock or water with garlic, turmeric, and cardamom (the meat is sometimes sautéed with the garlic and spices before simmering; sofrito is also the term used for an olive oil–based sauce made with garlic, onion, paprika, and tomatoes that is popular in all Latin-influenced countries, particularly Puerto Rico). There's a special Passover boreka that is made with soaked matzah instead of a flour-based dough. Fava bean soup (fava bean soups are called fuol) is often eaten, both because fresh fava beans are usually harvested around Passover time and because fava beans were eaten by the Hebrew slaves in Egypt. Another dish that usually appears, in some form, in most Sephardic communities during Passover is the savory pie known as meginah or mina.

MINA

Savory pies, with flour-based crusts, are often served in Sephardic homes on Shabbat and holidays; this tradition goes back to the time when Jews lived in Spain, and it was taken to countries all over the Middle East when Jews moved there after the Inquisition. On Passover, the crust is formed from matzah.

• • • • •

4 servings
INGREDIENTS

For the filling:
1 tablespoon olive oil
¼ cup chopped onions
½ pound ground beef or lamb
2 tablespoons chopped parsley
¼ teaspoon cumin
Salt and pepper to taste

For the assembly:
2 eggs, beaten
2 cups mashed potatoes, salted to taste
5 matzahs

Heat the oil in a skillet. Add the chopped onion and sauté until soften. Crumble in the ground meat and sauté until browned. Add the parsley, cumin, salt, and pepper to taste and toss to combine. Allow to cool slightly.

Preheat oven to 375°F. Grease a nine-inch by nine-inch deep baking dish. Prepare a plate lined with paper towels for the matzah.

Add one and a half eggs (reserve half an egg for brushing) and half a cup of mashed potatoes to the meat mixture to bind them.

Soak two of the sheets of matzah in water for about a minute; don't let them get too mushy and try to remove them whole. Drain for a minute on paper towels, then move them to an oiled baking dish, one on top of the other; brush the top lightly with egg. Spread half the meat mixture and half of the remaining mashed potatoes over the matzah. Soak two more matzahs the same way and brush with egg. Spread the remaining filling and potatoes over the matzahs. Crumble the last matzah into small pieces, soak in water, drain, and sprinkle over the top. Brush the top with the rest of oil.

Bake in the preheated oven for about thirty minutes until the matzah is soft and brown. Cut into pieces and serve hot.

• • • • •

Chocolate is not as popular with Sephardic Jews as it with Ashkenazim. The dessert more likely to appear in Sephardic homes is *Torta de Reyes* (Kings' Cake), a very moist egg-based cake flavored with orange zest, cinnamon, and almonds.

On Shabbat, it's made with bread crumbs, but that ingredient is changed to matzah meal on Passover. Wine biscuits, made with matzah, cake meal, potato starch, and sweet red wine, is another popular dessert. Marzipan, made with almond flour, sugar, and rosewater, was originally a Passover treat but is now served year round.

PASSOVER TRADITIONS AROUND THE WORLD

Surinam
Some of the Jews who fled the Spanish Inquisition in 1492 settled in South America; they found freedom and tolerance in Surinam, the oldest Jewish settlement in the New World. Jews in Surinam created their own *haroset*, which they eat at the Seder and for the whole week of Passover. It's called the "seven-fruit" *haroset*. Its main ingredients are coconut and cherries; originally the local Surinam cherry was used, but cherry jam can be substituted. It also includes other fruits such as peaches, pineapple, raisins, apples, prunes, apricots, and pears, plus walnuts, cinnamon, sugar, and wine.

Iran and Afghanistan
At Seders in these countries, during the singing of *Dayenu*, participants beat each other (lightly) on the shoulders with scallions to recall abuse that the slaves suffered in Egypt.

United States
In 1866, a group of Jewish Union soldiers found themselves in West Virginia on Passover and wanted to hold a Seder. They were able to find bitter herbs, lamb, eggs, and other items they needed for their Seder plates, but were stumped when it came to *haroset*. They ended up using a brick, which was not edible, but reminded them of the clay or cement used by their forefathers.

Ethiopia
Passover was an important holiday in the Ethiopian Jewish community. Ethiopian Jews made matzah from chickpea flour if they could not find wheat and slaughtered a lamb. The matriarch of the household would destroy all her earthenware dishes and make new ones for the holiday.

Yemen
Seders in Yemen (also in Iraq and Kurdistan) sometimes included little skits. The leader would put the *afikomen* matzah in a bag, grab a cane, and pretend to start

a journey. Children would call out questions, asking where he was coming from and where he was going—and the answers would be the recitation of the story of Passover.

Nepal
Every Passover, for the past several decades, the Chabad organization holds "The Seder on Top of the World," which often attracts more than one thousand participants and is considered one of the largest Seders in the world. They bring thousands of pounds of matzah and other Passover requirements to this location, and bring in many rabbis to lead the services. "Many young Jews travel to the Far East searching for meaning and spiritual identity," said Rabbi Yehuda Krinsky of the Lubavitch World Headquarters. "We hope that this positive Jewish experience and observance will help them find their true spiritual heritage in their own vineyard of Judaism."[11]

Poland
At their Seders, some Polish Jews re-enacted the crossing on the Red Sea by pouring water on the floor.

India
When the ten plagues are recited, Jews in Bombay's Bnei Israel community dip their fingers in sheep's blood and flick a bit of it onto a piece of paper; the paper is then hung in a doorway to ward off evil. In most other communities, wine is the liquid used for this.

Morocco
Many Moroccan families keep a chunk of *afikomen* and some shreds of meat from the shank bone as good luck charms. They store these amulets in cupboards, but take them out and carry them around when luck is needed, when they are going on a plane ride, for example.

North Africa
In many Jewish communities in north Africa, Passover is extended for an extra day called Mimouna, which celebrates the return to chametz. It's an interfaith holiday; Muslims bring treats made with honey and wheat to their Jewish neighbors, who prepare buffets for all to share. The traditional food is mufletta, a thin crepe that is rolled and fried and served with jam, syrup, nuts, and dried fruit.

8

❖ ❖

Yom Ha'Atzma'ut

Masters of Our Fate and Our Falafel

On November 29, 1947, millions of Jews all over the world, as well as the future government of a not-yet-created state, hovered over their radios as members of the United Nations voted to decide the fate of the Jewish people. For centuries, Jews had endured exile and statelessness; for decades, they been subjected to one of the cruelest episodes of genocide ever perpetrated. And for about fifty years, they had slowly returned to the land they considered their own, cultivating barren land and building institutions and infrastructure in the hope that they would live in that land as a free nation.

After days of political maneuvering and see-sawing by every country, including the United States, the votes were counted. Thirty-three countries approved the partition of Palestine into a Jewish state and an Arab one. Thirteen countries, including all the Arab nations, voted no. Ten countries, including Great Britain, abstained. And Thailand did not show up for the vote.

One the first tasks of the elated leaders was to find a name for their country. They considered "Judah," after one of Jacob's sons; "Tsabar," which means sabra, Israel's national fruit; and "Zion," which may have been rejected because its English pronunciation is slang for penis (in Hebrew, it's pronounced Tsion). The group voted seven to three for "Israel," another name for Jacob, whose root comes from the phrase "God fought."

Less than six months later, one day after the League of Nations Mandate that put Great Britain in charge of Palestine expired, the Jewish People's Council convened in the Tel Aviv Museum, where David Ben-Gurion read a proclamation that said, "By virtue of our natural and historic right and on the strength of the resolution of the United Nations General Assembly, [we] hereby declare the establishment of a Jewish state."¹ The declaration went on to plead with the world for help in building their country and to extend their "hand to all neighbouring states and their peoples in an offer of peace and good neighbourliness." And suddenly the dream of Israel was a reality.

REFLECTIONS

As long as in the heart the Jewish spirit yearns, with eyes turned eastward, looking towards Zion.—Hatikvah (the hope), Israel's national anthem

For the Jew, Israel is the center of the world. The longing for Israel, and still more for Jerusalem, that has been felt by Jews throughout their history is best described by the Talmud's comments on the text: "for your servants delight in her stones and love her dust." The Talmudic rabbis illustrate the meaning of "delight" and "love" in this passage by explaining that Rav Abba used to kiss the stones in Akko, Rabbi Haninah would mend Israel's roads, and Rav Hiyya bar Gamla would roll in the dust of the Holy Land (*Talmud Ketubot*, 12a–b).

Yom Ha'Atzma'ut marks the rebirth of the modern state of Israel, the Third Commonwealth of the Jewish people. It took place on May 14, 1948, which corresponded to the fifth of Iyar, 5708 on the Hebrew calendar. Since 1948, the miraculous return of the Jewish people to their homeland has been celebrated on the fifth day of the Hebrew month of Iyar. Although Yom Ha'Atzma'ut is usually translated as Independence Day, it is worth noting that *atzma'ut* comes from the Hebrew root for bone, and hints at the positive affirmation of an identity, at standing on one's own feet. So an alternate translation might be Identity Day or Self-Affirmation Day, and in this way the celebration is a celebration affirming one's identity.

Rabbinic authorities of various orientations in Israel have set out a variety of liturgy for the day, including the reciting of *Hallel* (*Psalms of Praise*), sounding of the shofar, and a special Torah reading. All mourning practices associated with the *omer* period are suspended as well. Eating a festive meal that includes foods from Israel is strongly encouraged.

Israel's Independence Day is preceded by *Yom HaZikaron* (Remembrance Day) for the approximately fourteen thousand Israelis killed in the Israeli-Arab wars. On this day, special prayers are said, cemeteries are visited, and memorial ceremonies take place. At 11 a.m., all of Israel comes to a stop—traffic, business, and conversation—and a two-minute silence is observed.

Yom Ha'Atzma'ut is for many Jews more than celebrating the birth of a nation. It is an opportunity to reflect on their responsibilities to the dream and reality of Israel, including the *mitzvah* (religious obligation) to live there. *Am Yisrael Chai!* Long live the nation of Israel!

CREATING A JEWISH STATE

When David Ben-Gurion declared that Israel was an official state, he ended almost nineteen hundred years of statelessness for the Jewish people. Before that—from about 1200 BCE, when the Jews conquered Canaan, until the first century CE, when the revolt of the army of the Jewish warrior Bar Kochba against the Roman army was put down and almost all Jews were forced to leave, sold into slavery, or killed, with several long expulsions in between—the land was under the control of Jews. The government was led by prophets and kings, governed under the rule of the Sanhedrin, a group of seventy scholars who created and enforced law. During their reign, population peaked at about a million people—some scholars say it could have been two million—and industries—including the making of clay pots and oil lamps, as well as agricultural products such as wine, oil, dates, and wheat—thrived. At various times, the Hellenic, Byzantine, and Roman Empires conquered and occupied Israel for different period of time; Jews were often exiled from their country, most notably by Babylonians who exiled them to Persia, where they thrived, and to many other countries where Jewish communities formed. But even after the Jews were expelled from Israel in the first century, small communities remained there; Jews never really left Israel or stopped longing for it. As Spanish poet Yehuda HaLevi wrote in 1121, "My heart is in the east, and I am at the end of the west."

The population of the land then known as Palestine didn't return to the population levels it maintained under Jewish rule until the middle of the twentieth century. Until the tenth century, there were under 250,000 people living there, a majority of them Christians with minorities of Muslims and Jews.

By 1890, there were about 532,000 people living there; about 432,000 were Muslims and under forty-three thousand were Jews.[2]

At the start of World War II, there were over seventeen million Jews living in Europe, most of them in central Europe and Russia.

Although Jews were thriving in Europe, an undercurrent of anti-Semitism always festered, showing up in anti-Jewish literature in the European press and exploding in pogroms in Russia. By the 1880s, ripples of emigration to Palestine, called the first *Aliyah* ("*Aliyah*" means rising; the term is used for emigration to Israel) were getting stronger. Several activists, including Moses Hess from Germany and Leon Pinsky from Russia, were writing about the possibility of a Jewish state in Palestine. For religious, economic, and political reasons, groups began to form to create communities in Palestine. In 1882, fourteen Russian university students, under the aegis of an organization called Bilu that aimed to establish agricultural settlements in Israel, arrived in Israel. (The name Bilu is formed from the first letters of a phrase from Isaiah: *Beit Yaakov, Lechu v'nelcha*—House of Jacob, let us go up.) After a stay in a farming school, they joined another group called *Hovevai Zion* (lovers of Zion) to found an agricultural settlement that they called Rishon LeZion (first in Zion), near what is now Tel Aviv. But lack of funds, skills, and preparation, plus bad weather and illness, caused it to fail after several months. The group then sought the help of Baron Edmond James de Rothschild and Maurice de Hirsch; with their financial assistance and business acumen, they bought land for a new settlement in Zichron Yaakov, where a vineyard and winery were established; the enterprise still flourishes today and Zichron Yaakov is a modern city, as is Rishon LeZion. By 1903, there were about ten thousand settlers in Israel, building homes and growing food.

The Zionist movement was given a strong push forward when a young Hungarian/Austrian journalist named Theodor Herzl attended the treason trial of a French captain named Albert Dreyfus whose main crime was being Jewish. The trial was accompanied by rabid anti-Semitism; naturalist novelist Emil Zola answered this intolerance with his rousing "*J'accuse*" essay and the whole incident put France on a more liberal path. But the young Herzl started thinking that a permanent solution was needed for what bigots called "The Jewish Question," and he wrote an article called "*der Judenstaat.*" A few years later, in August 1897, he convened the First Zionist Congress in Basel, Switzerland. Its purpose was "to create for the Jewish people, a home in Palestine."[3] He later wrote in his diary, "At Basel, I founded the Jewish state."[4] He mused that people would laugh if he said that, but that they would agree in five or ten or fifty years; just about fifty years later, Israel was declared a state.

Pioneers (also known as *halutzim*) continued to move to Israel; by the beginning of World War I, about ninety thousand[5] lived there. Palestine was a political football during the war; the Ottoman Empire was on the Axis side and Great Britain needed the help of the Arabs to fight it. In exchange for this help, the British pledged that they would support an Arab kingdom in the area. Palestine was not included in that pledge, but the Arab ruler, Sherif Hussein ibn Ali, decided that it was. But Jewish pioneers, under the leadership of Dr. Chaim Weizman, a major figure in the World Zionist Organization, also joined Britain's war effort, forming *HaG'dud HaIvri* (the Hebrew Legion). They too were promised support for a state of their own. In 1917, Dr. Weizman convinced the British governor to sign the Balfour Declaration, which stated that the British government supported the establishment of a Jewish state in Palestine. At the end of 1917, the British received a mandate from the League of Nations to become governors of Palestine.

Although the small communities of Jews and Arabs had lived and worked together in peace until that period, that peace fell apart in the 1920s and 1930s. That was partly because the numbers changed—new waves of immigrants from both groups were streaming in, doubling the Jewish population and raising the Arab population by 50 percent from 1914 to 1931—and because both groups had been promised by the British that they were entitled to control of Palestine. Incidents that included fatalities began to occur, and both groups became more militant. The *Hagana* and the *Irgun*, the first less violent than the second (run by future Israeli Prime Minister Menachem Begin), began to carry out protests and attacks. And Britain began to side with the Arabs, limiting Jewish immigration. At the same time, as it became clear to the Jews of Europe that Hitler's threats made it urgent that they leave, many were denied entrance to Israel (though many did manage to move there).

And then in the 1940s, the full impact of the Nazi regime was revealed. Suddenly, people realized that there were hundreds of thousands of homeless people who had survived the Holocaust and had no place to go. As the world struggled with their own responsibility for what had happened, and with deep empathy but without fully dealing with the future political implications, they voted to divide Palestine into two states. One of those states would officially be declared the State of Israel, controlled by Jews; the other would become an Arab monarchy.

Within days after the establishment of the State of Israel, all their Arab neighbors attacked them at once, from all sides. With only the beginnings of a government or an army, with a populace that was still scarred by years of torture, the Jews fought back and survived. Like the slaves of Egypt and the Maccabees who were stars of the Hanukkah story, they were vastly outnumbered by the people who were trying to kill them. But they survived. And then they had the enormous task of creating a land where they could live. It was time to eat—but where would the food come from?

CREATING A NEW FOOD CHAIN

When the first pioneers came to Israel, they faced a land that had not been nurtured and cultivated for centuries. The Arabs, along with and supported by Jewish investors, settlers, and technology, had installed and promoted the citrus industry, but had not worked on many other agricultural ventures to feed the rapidly expanding population. Those conditions remained after the State of Israel was formed.

But the infant state had an incredible resource in the chain of communal settlements, called kibbutzim, that had been founded by the earliest settlers and expanded through the war. The members of the kibbutzim had a guiding philosophy and a deep passion that made them able to overcome the difficulties of coaxing food from land that had been considered barren. When the first Jewish settlers arrived, the northern Galilee was a swamp, the south was a desert, and the hills of Judea were full of rocks. Diseases that attacked both plants and people, included malaria, were endemic, and the native Arab population was not always cooperative. Moreover, they started out with little knowledge of farming—they were students and philosophers, dentists and lawyers, born and bred in cities. No one farmer could have succeeded, but together they learned what they needed to know, and then accepted the backbreaking labor and lived through inevitable setbacks to grow the food that they needed. They sang and danced when they harvested and ate.

KIBBUTZ CULTURE

The word *kibbutz* (plural: kibbutzim) derives from the word *kvutzah*, which means group or gathering. It has no relation to the word kibbitz, which is Yiddish slang for a joker and comes from a German word for interfering interloper. The first kibbutz, Degania, was established in 1909 near the Sea of Galilee; its name means grain. Its founders were young pioneers from eastern Europe, steeped in socialist culture, who wanted to create a new way of life; their revolution was much more successful than that of Russian rebels, since they are still going strong today.

Not all kibbutzim were created equal. Although there is a union of kibbutzim that maintains a set of rules, they acknowledge several levels of communal ownership. In some kibbutzim, members, who are called *chaverim* (friends) or kibbutzniks, give up all personal property and receive everything from the kibbutz, based on their needs, not their productivity. In others, members receive salaries and in some they own their own homes. Moshavim (settlements; singular: moshav) are also communes, but allow much more flexibility in ownership and working off-grounds. On a *moshav shitufi* (participatory settlement), there is usually a business that all or most members work for, and each member usually owns his own property.

In order to be able to care for their families while they worked all day, many of the kibbutzim instituted a policy that was controversial and has been abandoned by most of them today: Children did not live with their parents. Instead, they spent days and nights in dormitories with other children from the kibbutz, cared for by some of the kibbutzniks. Meals were served in communal cafeterias, where parents sat with their children and enjoyed the harvest. To some, this was a necessary but unpleasant sacrifice, but others who grew up in the kibbutzim said that it resulted in unsurpassed maturity, social skills, and family bonds. The country turned to the people who matured on the kibbutzim, whose strength, courage, and enthusiasm had been forged in the idealistic, socialist world of communal settlements. After spending their youth farming, they became the prime ministers (David Ben-Gurion helped found Kibbutz Degania, Golda Meir lived in Merhavia, Levi Eskol spent time in Degania Bet, Yitzchak Rabin studied agriculture in Givat Hashlosha) and military masterminds (Moshe Dayan was born in Degania) who led Israel for generations.

By 1950, soon after Israel was established, there were close to seventy thousand people living on 214 kibbutzim. There are 270 kibbutzim in Israel today; only 25 percent of their income is from agriculture, but the kibbutzim still provide more than 30 percent of Israel's agricultural products.[6] Tourism, electronics, information technology consulting, manufacturing, and crafts are more popular than farming. But communal settlements are still responsible for many agricultural innovations—such as the hardy, delicious tomatoes and bug-free lettuces that were invented in Gush Katif, a group of settlements in Gaza (which was returned to the Arabs in 2005). These settlements also train soldiers, educate immigrants, and nurture artists; they remain an integral part of Israel's identity.

It was the kibbutzim that drained the swamps, cleared the rocks from the fields, and made the desert bloom. Out of necessity, all of the early kibbutzim were involved in agriculture. They grew food to eat and to get enough cash for the other necessities. They needed to do it efficiently and quickly; they could not make many mistakes—there was enough uncertainty provided by the elements. They combined hard labor, perseverance, and intelligence, applying new technology to grow more crops than anyone imagined could be grown on this land. (See pages 178–179 for more information on how Israel advanced agriculture in their own country and around the world.)

In the kibbutzim, members ate simply—some say that they grew up on cottage cheese and chopped salads. Members took turns in the kitchen, turning out solid, satisfying but unglamorous fare that could be made quickly. In a 2009 book entitled *Chederochel (The Dining Room)*, authors Ofir Vardi and Assi Haim collected recipes and the stories behind them from over one hundred kibbutzim. "People we met are connected to the food not so much from the belly but from the heart," they wrote. Each kibbutz had its favorites, often named for the *chaverim* who invented them.

The dining hall was the center of life on the kibbutz, and usually the first building erected on a new kibbutz. It's where parents met with children who lived in dormitories, where official meetings took place, where both arguments and friendships formed and deepened.

One dish that was common in kibbutzim was "Moses in a blanket"—a piece of sausage cooked in dough. Another was pashtida, a quick, filling dish that could be made with any ingredients that were around but often included potatoes and onions It's still a favorite for family dinners in Israel.

PASHTIDA

This endlessly adaptable recipe is similar to a quiche, but the egg custard has a white sauce base. The term *pashtida* may be connected to pasta—and noodles do often appear in pashtida, as in the noodle-and-cheese pasta that was served in Kibbutz Givat Brenner on Friday afternoon and called Sabbath Queen Pashtida. Other sources say it's a term used by Rashi, the thirteenth-century French biblical commentator, to refer to a casserole made of pigeons covered in dough. Other etymologists tie it to the word "pizza."

Pashtida can be made with or without a bottom crust. If you're skipping the crust, oil the bottom of the baking dish fully before adding the vegetables.

Use a nine-inch round or square ovenproof baking pan for this recipe.

• • • • •

6 to 8 servings
INGREDIENTS

For the crust:
1 cup flour
½ teaspoon salt
¼ cup oil (olive or vegetable)
¼ cup ice water

For the filling:
About 4 cups of vegetables and or grains; see below for suggestions
2 tablespoons melted butter
2 tablespoons white flour
½ cup milk, heated to scalding but not boiling (a microwave does this well)
4 eggs, separated
1 cup shredded cheese—your favorite or a mixture
Salt, pepper, herbs, and spices to taste

Prepare the crust: mix the crust ingredients with a fork until they form a dough. Knead for a minute or two until it is smooth. Press it into your baking dish, with the dough coming up the sides. (If you want to make it more uniform, roll out the dough to a ten-inch circle before pressing it into the pan.)

Cook the vegetables to tender-crisp—boil, microwave, roast, or braise them.

Melt the butter in a small saucepan. Add the flour and whisk until combined completely. Pour in the hot milk and keep whisking until the sauce thickens enough to coat the back of a spoon. Turn off the flame and allow to cool slightly. Beat the egg yolks and when the sauce is slightly cooled, add them to the sauce and whisk. Whisk the egg whites until frothy, and add them as well. Season with salt, pepper, herbs, and spices.

Spoon the cooked vegetables over the crust. Pour the sauce over the vegetables and smooth out the top; it should barely cover. Bake in a 375°F oven for twenty-five minutes or until the crust has browned and the sauce is firm. Cut into wedges and serve hot.

Some combinations:

Potatoes and onions

Noodles with thyme and paprika

Tomatoes and corn with basil

• • • • •

FOOD FOR A GROWING NATION

When Israel became a nation in 1948, about 872,000 people lived there. By 1950, that number increased to 1.4 million; by 1955 to 1.8 million, more than doubling in seven years. (The population had been higher before Israel was established, when over a million Arabs fled—but much of the arable land was no longer within Israel's borders.) Today, Israel's population stands at a little over eight million. All these people have to eat from a country whose area is about 60 percent of Rhode Island's, with roughly eight times as many residents—and 60 percent of the Israel's land is a desert. Living among hostile neighbors, Israel needed to produce most of their food on their own land—95 percent of the food that is eaten in Israel is produced there.[7]

WATER, LIKE BLOOD

Necessity became the mother of invention, and the first thing that Israel had to do in order to grow food was find ways to water their crops. They did it by recognizing and appreciating the value of every drop they could find. Levi Eshkol, Israel's second prime minister, said that for the land, water is as important as blood is to a human being.[8] As Seth Siegel points out in his book, *Let There Be Water: Israel's Solution for a Water-starved World*,[9] every home was aware of how they used water; every family recycled gray water and conserved carefully. Water engineers were considered heroes, and universities established departments to research ways to increase the water supply. Most important, in the early days, they passed laws that made water a national resource and never owned by individuals or companies. No one is allowed to drill or divert water except under government supervision.

To increase the amount of usable water, Israeli engineers advanced the science of desalinization so they could use salt water to feed their crops. They created or improved techniques like plastic tunnels and recirculating irrigation to use less water, to keep the crops cool, and to reduce evaporation. One of their greatest advances was drip irrigation—which is now used around the world. Drip irrigation was first imagined in 1939, when Simcha Blass—known as Israel's "Water Man"—noticed that one of the trees in his neighbor's yard was growing taller than others; he looked down and saw that there was a tiny hole in the irrigation pipe near that tree, so extra water was delivered directly to its roots without wasting any on nearby areas that had no trees. Twenty years later, he created plastic piping with tiny perforations that would deliver irrigation precisely to the spots where it was needed. It is one of the many ways that Israel has increased the ability of farmers to produce crops in a water-starved world.

MORE FOOD THROUGH MASS PRODUCTION

In the early days of Israel, farm-to-table dining was not a trendy idea; it was the only way to eat. Most people got most of their food directly from the farm. But as the country became more populated, more urban, and more industrialized, big food companies began to process and sell food in retail outlets. At first, most Israelis would buy their food in a *makolet*, a small store that carried fresh, unpackaged food and never supplied bags—it's strange to see that while the rest of the world is trying to cut back on bag production, Israeli stores now offer them (though they're starting to go back to the old ways and just passed a law that makes supermarkets charge for plastic bags). Modern supermarkets exist in every major city; the first was Supersal, which was founded in 1956 and currently has almost 250 stores and over twelve thousand employees.[10]

Food cooperatives such as Tnuva, which is responsible for distributing 70 percent of the dairy products in Israel today, was founded in 1926.[11] In 1956, Agrexco, which went bankrupt in 2011, began to market Israeli agricultural products worldwide, which is why European markets are filled with Israeli oranges, tomatoes, flowers, and other produce. A family of German-Jewish immigrants founded the Strauss Group in the 1930s and produced some of Israel's packaged dairy products, such as Dani chocolate yogurt. They merged with Elite Chocolate, started by Russian Jew Eliyahu Fromenchenko, who came to Palestine in 1933, when the Nazis took power. Elite's first products were ready for Passover in 1934, and the company remains a leader in the Israeli chocolate market and exports the Sabra brand of prepared foods all over the world.

In the early 1950s, Israel entered a period of rising population and austerity; food was rationed and became a luxury. Busy creating a country, with little income, families had no time to cook the traditional, labor-intensive ways. Prime Minister Ben-Gurion went to Osem, a food manufacturer founded in 1942 and now a producer of snacks, grains, and other products that are sold worldwide—it is Osem that makes Bamba and Bissli, the oddly addictive snacks that Israeli kids adore. Ben-Gurion explained that the country needed a fast, cheap food that could take the place of rice. They came up with an extruded toasted pasta in the shape of rice; they called it Ben-Gurion's rice. Later, they started to sell it as tiny balls that resembled couscous, a part of semolina wheat that took a long time to extract and cook. People, especially children, loved the new foods that could be on the table in fifteen minutes; they were considered somewhat lowbrow, but Israeli couscous has traveled the globe and is often mixed with exotic vegetables and appears on menus in upscale restaurants—though they're still fine plain, with just a bit of butter.

Israel's agribusiness uses science to keep it sustainable. One company, Pimi Agro, is working to cut back on food waste by making perishable foods last longer.[12] Rivka Elbaum, a scientist at Hebrew University, has developed a secret formula that keeps lettuce fresh, without refrigeration, for up to two weeks.[13] Israel's cutting-edge research in water management and pest resistance enables their food businesses to make the most of their inhospitable climate and small area; they are able to feed not only Israel, but the world.

THE INGATHERING OF EXILES

Before the start of the twentieth century, fewer than fifty thousand Jews lived in what was then Palestine. The movement called the *Aliya Aleph*—the first rising—swelled the population to just under one hundred thousand as settlers came to sink Jewish roots in the Promised Land. During the time that the British governed under the League of Nations Mandate, about another eighty thousand Jews arrived.[14] Most of them snuck in because the British didn't want them but they realized they could not remain in Europe. After the war, several hundred thousand more Jews arrived, many of them survivors of the Holocaust; some of them had been waiting in displaced persons camps for several years.

After the State of Israel was declared, one their first actions was to gather Jews from all over the world, a fulfillment of a biblical prophecy and a dream. The prophecy is from *Isaiah* (43:5–6): "I will bring your descendants from the east, and gather you from the west; I will say to the north, 'Give them up!' And to the south, 'Do not keep them back!' Bring my sons from afar, and my daughters from the ends of the earth." And Ben-Gurion remembered when he declared statehood for Israel, "The State of Israel will be open for Jewish immigration and for the In-gathering of the Exiles; it will foster the development of the country for the benefit of all its inhabitants; it will be based on freedom, justice and peace as envisaged by the prophets of Israel."[15]

The population exploded, from about nine hundred thousand to 1,800,000 (including Jews, Muslims, and others) by 1955.[16] Jews from other countries in the Middle East, where many were persecuted—Yemen, Iraq, Iran, Morocco, Egypt, Libya, Tunisia, Syria—were brought to Israel by any means possible. The fledgling government made a concerted effort to transfer most the Jewish populations of those countries to Israel, starting with the fifty thousand Jews from Yemen who were flown in on what is known as "Operation Magic Carpet." These new citizens were greeted with great enthusiasm but very little idea of what they needed in their new homes. The Yemenites who arrived on Operation Magic Carpet endured horrible conditions on their journeys from their villages— hundreds of them died. And the Ashkenazis who already lived in Israel were unprepared for the fact that the Jews living in the Middle East for centuries were not exactly like them; friction between the many cultures caused problems that still exist today.

But the food that each of these communities brought enriched Israel's cuisine with fabulous new tastes. The early settlers had brought with them all the culinary traditions of Europe—their gefilte fish and *cholent*, stuffed cabbages and kugels (see pages 16–18). Now, as Israel built a culinary base, cooks could add the tastes of north African countries (see pages 13–16)—both those that the Sephardim brought with them when they were chased from Spain during the Spanish Inquisition in the fifteenth century and those of the Mizrachim, Jews who had lived in Palestine or other parts of the Middle East since well before then. The fiery sauces, exotic spices, and intense sweets from these cuisines were sometimes combined with the Ashkenazi dishes and sometimes kept separate—but every family had many dishes from which to pick and choose.

They chose the sabra ("tsabar" in Hebrew) as their national fruit and icon, and honored it by calling the new generation of native-born Israelis sabras. Sabras are part of the *Opuntia* cactus family; they're not native to Israel, but were imported from New Mexico in the eighteenth and nineteenth centuries as barriers and are now a part of the landscape. Israelis recognize themselves in the plant—prickly on the outside, but soft and sweet inside. They're an acquired taste and are not often served because they are hard to peel and there's not much sweet flesh—but they can be made into jams and jellies, stewed in soups, or just peeled with a sharp knife and eaten raw. They're sold on roadside stands in Israel when a touch of history and identity is wanted.

Though sabras never made it as a popular food, some other native foods did. Probably the most visible are falafel and pita, which are probably the foods that are most connected with Israel.

PITA

Flatbreads like pitas, which rely on a sourdough-like starter, have been baked since around 5000 BCE; early humans had already domesticated wheat and invented beer by then, and they noticed that the sugar in the alcoholic beverage caused the wheat to rise (though they had no idea that the sugar was causing the change). They saved a bit of dough from each day's production and used it again the next day. Bread remained fairly flat, leavened only a bit by the starter dough, for thousands of years. The show bread that was used in the Temple was certainly flat. The ancient Israelites knew what leaven was—it was part of the Passover story—but they did not know that it was created by tiny organisms released by rotting food or sugar. It was not until the nineteenth century, when the microscope was invented, that the organisms in yeast were isolated and reproduced, and eventually sold in the little packets that we use to make big, fluffy breads.

Pita's name has multiple origins; the word "paht" means "slice" in modern Hebrew and was a natural choice when it became a popular bread in Palestine in the nineteenth century. But there was also a flatbread in Greece called pita in the first centuries of the common era; the name of that bread, which was used for toppings, was eventually changed to "pizza."

Today, packaged pita is available in most supermarkets. Some of it is made by big food companies—it's mushy and tasteless. Pitas from smaller bakeries, some of them pita specialists, can be found in higher-end stores and they're quite good.

The pita's main attribute is its pocket, which forms when dough is placed in a very hot oven. The top and bottom of the pita puff up, forming two layers that make it perfect for stuffing. If your pita does not puff up and form a pocket, it's probably because you didn't knead long enough or because your oven was not hot enough. No-pocket pitas are great to use as dippers or as the base for pizzas—but they will never regain their sandwich capability.

• • • • •

6 to 8 pitas

INGREDIENTS

1½ cups very warm water
1 packet active dry yeast
1 teaspoon sugar or honey
3 to 3½ cups white flour
1½ teaspoons salt
1 tablespoon oil (olive oil is preferred, but any good-quality oil will do);
    more for greasing
½ teaspoon chopped herbs or ground spices, such as za'atar, cumin, rosemary,
    or thyme (optional)

Place the warm water in a large bowl; add the yeast and sugar or honey and stir to dissolve. Let it sit in a warm place until frothy and/or bubbly.

Add three cups of flour, one cup at a time, stirring after each addition; add salt, herbs if desired, and oil, and stir again until it forms a rough dough. Gather the dough into a ball. If it is too loose or sticky to form a ball, add extra flour, a few tablespoons at a time, until it sticks together.

Place the dough on a floured board and let it sit for a few minutes while you wash, dry, and lightly oil the bowl. Knead the dough for about ten minutes or more until is smooth and elastic (or mix in a food processor for eight minutes).

Gather the dough into a ball again and place in the bowl, turning once so that it is lightly coated on all sides; cover with a damp cloth or plastic wrap. Let it rise until roughly doubled in bulk, about one to two hours.

While the dough is rising, preheat the oven to 500°F. Prepare a rack or platter on which to cool the baked pitas. Halfway through the rising time, place a baking stone (if you don't have one, use a cookie sheet turned upside down) on a rack in the bottom third of the oven.

Flour a baking board generously. Break the dough into six to eight pieces, depending on how big you want your pitas to be; form each piece into a disc and let them sit on the board for about ten minutes. Then use a rolling pin to flatten the discs, one at a time, until they are about a quarter-inch thick.

When you have two or three of the discs (as many as you can fit on your baking stone or cookie sheet) spray the oven with water or place a small, oven-proof bowl of water into the oven. Quickly but carefully place the discs on the heated surface—remember, it's very hot in there. Close the oven door immediately and go back to rolling out the rest of the discs, but keep watch over the oven.

It takes only two to three minutes to bake the pitas; they should puff up in less than a minute. If you want them well done, bake for another minute or two. When they're done, move them to the cooling station you've prepared, and repeat with the rest of the pitas.

Store in paper bags or storage containers; plastic bags are a last resort. They're best fresh, but will last a day or two. If you won't be using them by then, freeze them.

Variation: One cup of white flour can be replaced with whole wheat.

• • • • •

GOD BLESS THE CHICKPEA

Chickpeas are one of the oldest cultivated crops in the world; along with emmer and einkorn wheat, barley, lentils, peas, bitter vetch, and flax, chickpeas are known as a founder crop. Remnants found in Turkey have been dated back to 7500 BCE and by 6500 BCE, chickpeas were being eaten in French caves. Rice, which now feeds many more people than chickpeas, was not in common use until several millennia later. Chickpeas first appeared somewhere in the Middle East and spread throughout Mesopotamia, Asia, Africa, and Europe. They have double or triple the nutrient values of rice and wheat: a one hundred-gram serving of chickpeas contains 8.86 grams of protein, versus 2.69 for rice; chickpeas also provide loads (about 20 percent) of most of the other nutrients we need. Yet the worldwide consumption of chickpeas is about eleven million metric tons, while China and India alone produce almost four hundred million metric tons of rice. This is possibly because advances in rice cultivation have resulted in rice fields' ability to produce up to ten million metric tons per hectare, while the much-ignored chickpea is still hovering at the two million metric tons per hectare level.

It would make sense for the world to take notice of this ancient food; it's been a large part of the diet in the Middle East and other parts of Asia since biblical times, but it's just beginning to lose its status as an oddity elsewhere. In Israel, it appears in soups, stews, and salad, but it's most famous use is falafel.

FALAFEL

Falafel—the word is derived from "pilpel" the word for pepper in Arabic—is the national food of Israel; wherever you go within the country, there is always a falafel stand nearby. But it did not originate in Israel or by Israelis; most sources believe that it was first invented over one thousand years ago by Coptic Egyptians who ate it during Lent. It became popular in Alexandria, a port city, from which sailors took it to ports of call. Many countries, including Lebanon, Palestine, and Egypt, also consider it as their own, and they are quite resentful that Israel has appropriated it. In fact, in 2008, a group of Lebanese industrialists sued Israel in international courts to stop them from marketing falafel as an Israeli food. The suit was based on a successful 2002 case that stopped other European firms from calling cheese "feta" if it not did come from Greece, but the Lebanese suit went nowhere.

Though few people argue that Israelis invented falafel (it certainly existed before Israel became a modern state in 1948), some do say that it first found its way into a pita in Israel. It arrived there with immigrants from northern Africa and quickly flourished as a street food. Many new arrivals, especially Yemenites, started businesses that sold the treat—it was cheap, nutritious, delicious, and pareve (containing neither meat or dairy products), which made it perfect for the many observant Jews who were part of the new communities.

Though it's considered a street food, it can also be made quickly and easily at home. Chickpeas are not boiled for this recipe, just soaked overnight. Then they are drained, added to a food processor filled with herbs and spices, chilled, and deep-fried.

• • • • •

Yields about 10 balls, 3 to 4 servings

INGREDIENTS

1 cup (about 8 ounces, ½ bag) dried chickpeas—canned chickpeas won't work
2 tablespoons chopped cilantro
1 small onion, chopped roughly
3 large garlic cloves
1 teaspoon salt
¼ teaspoon cayenne pepper
1 teaspoon ground cumin
½ teaspoon baking powder
3 tablespoons flour, or more
Vegetable oil for frying enough to reach 3 inches high in your smallest pot

Place the chickpeas in a bowl and cover with water; the water should be six inches over the chickpeas. Soak overnight, or at least eight hours. Drain completely, saving about a quarter cup of the water.

Place all of the ingredients, except the chickpeas, flour, and oil, into the bowl of a food processor. Pulse until all are finely chopped. Add the drained chickpeas. Process until fully chopped, but not pasty. Add the flour and pulse a few times just to combine. If necessary, add the soaking water, a teaspoon at a time, if the mixture isn't well combined at first; if it's liquidy, add additional flour, a teaspoon at a time. The mixture will get firmer when it chills, so don't go overboard on the flour now, you can add more later. Taste and adjust seasonings. Chill for at least two hours.

Heat oil in a small pot—the oil should come at least three inches up the sides of the pot. Form the falafel mixture into balls, using about a tablespoon for each. If it's still too wet to form balls, add flour, a teaspoon at a time (too much flour will make your falafel hard). When the oil reaches 225°F on a frying thermometer, drop the balls into the oil. (If you don't have a frying thermometer, drop a smaller ball, about one teaspoon of batter, into the oil; if it immediately begins to fry, the oil is ready.) The balls should not touch in the oil; you may need to do two or three batches, depending on the size of your pot. Watch the balls carefully; they should begin to color and fry immediately, and then turn over. If they don't turn over themselves, turn them with a wooden spoon. They will be done in about five minutes—dark brown and crispy all over. Use a slotted spoon to remove them and place them on a plate lined with paper towels to drain. Allow to cool slightly before eating.

Variations: Many other herbs and spices can be added; choose your favorites. Cardamom, coriander, and parsley are often used.

Some people use fava beans instead of chickpeas; prepare them the same way as chickpeas. The inside of the falafel will be green instead of beige.

Add-ons: Once you stuff three or four falafel balls into your pita, it's time to add salads and sauces to make it awesome.

Techina: A simple sauce made from tahini paste, which is essentially ground sesame seeds. Most supermarkets carry some kind of packaged tahini paste, usually in plastic bottles. Look for a brand that was imported from a Middle Eastern country—if your supermarket doesn't have it, find a specialty store that does. There will be a layer of oil on top of the paste, which settles to the bottom. Use a long spoon to mix it; you want to get some of the thick paste. Scoop about three tablespoons of the mixed tahini into a small bowl and add an equal amount of water. Stir vigorously for a few minutes and you'll suddenly have a smooth, syruplike sauce. Add finely minced or roasted garlic, lemon juice, salt, and red pepper to taste, a little at a time until you've done this several times and know what you like. You now have techina, great over falafel and also in salad dressings and as a dip.

Hot sauce: Add more cayenne pepper to the tahini sauce—as much as you can stand—to fire up your falafel. Do not serve to unsuspecting guests.

Chopped salad: Dice a large tomato and a small cucumber. The traditional salad uses very small dice, but saving time by using large dice works also. Add two tablespoons chopped parsley, two tablespoons chopped onion (or scallion, chives, or shallot), a finely chopped garlic clove, salt, and pepper. Mix well, then add a tablespoon each of olive oil and your favorite vinegar or lemon juice. Mix and adjust the seasonings. This chopped salad is used in pita but is also a staple for meals and all purposes in Israel. Chopped salads, which were rare outside the Middle East, are now trendy. Everything imaginable is added to the mixture, making it a full meal. There's even a chain of fast-foods call Choppt in the northeast.

Chiffonaded lettuce: Dressed, if you like it that way.

Fried eggplant: Fry sliced eggplant, breaded if you prefer, and stuff into the pita.

Pickles: Any type of pickled vegetables—capers, cucumber, beets. Chopped olives and pickled mango are also good.

• • • • •

SHAKSHOUKA

In Israel, and throughout the Middle East, this recipe is as common as mac 'n' cheese is in America. Few people shop for the ingredients—you use what's in the refrigerator. Tomatoes and eggs are the only constants. Lately, this dish has been popping up in recipe columns and restaurants, usually with complicated ingredient lists and instructions. But it can be made simply and with whatever you happen to have.

Shakshouka has been around since the Middle Ages; most sources say that it originated in north Africa, others claim it for Turkey. In any case, it was brought to Israel by Mizrachi immigrants and became an important menu item.

• • • • •

4 servings

INGREDIENTS

Oil for frying
2 cloves garlic, minced
About ¼ cup of chopped onion, shallots, leeks, or scallions
¼ cup chopped parsley, or whatever herbs you have
Spice mix—cayenne pepper, cumin, coriander, cardamom—about 1 teaspoon
   of your favorites
About 4 cups of any mixture of vegetables—summer squash, peppers,
   mushrooms, eggplant, carrots, string beans, greens
¼ to ½ cup vegetable stock or water, optional
About 2 pounds of tomatoes, chopped, or 2 cups of homemade or canned
   tomato sauce
Salt and pepper to taste
4 large eggs

Heat oil in a large skillet. Add garlic and chopped onion/shallot/leek/scallion, parsley, and spice mix to flavor the oil. Sauté for a minute or two, until the garlic and onions are soft and fragrant.

Add the vegetables. If you're using firmer vegetables, such as carrots, pre-cook them or put them in first and give them more time. Eggplant also needs more time to lose its sponginess. The greens can be added in the last minute or two. Cook the vegetables, stirring every minute or so, until they are all soft. Add a quarter to half a cup of vegetable stock or water if it starts to stick.

Add the chopped tomatoes. Stir until the tomatoes lose their shape and the whole things becomes sauce-y. It needs to be fairly loose—add more broth/water if it's too thick to hold the eggs that will be added in the last step. Or, if you're using tomato sauce, add it and stir for a few minutes to combine.

Add salt, pepper, and other herbs. Stir, taste, and adjust seasonings.

Crack the eggs for each serving into the hot mixture. The eggs will begin to set right away. It will take about four to five minutes until they are fully poached. By this time, the vegetable mixture will be firm as well; if it's not firm enough to cut, allow it to cook for a few more minutes. Cut into wedges, with one egg in each wedge, and transfer to plates. Serve over couscous, rice, or another grain for a full meal.

Variations: Add grated cheese during the last minute or two of cooking.

Some people move the skillet (if it is an ovenproof skillet) to the oven for the final poaching of the eggs, instead of doing it on top. If you prefer that method, preheat oven to 350°F.

To heat it up, add hot sauces such as harissa or schug, or spicy sausages. Most children won't eat the spicy versions, though unspiced shakshouka is usually a favorite among children.

• • • • •

THE COMING OF AGE OF ISRAELI CUISINE

For the first thirty or forty years of Israel's statehood, knowledgable tourists agreed: Stick to the simplest foods you can find, like fine, fresh produce (especially tomatoes and cucumbers, citrus, and strawberries), just-baked breads, and phenomenally rich dairy products (like the cottage cheese). And if you're near the Sea of Galilee (Yam Kineret), try one of the dockside restaurants where someone will catch a St. Peter fish for you and cook it as you watch. Otherwise, Israelis, including restaurant owners, were just not into fine food.

That's all changed. A few incredibly talented and camera-ready chefs created sensational restaurants in Israel, then took them around the world, publishing bestselling cookbooks along the way. *Jerusalem: A Cookbook* by Yotam Ottolenghi (a Jew) and Sami Tamimi (a Muslim) and *Zahav: A World of Israeli Cooking* by Michael Solomonov and Steven Cook both won prestigious James Beard Best Cookbook Awards and both are the creations of chefs from revered Israeli restaurants that named their books after their restaurants. (Ottolenghi and Tamimi have moved their restaurant to London, and Solomonov's is now in Philadelphia.) Both cookbooks include standards, like Solomonov's kugel and latkes and Ottolenghi's hummus and chicken soup with knaidlech, as well as more sophisticated fare like Solomonov's Chocolate Situation, a flourless chocolate cake, and Beluga Lentil Soup with Marrow Bones and Ottolenghi's Clementine and Almond Syrup Cake and Portobello Mushrooms with Pearled Barley and Preserved Lemon. Many modern Israeli cooks don't restrict themselves to one type of cuisine. One example of that is a thirteen-course dinner that Ottolenghi staged, along with food writers Maggie Schmitt and Laila El-Haddad (authors of *The Gaza Kitchen*) at New York City's Metropolitan Museum of Art. They avoided the foods of Jerusalem, which during the Middle Ages was somewhat backward in a culinary sense, and instead presented the "richly thick dining experiences"[17] of Gaza during the Abbasid Dynasty in the time of the Crusades, when Gaza's location as a busy port made available spices such as ginger, cinnamon, and galangal.

More and more restaurants in Israel have reached celebrity status, winning international awards and serving exquisite fare that can compete with that of any city. They include Haim Tibi's Muscat, in the Galilee, where he uses produce from a local organic farm; Jem's, a microbrewery in Petach Tikvah; Omar Iluwan's Haj Kahil, which serves traditional Arab food in Jaffa; and Eucalyptus in Jerusalem, where Chef Moshe Basson offers food from biblical times. There's also Machneyuda, located near the sprawling Machneh Yehuda open-air market and run by Yossi Elad, Asaf Granit, and Uri Navon.

Machneh Yehuda, an exuberant but not very clean sprawl of produce vendors and cafes, is also the source of a dish that was unquestionably invented in Israel, *Meorav Yerushalmi*, or Jerusalem mixed grill. There are debates over where it was invented and by whom; many restaurants in the neighborhood claim it. But it is indubitably a delicious combination of Jewish values: a delicious, cheap concoction that uses scraps (chicken livers and other innards and offal) that would have been thrown away and a diverse mix of vibrant spices to form a filling meal that is truly Israeli.

CELEBRATE!

In Israel, the entire country celebrates the Independence Day with parties, singing, dancing, and a variety of professional performances. There is also a ceremony at Mount Herzl in Jerusalem on the site of the grave of Theodor Herzl. The speaker of the Knesset, Israel's Parliament, lights a torch from which twelve other torches are lit, one for each of the twelve tribes of ancient Israel. The ceremony is concluded by a gun salute, one round for each year of Israel's existence as a modern state, and the awarding of the Israel prize for outstanding contribution to art and the humanities. For the first twenty years, there were military parades. These have been replaced by a march of Gadna, Israel's Youth Corps. In the city of Haifa, a dance parade is held, and there are official receptions throughout the country.

Apart from the official celebrations, many families flock to the forests, beaches, and historical sites to embrace the beauty of their country. Schools sponsor picnics and barbecues, families join with relatives from distant cities, and army bases open their doors to display their new inventions.

In America, the celebration has also included films, Israeli fairs, and parades. In New York City, the Celebrate Israel Parade (the name was changed from Salute to Israel) is celebrated with many religious school students, high school bands, Jewish organizations, and political dignitaries taking part in both marching and song. Many communities also sponsor Israeli folk fairs in which Jewish arts and crafts and music are featured. Of course, the celebration also includes the chanting of Israel's national anthem, *Hatikvah*, the Song of Hope.

And all over the world, Jews enjoy the immense diversity of Jewish food, from the plain grains eaten in biblical times to the foods of the dozens of cultures that joined together in Israel, simple to sensational creations from the Middle East, India, Europe, and America—and foods that were invented by the talented cooks of modern Israel.

9

Shavuot

From Barley to Blintzes

S havuot is a holiday with several facets. It marks an agricultural event, the harvest of the first sheaves of wheat. The Torah names it "the Feast of Harvest" and states (*Exodus*, 23:19) that "The choicest first-fruits of your land thou shalt bring into the house of the Lord thy God." It's also generally accepted to be the date that the Torah was given to the Jewish nation, newly freed from slavery. Therefore, it marks the date that the Jews were told the rules of the Torah. The verse above that describes the bringing of the first fruits ends with a puzzling non sequitur that includes a rule that has ended up as one of the most complicated and hard-to-follow culinary laws of Judaism: "You shalt not seethe a kid in its mothers' milk." And the day is connected to the story of Ruth, a tale that involves many Jewish values, especially those relating to farming. Shavuot is a holiday in which food—its production, preparation, and enjoyment—is integral.

REFLECTIONS

It is a tree of life to those who grasp it.—*Prayerbook*

Shavuot, the Festival of Weeks, was celebrated primarily as a thanksgiving for the wheat harvest. It falls seven weeks after the barley harvest when an *omer* of grain of the new produce was produced. The Torah refers to Shavuot as *Hag HaKatzir* (the feast of the harvest) and *Yom Ha Bikkurim* (the day of first fruits), observed by offerings of the best ripe produce of the fields. Beginning with the second day of Passover, seven weeks were carefully counted, and the fiftieth day was celebrated as the beginning of the wheat harvest or the festival of the first fruits.

In the course of time, as a result of the transformation of the agricultural festivals into historical commemorations, the additional significance of Shavuot as the festival of the giving of the Torah at Mount Sinai completely overshadowed its original significance. Though the Torah does not identify Shavuot with the anniversary of the giving of the Ten Commandments, Jewish tradition has held that the Torah was given on the sixth day of the Hebrew month of Sivan (i.e., Shavuot).

Shavuot is the only holiday the Jewish people look forward to by counting the days until it arrives. It is done by counting down to Shavuot each night, beginning from the second night of Passover, thus heightening the anticipation of the day.

For some people, the most important preparation for Shavuot is a lengthy nap on the eve of Shavuot. This is because many communities sponsor a *tikkun leil Shavuot*, an all night study session. Originating with the Jewish mystics, there is a passage in the mystical work called the *Zohar* that praises those that stay awake all night in anticipation of receiving the Torah. Each Shavuot in Jerusalem, tens of thousands of Jews who have stayed up studying the Torah walk down to the Western Wall at the break of dawn to recite the morning service.

In some European countries, it was the custom to begin teaching children Torah on Shavuot. As the letters of the Hebrew alphabet were being taught and mastered, the teacher would give the students some honey symbolizing the sweetness of Jewish education. Today in many Jewish religious schools, students are often presented with their own book of the Torah on Shavuot. Many religious schools hold their confirmation exercises of Jewish teens at one of Shavuot's worship services.

The Sephardic Jews developed a beautiful ritual for Shavuot. Immediately after opening the ark on Shavuot morning, they read a specially designed *ketubah* (Jewish marriage contract), a contract between God (the groom) and Israel (God's bride). In the *ketubah*, God invites the bride to the palace and promises to bind to her forever. The bride responds, "We will do and we will listen," the exact words that were used by the Israelites at Mount Sinai.

In Israel, some *kibbutzim* (collective farms) and other agricultural settlements have revived the first fruits aspect of Shavuot. A procession of tractors, trucks, and dairy workers arrive from the fields carrying grain, milk, eggs, and honey. All join in parading to an open air makeshift theater, where the fruits of the settlement's labor are presented to the community. The children read poems, show drawings, and dance a circle dance. Some of the community's income may be dedicated to charity, a help for those in trouble.

No doubt the receiving of the Torah on Mount Sinai changed the course of Jewish history and gave the Jews the most valid reason for living a Jewish life. The medieval Jewish scholar Saadia Gaon has said that "Jews are a people because of our Torah." This fact alone would be sufficient reason to make Shavuot one of the mightiest pillars supporting Judaism's structure. The Torah for the Jewish people has become its Tree of Life.

FIRST FRUIT

During the time that the Temple stood in Jerusalem, the first shoots of barley were brought to the Temple on the second day of Passover. On that same day, a count-down began to the day that the first wheat would be harvested, exactly fifty days later, on Shavuot. There was a ritual surrounding the harvesting of the first wheat, intricately laid out in the *Mishnah*, right down to the kind of baskets that were to be used. When the first plant would show signs of ripening, the owner of the field would tie a band around it and declare that it was the first fruit. Once they were ready for harvest, these sheaves would be packed in special woven baskets, laced with silver and gold. In the time of the Temple, the baskets were brought with great fanfare. Farmers were obliged to bring a tenth of their crop to donate to the *koha-nim* (priests). From all over the country, citizens converged on Jerusalem, baskets on their shoulders or on the backs of donkeys and oxen. Even the animals were decorated—garlands of flowers were flung around their necks and the horns of the oxen were gilded. When the story is presented today, it is usually accompanied by images of baskets laden with luscious fruit. Wheat is a less appealing graphic, but that is what was actually brought.

During Talmudic times, someone realized that the fiftieth day of the countdown (which is called *Sefira*, or counting) would also have corresponded with the day the Torah was brought down from Mount Sinai and given to the Jews, who had left Egypt fifty days before. After fleeing their enslavers, jumping into the raging Red Sea, and being amazed when God parted it so that they could walk safely to shore, they were offered the Torah and accepted without hesitation. "We will do and we will listen (*Na-aseh v'nishmah*)" is what they said—they meant that first they'd agree to follow, then they would find out what they were agreeing to. The fifty days between the Exodus and Moses' return to Mount Sinai with the Ten Command-ments gave them time to prepare for the life-altering event.

LAG B'OMER

Both end-dates of the countdown (the bringing of the sheaves and the acceptance of the Torah) are joyous, but by the time of the Talmud, the counting of the *omer* had turned into a time of mourning. The sadness is in respect for thousands of students of Rabbi Akiva who died suddenly. Some sources believe the deaths were due to an epidemic; others theorize that they were attacked by Roman forces. Only five of Rabbi Akiva's students—including Rabbi Shimon Bar Yochai (see page 114)—were alive at the end of whatever caused the deaths; the dying stopped on the thirty-third day of the *omer*, which has become a holiday known as Lag B'omer—the "L" in Lag is for lamed, the thirtieth letter in the Hebrew alphabet, and "g" is for gimel, the third letter.

The mourning in the first weeks of the *omer* is expressed by traditional Jews in several ways—people don't shave, wear new clothes, listen to music, or get married. Then, on Lag B'omer, celebrations blaze in the form of bonfires throughout Israel and other Jewish communities. Fire was chosen as the essential element of Lag B'omer to honor Rabbi Shimon Bar Yochai, whose saintliness imbued him with a light that was visible to everyone around him and who was one of the five surviving students of Rabbi Akiva. He also died on a later Lag B'omer. On the day of his death, he revealed many of the Kabbalistic secrets (see pages 113–116) that he had learned during his many years of study. The light of the bonfire symbolizes the light that Rabbi Shimon Bar Yochai brought to the world.

The first mentions of the Lag B'omer celebration appear in Jewish writings in the thirteenth century. From then until modern times, the celebrations have grown. In Israel, children collect firewood for weeks and pile it up into huge structures—in both secular and religious neighborhoods, fires rage and parents worry about accidental burnings. Nowhere do the flames burn brighter than in Meron, where Rabbi Shimon Bar Yochai lived while he was hiding from the Romans. Hundreds of thousands of Hasidic Jews converge on the small town, bringing their whole families and laying out feasts that they cook on the hot fires. Hasidic rabbis lay out *tisches* (tables) with food for their followers. In less pious families, typical barbecue recipes are prepared—hot dogs, hamburgers, and s'mores that Rabbi Shimon Bar Yochai never dreamed of. Another custom at Meron is to cut a boy's hair for the first time—it's a tradition not to cut a boy's hair until he is three years old—at this huge event. Although it does not appear in the Torah, Lag B'omer is a much-anticipated holiday in Israel.

SHAVUOT FOOD

Food is a theme that is carried through all the rules and customs of Shavuot. When those sheaves were brought to the Temple, the Torah states that two loaves of bread—made from flour ground from a small part of that early harvest—should come with them. These loaves were sacrificed in the Temple along with two rams, nine lambs, a goat, and a bull. Seven of the lambs, the bull, and the rams were burned, but the goat, two lambs, and the loaves were eaten by the *Kohanim*.

Considering its primary purpose—the bringing of the first sheaves to the Temple—one would think that Shavuot food would have a firm connection to wheat. And although dairy is the go-to ingredient for the holiday, there are several wheat-based Shavuot dishes, some of which include dairy products. In Kurdistan, a ground wheat pudding cooked with soured milk is a popular Shavuot dish. In eastern Europe, a cheese challah (*kauletsch*) was served. In Greece, the challah was made with yogurt and honey. Tablet and ladder-shaped loaves and cakes are eaten in Tunisia and Morocco. But the most elaborate bread served on the holiday—probably the most elaborate and symbol-laden dish found anywhere—is the Bread of Seven Heavens that is served in many north African countries as part of the *tikkun leil Shavuot*.

Christian bakeries concocted several symbol-laden breads for the Easter holidays. During the Golden Age of Spain in the Middle Ages, this tradition was picked up by Jewish bakers for hundreds of years—in Spain until the Jews were expelled from Spain and in countries such as Greece until Jews were deported or killed during World War II. The custom has been revived in Sephardic countries and in Israel. The bread is a typical challah dough (see pages 33–34). Tiny shapes baked into this loaf symbolize body and soul, life and death, the physical world and spiritual. The center of the bread is a lump of dough that stands for Mount Sinai. It is surrounded by seven rings of dough, each symbolizing one of the rings that the soul climbs on its way to heaven. Bits of dough are shaped as the tablets of the Ten Commandments; a fish that symbolizes the coming of *moshiach* (the Messiah); Miriam's well; a snake; a Torah; and a tiny ladder—known as Jacob's ladder—to aid in the climb between Earth and Heaven.

A baklava-style, phyllo-based dough is used for a similar, sweeter version, laced with honey and studded with raisins and nuts.

DAY OF DAIRY

Dairy is the food one thinks of first on Shavuot. Though not quite universal—Yemenite Jews, for example, eat meat and other Shabbat foods on Shavuot—dairy dishes are incorporated into Shavuot meals in most Jewish communities, which is a departure from the norm of eating meat and fish to make a holidays special.

The association of dairy foods with Shavuot may have originated on Mount Sinai, but it's first mentioned in Jewish literature in a commentary on the Torah by Rabbi Avigdor Tzarfati in 1270. Rabbi Tzarfati wrote that French Jews asked why we eat dairy on Shavuot. He answered by quoting a verse in *Numbers* (28:26). The verse has no clear connection to eating dairy, but it seems that there is a complicated numerical association to the word "milk."[1] The next references are easier to understand: Rabbi Aaron HaCohen of Lunel (1300) said that "it is customary to eat honey and milk [on Shavuot] because the Torah is compared to honey[2] and milk, as it is said 'Honey and milk are under your tongue'" (*Song of Songs*, 4:11). Rabbi Kalonymus ben Kalonymus (1286–1328)—the rabbi who popularized latkes on Hanukkah and hamentaschen on Purim—also mentioned numerical hints (the numerical values of the letters in *chalav*, the Hebrew word for milk, add up to forty, the number of days that Moses stayed on Mount Sinai to learn the Torah from God) and verses in the Torah that suggest milk and honey as Shavuot foods. References appear in several other Middle Age treatises; in the fifteenth century, the *Shulchan Aruch* included a section on the halachic logistics of eating a dairy meal before a meat meal. By the eighteenth century, the custom of eating dairy on Shavuot was accepted throughout the world.

In some cases, a bit of dairy is added to common dishes—an extra dollop of sour cream to a bowl of borscht in Russia, some cheese in a German noodle kugel, butter and yogurt instead of oil on couscous. In Greece, cheese is added to fried bread rings and filled phyllo pastries on Shavuot. And in modern homes, standard dairy dishes—quiches, vegetarian lasagnas, gratins, cream soups—are incorporated into Shavuot meals.

THE HISTORY OF DAIRY IN THE WORLD AND IN ISRAEL

Milk came to Earth when the first mammals—small, furry animals that looked like mice—developed mammary glands from hair follicles, which probably occurred in the Triassic period (about 250 million years ago). This unique nutrition system for offspring gave mammals an advantage and may have helped the mammal class survive when the dinosaurs who co-existed with them became extinct. In about 10,000 BCE—the time at which the climate on Earth stabilized—Neolithic humans began to form communities. The agricultural revolution followed. Once they could stay put and not have to flee or be killed by glaciers and wildly fluctuating temperature, people looked for ways to acquire food that didn't have to be foraged or hunted. They learned to plant crops and domesticate animals (there is archaeological evidence that cattle were raised in Turkey around 7000 BCE), and it didn't take long for them to realize that they could extract and use milk from other species. Milk was not commonly available in the ancient world—most of it went to the upper classes—but it was highly revered. For example, the best recommendation for Israel was that it was flowing with "milk and honey" (*Exodus*, 33:3).

Creating cheese from milk was inevitable. Mesopotamians carried their milk in vessels made from the stomachs of the animals that produced it. The stomach linings contained rennet, an enzyme. As the milk soured and curdled, it reacted with the rennet, and curds separated from whey. The process that took place in those Mesopotamian stomach vessels is roughly the same as the ones that are used by today's cheesemakers. In the millennium between 7000 and 6000 BCE, several developments made cheesemaking feasible: Domestication of mammals (cows, sheep, and goats) was thriving, so there were enough animals to use for meat, with plenty left over for milking. Humans learned to control fire. Pottery to store the cheese was invented, and somewhere along the line, someone observed that the curds formed in the stomach vessels were more stable than plain milk and tasted very good, and that heating the milk over fire made the process faster. Separating cream from cows' milk to form butter happened a little later.

Over the next several thousand years, cheesemaking progressed and cheese became a staple food. Several early artworks from the third century BCE depict cheesemaking. Records show that cheese was popular in Sumeria and Egypt. There was also cheesemaking in India, though most were made without rennet because cows were considered sacred and never slaughtered. When Abraham wanted to entertain the angels that God sent to him, he "brought some curds and milk" (*Genesis*, 18:6–8). When young King David's father Jesse sent him to find his brothers, who were fighting Goliath in King Saul's army, Jesse told him, "take along these ten cheeses" (*1 Samuel*, 17:18) to give to the generals.

Cheesemaking flourished in the Roman Empire—over one hundred varieties appeared—and its territories, but never took hold in the Americas. In Asia, Mongolian and Tibetan cheeses started to show up in Chinese markets, but cheese is not an important ingredient in most Asian cultures. In western Europe, cheeses became more sophisticated—brie was created by French monks in the eighth century. About five hundred years ago, a slew of new cheeses—cheddar in England, gouda in Holland, parmesan in Italy—appeared. When settlers began raising animals in the great open spaces of America, several regions became famous for great fresh cheeses, including the lake counties of Wisconsin, New York, and Ohio (Ohio's nickname was "Cheesedom" in the nineteenth century).

Historically, the dairy industry was not particularly active in the Middle Eastern region, even though it was discovered there. Cows don't produce much milk in hot, dry climates, and it's hard to provide enough grass for them. But when the kibbutzim became established in the early twentieth century, they found that they could improve yields and make dairy farming profitable. In 1926, hundreds of farms, mainly kibbutzim, joined in the Tnuva Dairy Cooperative (the word "*tnuva*" is Hebrew for fruit or produce). Together, they found ways to cool and hydrate the cattle and to breed heat-resistant cows. Today, specialists monitor every phase of production, visiting farms to ensure that the animals are treated humanely, that the environment is protected as much as possible, and that antibiotics are rarely used. Israeli dairy practices are replicated worldwide. The Israeli Holstein cows produce the most milk per cow of any in the world. And Israeli dairy products are among the most delicious and nutritious to be found (their cottage cheese is divine). In 2014, the majority interest of the Tnuva collective was bought by a Chinese conglomerate.

WHY DAIRY?

Dairy is connected to the Torah and thus to Shavuot through many Torah verses and numerical references. But the use of dairy food on Shavuot may have had a more practical provenance: Dairy animals give birth and produce milk in the spring, around Shavuot. There is a lot of milk available on Shavuot and, with their congenital frugality, Jews would naturally want to put it to use. Delicious recipes were created to use an available resource.

There's another reason that is often given for avoiding meat and using dairy products on this holiday. After receiving the Torah, the Jews realized that preparing meat according to its rules was not going to be easy; in fact, it took centuries to extract and understand the rules of kashrut as outlined in the Torah. There's no evidence that their immediate reaction was "let's just have blintzes tonight." As previously noted, the first written connection between Shavuot and dairy came in the thirteenth century. But later generations may have honored the complexity of the kashrut rules (and the generation that first had to deal with them) by simplifying the meals served on the day we celebrate receiving them.

WHAT DOES KOSHER MEAN?

The word "kosher" means proper or appropriate and applies to many things in addition to food; food that is not kosher is called "*treif*," which is derived from a word that means "torn." The foundation for the laws of kashrut appear in the Torah. In *Leviticus* (11:3–8) and *Deuteronomy* (14:3–21), the characteristics required for mammals, fish, and birds to be kosher are listed. Mammals must have cloven hooves and chew their cuds. Cows, goats, sheep, deer, and oxen fall into this category, whereas pigs, all carnivorous animals, primates, and rabbits do not. Marine mammals, such as seals, dolphins, and whales, are also non-kosher, as are bats and marsupials. Kosher fish must have scales and fins, making salmon, flounder, tilapia, whitefish, cod, and snapper kosher. Catfish, swordfish, and all shellfish and mollusks are non-kosher. Some fish, such as sharks, have some form of scales and fins, but it's been decided to keep them in the non-kosher column. Birds that are not kosher are listed in *Deuteronomy*: all birds of prey (eagles, hawks, vultures), owls, pelicans, ostriches, sparrows, swans, gulls, ravens, kites, and many that are no longer common. Birds that don't appear on the proscribed list—chickens, ducks, geese, turkey, pheasant, quail, partridge, pigeon—are traditionally considered kosher. Things that creep or swarm—insects, all invertebrates, reptiles and amphibians such as frogs, crocodiles, alligators, lizards, and worms are all deemed "detestable" in *Leviticus* (11:29–30).

A few other specific foods are prohibited in the Torah. In chapter 9 of *Genesis*, Noah, his descendants, and everyone else were forbidden to eat limbs pulled from living animals—which is usually not something casual diners want to do anyway. Chapter 32 of *Genesis* relates the story of Jacob's fight with an angel. Because Jacob's sciatic nerve was damaged, the sciatic nerve of every animal became *treif*—which is why certain cuts of beef, including sirloin steaks, are not available in kosher stores. Because the sciatic nerve is difficult to extract, many kosher butchers choose to avoid the whole back part of the cow—and non-kosher meat purveyors are happy to take that part. (In Israel, where non-kosher meat is hard to sell, *shochtim* have learned the skill of extracting the sciatic nerve, so they salvage the sirloin and other steaks. If you want kosher sirloin, go to Israel.)

Other prohibited foods include harvested crops that have not been tithed. Food should not be eaten until a portion has been donated—and fruit from a tree that is less than three years old.

A PAINLESS DEATH—KOSHER SLAUGHTER

Even meat from kosher animals is not kosher until and unless it is slaughtered "as I have instructed you" (*Deuteronomy*, 12:21)—but the instructions are nowhere to be found in the written Torah. The complicated rules of ritual slaughter appear in the oral tradition—a comprehensive code that was memorized and passed down from generation to generation "by mouth" until it was finally written down in the *Mishnah* in the third century CE.

As with all the rules of kashrut, the reasons for the regulations of kosher slaughter, which is called *shechita*, are not given. Nevertheless, three ideas seem to underlie most of the instructions regarding kosher *shechita* and what makes an animal non-kosher: all blood should be removed, the animal must be healthy at the time of slaughter, and the slaughter must be swift and result in as little pain as possible to the animal. (Cruelty to animals is deplored in Judaism—even non-Jews are prohibited from causing pain to animals. If practiced correctly, animals lose consciousness almost immediately and their suffering is quickly over.) To adhere to these regulations, meat is salted and soaked to remove blood; knives must be sharp and wielded by trained *shochtim* (slaughterers); inspectors must make sure that the animals are disease-free before slaughter (downed cows, which may be causing disease in humans in today's factory farms, would not be kosher). The part about the blood may be connected to avoidance of idol worship that used blood in ritual—but the other two ideas result in healthy, practical, and humane food production.

There's one more brief mention of prohibited foods in the Bible—a verse that makes kosher much more difficult to keep. The verse states: "You shall not seethe a kid in its mother's milk"—and it must be important, because appears three times (*Exodus*, 23:19 and 34:26, and *Deuteronomy*, 14:21). Though it seems quite innocuous—it says nothing about seething a kid in the milk of a goat that is not its mother, let alone cheeseburgers. But the verse has been expanded to include the mixing of any milk and meat and has been used as the foundation for a rigorous segregation of any utensils that ever come in contact with either.

In fact, the kid that was not to be seethed in its mother's milk has morphed into a whole industry. Kosher homes keep milk products (known as *milchig* in Yiddish, *chalavi* in Hebrew) and meat (*fleishig* in Yiddish, *besari* in Hebrew) totally separate. They have separate dishes, pots, food processors, dishwashers, counters, and electric can openers for each. Using the *fleishig* knife on a bread that has a bit of butter in it or mixing up the silverware are heinous transgressions. If a single drop of milk is accidentally added to a meat dish, the whole thing is sometimes tossed (though many Orthodox rabbis will find halachic loopholes—because no one wants to waste food) or offered to a non-Jewish neighbor. Commercial manufacturers are not trusted to follow the laws, so specially trained inspectors, called *mashgichim*, watch over the production process. They make sure that no *treif* ingredients (such as lard) are used, but also that no equipment that has ever been used for meat is used for dairy or vice versa. If the food passes muster, the manufacturer is allowed to print their seal of approval on the package. The tiny symbols on packages such as OU and Star-K are called *hechshers*, or kosher guarantees, and each belongs to a specific monitoring organization of which there are hundreds in the United States alone. Manufacturers are willing to pay significant fees for the inspection seal, not only to appeal to kosher clients but because many consumers consider the symbol an indication that the food is pure and clean.

When did that simple phrase become so pervasive? A joke told by borscht-belt comedians assumes that it happened on Mount Sinai. God was explaining the Torah to Moses before it was presented to the Jews. When God came to the verse about not seething a kid in its mother's milk, Moses nodded. "I understand—we are never to mix milk and meat, in any form, not even a drop." "No," answered God. "Just, you shall not seethe a kid in its mother's milk." Again, Moses chimed in. "And we'll get two sets of dishes, and pots, and pans, and knives, and we'll wash them separately and never ever mix them." God interjected. "Moses, Moses—thou shall not seethe a kid in its mother's milk; that's all." That didn't stop Moses. "And when we eat meat, we'll wait six hours before eating dairy. And if we accidentally mix up the silverware, we'll boil them. And . . ." God sighed. "Moses," He said. "Do what you want."

Obviously, it didn't happen that way. The verse was expanded to cover all meat and milk almost immediately and that is reflected in the Oral Torah and in the *Mishnah* that codified it. From the times of the Talmud, milk and meat were not combined in any dish.

But the use of separate dishes came later; there are debates about when it happened. Orthodox rabbis point to a verse in the Torah (*Numbers*, 22–23) that states that vessels that are acquired as spoils of war must be purified before they are used. There are also numerous medieval commentaries that demand two sets of dishes. On the other side of debate, in "Separating the Dishes: The History of Jewish Eating Practice," David Kraemer writes: "Nowhere in all of Talmudic literature is there a hint that the Rabbis demanded a systematic separation of dairy and meat utensils."[3] He points out that the *Shulchan Aruch* (written by Rabbi Yosef Caro in 1564) shows that though some further rules are in place, meat and dairy dishes were not rigorously separated: "plates used for meat that were washed in a kettle used for milk, in water hot enough to scald one's hand, even if they had both been used [for meat and dairy] on the same day, it is permitted" (*Yoreh Deah*, 95:3). But the previous sentences in the *Shulchan Aruch* say that this only applies to clean dishes, and only in circumstances that can't be avoided.

For the next few hundred years, the rules became more stringent and more and more sources suggested keeping dishes separate. By the eighteenth century, the two-sets-of-dishes law was firmly in place. And today, families about to start kosher homes have many extra lines on their bridal registries as they assemble double equipment; kitchens in kosher homes include extra cabinets and two dishwashers.

What is the reason for kashrut in the first place? Many people believe that the rules are based on cleanliness. There's no basis for that belief. Dirty and spoiled food can be quite kosher. There's also a common misconception that kosher food is blessed by rabbis and confers a sanctification; there are no such blessings. Other theories involve health criteria. Indeed, some *treif* foods hold health risks. Pork, during the time of the Torah, was often infected with trichinosis that could be deadly to humans. Shellfish, then and now, can be contaminated by marine waste that makes it toxic to humans. And the mixing of meat and milk was considered unhealthy by many people around the time the Torah was written.

The fact is, though—the reasons behind the laws of kashrut are a mystery. They have never been revealed and Jews are expected to accept them on faith. That acceptance is a reason in itself. When we self-impose the discipline of kashrut on ourselves, we carefully watch everything that goes into our mouths. The mindfulness of keeping kashrut, while not an explicit reason for doing so, is a beneficial result. And accepting the fact that not everything we do has a clear and practical reason is a way to increase our understanding of a world that we don't fully understand.

For many, keeping kosher makes us feel that we are part of a community, a member of a like-minded group—we're not narrowing our horizons by avoiding certain foods, we're joining with others who believe as we do. The fact that this particular quest has ancient roots and is tied to an extraordinary system of values and morals makes us happy to be part of it.

There's one more result of keeping kosher, one that might not be considered an advantage. And it's never been proven that this was a deliberate, intended result predicted by the leaders who expanded the rules of kashrut. Being forbidden to share the food of all our neighbors—to eat in their homes and on their dishes, to taste their traditional foods—drives a wedge between us. It's almost impossible to fully share in the lives of those who don't keep kosher when you're so restricted. There's debate in the Talmud that concludes: "Avoid their food because of their wine, avoid their wine because of their daughters" (*Gemara Shabbat*, 17b)—in other words, when we stay away from food that is not specifically appropriate for us, we'll stay away from drinking with our gentile neighbors and be less inclined to marry out of the faith. A religion that seeks to survive intact for thousands of years without a huge population and without a constant state needs a way to keep its members within the fold. And kashrut serves that purpose.

The laws of kashrut are connected to other more understandable Jewish values, but in some cases these connections are not binding. The rules of kosher slaughter are meant to reduce the pain felt by animals, but to some observers in modern times, *shechita* seems more painful than other forms of slaughter—it has been called barbaric. Some rules of kashrut help protect the environment—refraining from eating fruit from new trees strengthens the rootstock, for example. But, despite the fact that the Talmud recommends sustainable farming practices, crops that are grown in ways that harm the environment can still be kosher. And respect for our fellow humans, especially those who are poor, is present in rules about what we can eat. We are told to contribute a portion of every harvest to the community and to the poor. But some strictly kosher manufacturers have been found to abuse their workers, even under-age employees. A movement has started to label food with not only a general *hechsher*, indicating that it has been prepared under the rules of kashrut, but also a *hechsher* of goodness and/or justice, guaranteeing that it has been produced in a way that does not torture animals, destroy the environment, or oppress workers. In 2008, Magen Tzedek (Shield of Justice) was organized by conservative Jewish leaders "to develop and apply a set of standards that would certify that kosher food manufacturers operate according to Jewish ethics and social values."[4] Though still ongoing, the project has not caught fire, in part because of politics.

The rules of kashrut have been interpreted by thousands of experts since the Torah was presented on Mount Sinai. No one can point to a system and insist that it's exactly what God prescribed. Actually, they can and do insist, but that doesn't make them right. These variances make it quite reasonable for everyone to find his or her own way to keep kosher, whether it's avoiding a specific food or avoiding the slightest possibility that a food might be *treif*. Some people are rigorous in keeping their own dishes kosher, but more lax when eating in restaurants. Some who are very serious about kashrut have found a valid halachic basis for accepting certain ingredients (gelatin made from animal bones, for example). It is, however, hard to find a rabbi who would agree that all Chinese food is kosher as long as it is eaten on paper plates.

DAIRY

The focus on dairy on Shavuot is remarkable mostly for the fact that it is unusual. Although humans and other mammals are nourished with milk for the first months of their lives, it is usually relegated to secondary status after infancy, which is a shame, because it is healthy, easily available, and delicious. Along with vegetables and eggs, it can be the centerpiece of satisfying meals without depending on meat, which is more expensive, harder to digest, and more harmful to the environment.

One of the nice parts of Shavuot is the focus on dairy meals, which often are simpler and more creative than meat meals. Without a hunk of flesh at the center of the meal, combinations of lighter, fresher vegetables and grains are combined with cheese to create dishes that are usually not served at formal meals. It helps that Shavuot arrives at the same time that crops begin to flood the market— greens, asparagus, new potatoes, and tender young summer squash and eggplants show up in farmers' markets just in time to become delicious additions to traditional recipes.

In many Jewish homes, there is a dairy dish that exemplifies Shavuot; there's no rule that you can't eat these dishes at other times of the year, but we begin to salivate for them when the calendar turns to the sixth of Sivan. In Ashkenazi homes, pierogen, cheese *kreplach*, noodle and rice kugels with cheese, and especially blintzes are Shavuot favorites. There's also a very old eastern European recipe for a layered cheese tart called floden that was one of the first dairy dishes recommended for Shavuot in Jewish literature. Pashtida (see page 176), the Israeli version of quiche (the name is probably derived from pasta), is made with cheese for Shavuot. Rugelach, strudels, and cheesecakes (see pages 87, 226, and 210) filled with fruit and cheese were served for dessert. But the blintz is the go-to food for many people on Shavuot.

THE BIRTH OF BLINTZES

Many countries claim to be the originators of blintzes. There were many types of filled pancakes in central Europe. They were called "palacsinta" in Hungary, "blini" in Russia—the name blintz is probably a combination of the words blini and palascinta. Stuffing dough with savory fillings and then frying it is common to many cuisines: Italian ravioli, Chinese dumplings, Indian samosas, South American empanadas. What makes the blintz different is the thinness of the pancake that envelopes it and the light, soft fillings that stuff it. The thin, crepelike pancakes came from Turkey. When the Turks invaded the Balkan countries, they made life a little better for the people they conquered by introducing them to thin wheat pancakes made in shallow pans. The fillings evolved separately, based on available ingredients. Cheese was an early favorite. As with Hanukkah latkes, potatoes were not used until the seventeenth century because that's when they were brought to Europe from the Americas. When Jews came to America, blintzes became a little touch of home. Restaurants that catered to immigrants kept them coming. Today, chefs get creative, filling them with all kinds of vegetables, grains, and cheeses, and creating pancakes laced with herbs, spices, and other flavorings.

• • • • •

8 to 10 blintzes, 3 to 4 servings
INGREDIENTS

For the Wrappers:
2 large eggs
2 cups milk or buttermilk
2 cups all-purpose flour
½ teaspoon baking powder
1 teaspoons sugar
½ teaspoon salt
3 tablespoons unsalted butter, melted

For Potato Filling:
2 cups mashed potatoes, made with butter, salt, and pepper
¼ cup fried onions (optional)

For Spinach-Cheese Filling:
2 cups ricotta cheese
2 cups steamed, boiled or sautéed spinach or other greens
Salt and pepper to taste
2 tablespoons toasted chopped almonds, pecans, or pine nuts (optional)

For Fruit and Cheese Filling:
1 cup chopped fruit such as peaches, pineapple, plums, pears, mangoes
2 cups ricotta cheese
1 tablespoon brown sugar (optional)
½ teaspoon cinnamon (optional)

Combine all the wrapper ingredients except for two tablespoons of the butter in a food processor bowl. Pulse briefly until combined, but do not overmix.

Prepare a plate and eight-inch pieces of wax paper. Heat a seven- to eight-inch frying pan until hot but not smoking. Brush lightly with melted butter—you're going to use your melted butter for eight to ten wrappers. Measure a quarter cup of batter and pour into the center of the heated pan. Let it cook for about a minute until the edges start to crisp. Then run a spatula around the crepe so that it lifts from the pan. Shake the pan so that the formed crepe does not stick; if it is sticking, run the spatula under it. Quickly flip the crepe to the other side and let it cook for just about thirty seconds, then slide it onto the plate and cover with the wax paper.

If you're not comfortable with flipping—even though it's really not hard once you have a little practice—let the first side cook for about a minute longer; the crepe will cook through and you won't have to flip before you slide onto the plate.

Continue to cook the rest of the crepes; you should have a stack of eight to ten crepes by the time you're done, depending on the size of your pan.

Choose your filling; combine the ingredients. If you're using a cheese filling, place the filling in a strainer so that most of the liquid drains out.

To assemble: Place about two tablespoons of filling in the center of each wrapper; shape the filling with a spoon so that it extends in a vertical line down the center of the blintz, about an inch from the top and bottom. Fold the top over the filling, then roll up the sides one at a time, tucking in the first side and overlapping the second side over the first. You should have a neat little package.

To cook: Blintzes can be boiled, baked, or fried. To boil, add a few at a time to a pot of salted boiling water; remove after three minutes with a slotted spoon and place on paper towel to drain. To bake, place on a cookie sheet and put in an oven pre-heated to 350°F for fifteen minutes, until the edges brown. To fry (not the healthiest method, but probably the tastiest), heat a tablespoon of vegetable oil in a pan over medium heat. Place the blintzes in the pan and let them fry, checking them frequently until golden on one side, then turn over and fry the other side. Drain on paper towels.

• • • • •

SEPHARDIC DAIRY DISHES

Instead of blintzes, Sephardic dairy delights include cheese-filled borekas (see pages 140–142) and sambouseks, sfongo, a spinach-cheese nest, and a Syrian cheese-filled pancake called atayef. A milky rice pudding that originated in Persia, called sutlach or muhallabeya, is one of the most popular Shavuot dishes. A mound-shaped cookie, called Mount Sinai, is often served for dessert.

SUTLACH

If blintzes are the go-to Shavuot recipe in Ashkenazi homes, sutlach is the food that conjures up Shavuot for Sephardim. This milky pudding, made with ground rice or rice flour, probably originated in Persia, where the technique for grinding rice into flour was developed in the thirteenth century. The dish was called "ferni." It spread throughout the Ottoman Empire (sutlu means "with milk" in Turkish). A similar dish called muhallabeya is popular in Arab countries.

Sutlach is a fairly easy dish to prepare. A basic sutlach is made from just three ingredients—and a lot of patience. The mixture must be stirred constantly or lumps will form and the bottom will scorch. It takes about twenty to twenty-five minutes to achieve a smooth, thick pudding. Different countries have their own variations, but adding rosewater or orange blossom water and chopped almonds or pistachios are common. Rosewater is especially appropriate for Shavuot, the Feast of Roses, and rose petals are sometimes used as garnish. In Spain and Turkey, vanilla, lemon, and cinnamon are used as flavorings; in India, Iraq, and Iran, cardamom and rosewater are added.

• • • • •

6 servings

INGREDIENTS

4 cups milk, preferably whole or 2 percent
3 to 4 tablespoons sugar or honey
½ cup rice flour; ground rice cereal can be substituted
Optional flavorings and garnishes: see note above

Combine all ingredients in a heavy pot. Slowly bring to a boil and stir constantly until the mixture becomes thick or creamy, about twenty to twenty-five minutes.

If you are adding flavorings, add them in the last five minutes of cooking. Pour into bowls and add garnishes. Serve hot or cold.

• • • • •

FRUIT FOR SHAVUOT

There is some evidence that the *bikkurim*, or first fruits, also included samplings from all the seven varieties for which Israel is famous—barley, wheat, grapes, figs, pomegranates, olives, and dates—so fruit is appropriate even though the "first fruits" that have a starring role in the holiday of Shavuot are sheaves of wheat. Using succulent peaches, cherries, and plums are a bit of a stretch—but because they ripen around the time of Shavuot, and because they are delicious, they are common on the Shavuot menu, especially in recent years. Sometimes, they're combined with dairy in cheesecakes, blintzes, and strudels.

Jews in Hungary appropriated a popular fruit soup to start the Shavuot meal. In Hungary, this soup is known as meggyleves (meggy means sour cherries, leves means soup). The soup was served with spring meals, using the sour cherries that were among the first fruits to ripen.

Though it's still known as a Hungarian/Czech and Jewish favorite, cold cherry soup spread throughout eastern Europe when it was served in Baltic resorts—it's on the menus in Germany, Poland, and Austria, and was brought to North America and Israel in the early twentieth century.

Although meggyleves means sour cherry soup, sweet cherries (which are easier to find) can also be used. For variety, add other stone fruit (peaches, plums, nectarines) or berries (strawberries, raspberries—blueberries don't work). If you're using sweet cherries, mixing in a half cup of diced rhubarb will bring a bit of the original sour cherry flavor; make sure you cook the fruit until the rhubarb is very soft, and add more sugar to taste.

COLD CHERRY SOUP

• • • • •

4 to 6 servings

INGREDIENTS

1 quart fresh, frozen, or jarred cherries, sweet or sour
3 cups juice, see note
¾ cup sugar if you are using sour cherries; reduce to ½ cup if you are using
    sweet cherries and to ¼ cup or none if you are using sweetened cherries
½ teaspoon cinnamon, more or less to taste
2 cloves (optional)
1 cup sour cream

Remove the pits from the cherries, using a cherry pitter if you have one. Bring a cup of water to a boil and add the cherries; cook until they are very soft and have released their juice. If you are using fresh cherries, this will take about ten minutes; frozen or jarred cherries will take about half the time.

Add the juice, sugar, cinnamon, and cloves, if you are using them. Stir over low heat until the sugar is dissolved and the liquid is thoroughly mixed. Allow to cool slightly. Add a few tablespoons of the cooking liquid to the sour cream and mix thoroughly; add a few more tablespoons and mix again—the sour cream should be room temperature or warm before adding to the soup. Add the sour cream mixture to the soup and stir until combined.

Transfer the soup to a container with a tight lid. Chill the soup for several hours. It may separate, but will recombine if shaken vigorously. Serve chilled.

The soup is better after a few days in the refrigerator and will last for up to a week in a full, tightly closed jar in the refrigerator. If you use some of the soup, transfer the rest to a smaller jar; air in the jar will make it deteriorate faster.

Note on juice: Traditionally, cherry juice is used for this soup, sometimes with the addition of a tablespoon of lemon juice. But changing the juice can provide a more complex flavor. Many people replace half of the juice with red wine or add a tablespoon or two of liqueur. Orange juice can also be used in place of part or all of the cherry juice.

• • • • •

SHAVUOT SWEETS

Since fruit and honey are appropriate for Shavuot—fruit for the "first fruits" connection, honey as one of the *sheva minim* and for the "milk and honey" quotes from the Torah—there is no dearth of desserts to close Shavuot meals. But one treat is favored: For many, Shavuot means cheesecake and if the cheesecake is not as important as the Torah, it's a solid second.

Cheesecake has a Jewish flavor, but it was popular in many countries. Ancient Greeks and Romans loved their cheesecakes—archaeologists have found cheesecake molds that date back to 2200 BCE and Romans added eggs to make them fluffier. By the Middle Ages, cheesecakes had improved tremendously. Henry VIII's chef had a special recipe—he soaked the cheese in milk, then strained it and added sugar, butter, and eggs.

Cheesecake took a huge leap forward with the invention of cream cheese in the late nineteenth century; the higher fat content resulted in a softer, richer cheesecake that was easier to prepare and to vary with additional flavorings. Although there were various cream cheeses in Europe, they didn't come near the fat content of the American ones, which were invented by a dairyman named William Lawrence in Chester, New York, who successfully created a higher-fat cheese at the request of a specialty store in the city. Lawrence was not Jewish, but many of the dairies in upstate New York were, as were many of the people who marketed the new product. Cheesecake is considered to be a Jewish product, and William Lawrence rarely gets credit for it.[5]

In the United States, cheesecake has always been associated with Jews and with Jewish neighborhoods, probably because of the cream cheese connection. Among the most famous Jewish cheesecake purveyors were Lindy's in New York and Eli's Cheesecake in Chicago (which provided cheesecakes for the inaugural balls of Presidents Clinton and Obama). Sara Lee, the company that brought frozen cheesecakes to millions of homes, is also Jewish-owned.

Ratners, a Jewish dairy restaurant on the Lower East Side, was famous for its cheesecake as well as for its blintzes, its mushroom barley soup, its vegetable cutlets, and its charmingly nasty waiters. It was patronized by politicians, jazz greats, and movie stars. Ratners closed in 2002, but it has been immortalized on film (in scenes from *The French Connection* and *Mad Men*) and recipes such as the one below.

RATNER'S CHEESECAKE

There are many versions of cheesecake; some include fruit or flavorings such herbs, olives, ginger, lemon, nuts, chocolate, and liqueurs.

• • • • •

Makes one nine-inch by thirteen-inch cheesecake
INGREDIENTS

For the Cookie Crust:
½ cup sugar
½ cup shortening
½ cup (1 stick) butter
1½ cups sifted cake flour
1 cup all-purpose flour
½ teaspoon vanilla extract
½ teaspoon lemon extract
1 egg
¼ teaspoon salt
½ teaspoon baking powder
Sugar (optional)

For the Filling:
1 pound cream cheese, at room temperature
1 pound farmer cheese
1⅓ cups sugar
6 tablespoons soft butter
1½ cups sour cream
3 tablespoons all-purpose flour
4 eggs
2 teaspoons vanilla extract

Preheat oven to 350°F.

Prepare cookie dough: In a bowl, combine all ingredients with an electric mixer or by hand. Refrigerate for three or four hours, preferably overnight. (Dough may be wrapped and stored in the refrigerator for up to two weeks.)

Press enough dough into an ungreased nine- by thirteen- by two-inch baking pan to form a thin layer over the bottom and sides of the pan (see note below).

Prepare filling: Combine all ingredients and beat with an electric mixer until smooth.

Pour cheesecake filling into pan and bake for one hour. Cool on a rack.

If desired, when cheesecake has thoroughly cooled, sprinkle granulated sugar in a crisscross over the top of the cake.

Note: If there is any leftover dough, bake according to cookie dough recipe.

• • • • •

THE BOOK OF RUTH

The Book of Ruth, one of five Megillot (revelations) that are part of the Jewish Torah, is read on Shavuot morning.

The story starts with Naomi, her husband, and two sons leaving Israel and traveling to Moab. The sons married Moabite women—Ruth was one of the wives. Then the husband and sons all died (which is seen as punishment for leaving Israel). Destitute, Naomi decides to return to her homeland and leaves with both daughters-in-law. The journey is tough, and one of them goes back, but Ruth accepts the religion of her husband and mother-in-law. She says, "Do not entreat me to leave you. Whither you go, I will go, wherever you lodge, I will lodge, your people will be my people, and your God will be my God."

When they arrive in Israel, Naomi sends Ruth to glean food on the land of her cousin, Boaz. Jewish law states that gleaners are entitled to three forms of free food from farmers: one corner of every farm is to be left for them. Any food that falls from the harvesting equipment belongs to the gleaners, and any baskets that are forgotten by the harvesters are to be left in place. Ruth gleans gracefully and catches the eye of Boaz, who tells her, "daughter, don't glean in anyone else's field." (This phrase is used as a motto of the Beth Jacob Schools, a system of Orthodox elementary and high schools for girls all over the world.) Ruth decides to see if the attraction can be taken further. She visits Boaz at night, while he is sleeping and "uncovers his legs." The leg uncovering is successful. They marry and have several children. The union is obviously acceptable, as King David descended from Boaz and Ruth.

There are several reasons that the Book of Ruth is read on Shavuot: Ruth's descendent, King David, died on Shavuot; Ruth accepted the Torah, just as the Jews did on Shavuot; and Ruth's story happened around harvest time, the same season as Shavuot. And one more: The efficient and compassionate method of distributing food to the needy that is employed by Ruth is a significant example of the morality taught in the Torah that the Jews received on Shavuot. Farmers automatically donated some of their crop to those who needed it. There was no complicated tax system, no humiliating distribution. By the work of their hands, the poor collected enough to get by. If Shavuot celebrates the acceptance of the Torah, then reading about how Ruth prospered from its teachings is the perfect way to understand its precepts.

SHAVUOT CUSTOMS AROUND THE WORLD

Italy
Edda Servi Machlin writes about a Shavuot ritual in her town of Pitigliano, a way of using up matzah left over from Passover. No one wanted to keep matzah after Shavuot, but no one wanted to waste it—so they fed it to the fish. Families would gather all the leftover matzah, break into bits, then gather near the river and throw it in and watch hundreds of fish eagerly devour it.

Libya
On Shavuot, Jewish Libyan parents made cookies and other baked goods in symbolic shapes and strung them onto twine so that their children could wear them as necklaces.

Morocco
On Shavuot, Jews in Morocco and other north African countries playfully spray water on each other, referring to the way that the Torah is often compared to water, with both being vital to life.

Persia/Iran
Iranian Jews think of Shavuot as the time that Jews joined with God in a relationship similar to a marriage. They therefore eat foods that are traditionally served at weddings, such as sweetened grains and dried fruit.

Ethiopia
Most of the Jews from the Beta Israel communities in Ethiopia emigrated to Israel in two waves, in 1984 and 1991. There are now more than 125,000 Jews of Ethiopian descent living in Israel. Most live in neighborhoods near other Ethiopian Jews, under the guidance of a spiritual leader called a Kes. On Shavuot, Ethiopian Jews from each group gather and bring bread and other food; the Kes blesses the food and then the entire community eats together.

Turkey
Muhallebi, or pudding shops, were popular in Turkey, and one creamy pudding, called Mallabi in Israel, is served on Shavuot. Mallabi is made from cornstarch, milk, and sugar, and topped with cinnamon, shredded coconut, chopped nuts, and dried fruit.

India
Indian Jews think of Shavuot as the holiday of milk and honey; around Shavuot, they order extra milk and cream so that they can cook Basundi, a recipe that includes sugar, raisins, cardamom, and almonds.

Algeria
Before Shavuot, Algerian Jews buy green corn and hang it from their ceilings. They eat it with a pancake on Shavuot, dipping both in milk, after counting the *omer*.

Eastern Europe
Shavuot was known as the holiday of roses. Bukharan Jews would decorate their synagogues with red roses. In many eastern European synagogues, congregants would cut paper roses, called *reizalach*, and hang them near windows to catch the sun.

10

Life Cycle Events

Mitzvah Meals

A t the most important moments of our lives, we need wisdom, maturity, and faith to keep ourselves grounded and ready for whatever comes next. And, if we're Jewish, we also need chopped liver, strudel, chickpeas, and hard-boiled eggs. Throw in some fancy cookies and pistachios nuts, and we're all set.

Every life cycle event is marked with a *seudat mitzvah*, a meal of good deeds. We don't celebrate mindlessly, and we don't get drunk and stuff our faces (or we do, but that's not all). We raise a glass of wine and make a blessing; someone makes a speech that reminds us of the Torah; we remember previous generations. Even at a wedding, we don't shout mazel tov until we first shatter a glass to remind ourselves of the destruction of the Temple.

And no matter how joyous or somber the feast, we don't forget that it is our obligation to do our part to engage in *tikkun olam* (repairing the world). There's a *pushkah* (charity box) at every Orthodox shiva house; the poor are invited to every wedding and circumcision, where they are encouraged to eat and ask for donations; and as part of a boy or girl's Bar or Bat Mitzvah, he or she is expected to find a project that makes a small part of the world a little bit better.

REFLECTIONS

There can be no joy without food and drink.—*Talmud, Moed Katan* 9a

"Be fruitful and multiply" (*Genesis*, 1:28) is the first of the 613 commandments in the Torah. In Judaism, having children is not only a religious obligation but undoubtedly one of the crowning achievements in the life of parents. Jewish life cycle events are all special celebrations of children. Each rite of passage is marked by a pageantry of ritual and custom, law and folklore, celebration and feasting with festive food.

The quantity of meals that one chooses to eat in a day is strictly voluntary. However, in Jewish life the meal following a rite of passage is a required religious act. In fact, the meal is intimately associated with the act itself and is set down as a religious requirement, known as a *seudat mitzvah*, the celebratory meal. This special meal, mandated by Jewish law, was originally instituted for the day of the circumcision of an infant boy as this was the day on which the infant entered the covenant of Israel. By medieval times, many Jewish authorities had drawn a bond between the ceremonies of circumcision and Bar Mitzvah, not only because they serve as the beginning and end of Jewish childhood, but also because both are concerned with covenant. In the case of circumcision, parents determine to raise their child as a Jew, and in the case of Bar/Bat Mitzvah, boys and girls assume responsibility for themselves as Jews. The festive meal following these rites of passage becomes an instrument of community, bringing people together in sacred celebration.

Scholars have a field day in locating the genuine seed of the custom of serving food after a milestone event. Some say it goes back to Isaac's weaning (*Genesis*, 21:8) when Abraham throws a feast to celebrate that event. One ancient source (*Genesis Rabbah*, 53:10) suggests that Isaac was weaned at the age of thirteen, thus connecting food with the today's custom of throwing a party on the occasion of a Bar or Bat Mitzvah.

All religions have their moments of becoming, when an individual moves from one status to another in sacred initiation. Anthropologists refer to these moments when an individual moves from one status to another as liminal moments. Liminality is the quality of ambiguity or disorientation that occurs in the stage of a rite of passage when participants no longer hold their pre-ritual status but have not yet begun the transition to the status they will hold when the ritual is complete. During a ritual's liminal stage, participants stand at the threshold, where they are considered to be the most vulnerable to outside forces. Judaism has developed its own peculiar folklore within which one will find a variety of superstitions, some of which are related to Jewish rites of passage. As strange as some of these might sound, they were initiated with the goal of safeguarding a person in a liminal moment from the danger and the evil that was lurking in the air.

For example, before her son's circumcision, there is a custom of placing candy under the bed of the mother to draw the attention of the so-called evil spirits away from her and her baby. In eastern Europe, it was customary to throw sugar, raisins, and cake into the baby's cradle before the child was placed into it, an omen for a sweet and abundant life. It has become customary to throw sweet things (marshmallows, candy, and the like) at a Bar or Bat Mitzvah as a way of symbolically wishing them a good life.

Not only is food essential to Jewish life cycle events, it is essential to the Jewish experience itself. The very first act that the Israelites in Egypt are commanded to do is to have a communal meal—roasted lamb and herbs. And with that, the beginning of the Jewish people is through a meal. With the destruction of the Jerusalem Temple nearly two thousand years ago, the ancient rabbis transferred its rituals, food, and blessings to the family and its home and the act of eating becomes hallowed. The ancient Temple altar became the family table, libation wine became *Kiddush* (the wine blessing), and the show bread offered to the Jewish priests in Bible times became challah. Abraham Joshua Heschel gave classic expression to this thought when he wrote that "perhaps the essential message of Judaism is that in doing the finite, we can perceive the infinite." By saying a blessing over one single slice of bread, one can hallow the act of eating and discover the infinite!

PRE-CRADLE TO GRAVE

Judaism provides a plethora of guidance on how to handle the high points and transitions in our lives; some of it is profoundly intelligent and some of it is superstitious twaddle. The Torah points this out right from the start, in a story in *Genesis* (29–30). Leah, one of Jacob's wives, bore him six sons. Rachel, whom he preferred and upon whom he lavished much more attention, was barren. Rachel looked for ways of increasing her chances of getting pregnant. One day, she saw Leah's son Reuben carrying a batch of mandrake, which was supposed to increase fertility. She asked Leah to tell Reuben to give it to her, but Leah refused, pointing out that Rachel had already taken her husband, she was not going to get her son's mandrake. Rachel made a deal: She traded a night with Jacob for the mandrake and Leah approached Jacob and explained that he was hers for the night. Leah got pregnant; Rachel didn't—which shows that the authors of the Torah knew where babies come from, and it's not mandrake.

That hasn't stopped the proliferation of beliefs that certain actions and foods affect our lives, our fertility, and our health. The *etrog*, the citron that is used on Sukkot, is one of them; many people believe that eating the top of the *etrog* (the part that was attached to the tree, called a *pittum*), the *etrog* itself, or a jelly made from an *etrog* will improve chances for conception and/or a healthy pregnancy, easy labor, and successful birth. This is discussed, quite incomprehensibly linking Eve's guilt in the Garden of Eden episode to the biting of the *etrog*, in a book about customs called *Taamei Minhagim* (The Reasons for Customs) by Rabbi Yitzchak Avraham Sperling: "The reason is that our sages say that (according to one opinion) the forbidden fruit that *Adam* and *Chava* ate was an *etrog*. Therefore she bites the *pittum* in order to show that 'just as I have no benefit/pleasure from biting a *pittum* so, too, I had no benefit/pleasure from the sin.'"[1]

There are other traditions regarding conception and birth, some involve food, some don't. Some of them are called "*segulot*," which means omens; some were suggested in the kabbalah, others were picked up from other cultures. Eating the piece of the challah that sticks up from the braid is supposed to spur conception; eating food from the meal at the conclusion of Shabbat (*Seudah Shlishit*, or third meal) is supposed to make pregnancy easier. Some pregnant women keep a special stone in their beds to ward off miscarriage and avoid stepping on discarded human fingernails.

In fact, there are some foods that scientists say will increase fertility and sperm count, and some were available in biblical times—for women, foods rich in folic acid (such as lentils, peas, and nuts) and high-fat dairy; for men, beef and pumpkin seeds, but none are part of the superstitions.

Many Jewish women, even in modern, non-observant families, won't buy clothes or furniture for the baby-to-be or discuss his or her name before the baby is born. There's a belief that an "evil eye" is waiting for a time when people are too happy so it can swoop in to destroy that happiness. Saying *bili eyin hara* in Hebrew or *kenohar*a in Yiddish—which is a contraction of the Yiddish *kein eyin hara*, or without the evil eye—supposedly has some power to defer the effects of this evil.

Once the baby is born, the partying starts. There are many names for the gatherings that occur in the first week of a baby's life. One theme that runs through all these events (in addition to chickpeas) is that the birth of a baby is a time for joy and a time for people to gather to protect this new member of the community. Some Ashkenazim hold a *vakhnakht* (watchnight or vigil). Sephardim hold a similar *shasha* or *blade*, in which they read prayers and invite the prophet Elijah, who promoted circumcision, even bringing a chair dedicated to Elijah into the baby's room. The *mohel* (who will perform the circumcision) sometimes comes to make sure the baby is healthy and the guests stay all night, reading sections of the Torah to ward off evil spirits.

Most of these parties were only held for boys. But that's starting to change, and indeed there were always people who celebrated girls. Almost a hundred years ago, an ultra-orthodox man came to the Lower East Side of Manhattan from Europe, leaving his wife and three children behind, expecting that he would bring them over in a few years. But war and other difficulties lengthened the separation to almost a decade. His wife gave birth to a baby girl a little over a year after she arrived, and he prepared a huge celebration on the first Shabbat eve of her life. His neighbors laughed at him and told him that such celebrations are only made for boys, and he answered that no boy could make him as happy as his daughter; besides, it just wasn't fair. That man was this author's grandfather and the baby girl is her mother.

The most common event that is held in Ashkenazi families to celebrate the birth of a baby is called the *"Shalom Zachor,"* which means "Hello, male." Recently, the precedent set by the man on the Lower East Side has taken hold, and a parallel party, called a *"Simchat Bat"* is held for baby girls.

The *Shulchan Aruch* mentions these events (*Yoreh De'ah*, 265:12) and says they are made to console the infant, just as one visits a mourner. The infant has just left God's company, where legend says that he was taught all of the Torah by an angel. Right before birth, an angel strikes him just above the mouth (that indention between your upper lip and the bottom of your nose—that's where the angel struck you) to make the baby forget all that he has learned. But the baby feels the loss and is presumably cheered by people coming to visit and drinking beer and eating salty snack food. Some people say that the *"Zachar"* in *Shalom Zachar* is really *"zachor,"* exhorting the baby to remember.

These are usually casual, makeshift events held on the Friday night after the birth. Popcorn, chips, peanuts, and beer are the usual fare, along with store-bought cakes and cookies. The food is super-simple, cheap, and easy to prepare. No one wants to prepare food before the baby is born (remember, the evil eye is watching); besides, the mother is exhausted, having just given birth, and there is now a new mouth to feed. The only constant is chickpeas, served in big bowls with salt and pepper—they are considered to be the food of mourners because they are round and remind us of the circle of life and are therefore right for a baby mourning his separation from his place in God's heaven. Actually, the *Mishnah* mentions that *"adashim"* (lentils) have this quality, but chickpeas are used because who wants to eat lentils?

Sephardic Jews hold a similar event on the night before a baby's circumcision, called a *Brit Yitzchak* (covenant of Isaac) or Zohar (after the Kabbalah book written by Rabbi Shimon Bar Yochai). The food is much better at the Sephardic gatherings, with full meals and elaborate sweets and cakes; the typical mezze is usually laid out (see page 14). People read from the Zohar and other holy writings and hang Kabbalah charts and other good luck charms in the baby's room. The purpose is protection, giving this newborn support before he is officially welcomed into the Jewish faith.

Also on the night before the circumcision, in Sephardic and in many Ashkenazic communities, particularly in Israel, all the small boys in the neighborhood gather in the baby's room for *Kri'at Shema* (the reading of Shema—"Hear, O Israel, the Lord is our God, the Lord is One" [*Deuteronomy*, 6:4]). They are rewarded with bags of candy. In some communities, it is the men who gather to study the Torah and guard the baby.

THE COVENANT

When Abraham was ninety-nine years old, God appeared to him and made him a deal. God would make Abraham the father of many nations; he would lead his descendants to the Promised Land, which was then called Canaan, and he would increase his descendants. In return, Abraham would a) be faithful and pure, and b) as a sign of the covenant, "every male among you who is eight days old is to be circumcised" (*Genesis*, 17:10). In Hebrew, the circumcision is called *brit* or *bris*, which means covenant. Despite much discussion, no one has come up with a concrete answer on why removing this particular bit of skin was an appropriate way to seal the bargain. Circumcision was a common practice at the time and many physicians today agree that it is a healthy thing to do—but its connection to the deal between God and Abraham is still a mystery. In any case, to this day, sons born to parents who have even the slightest connection to Judaism circumcise their sons, and many do it with great pomp and fanfare, and a lot of food.

Ashkenazi families in eastern Europe had a set of special foods that were served at major events, including circumcisions. One of most elaborate was reshinke (also called *chosnbroyt*) and was probably derived from the Sephardic reshika and brought to Romania and Poland when the Ottoman Empire dominated the region. It was a flat cookie, decorated with colored sugar, flowers, coils, and garlands of dough and almonds. On the center of the cookie, bits of dough were arranged to form the words "mazel-tov"; after guests nibbled off the edges, that centerpiece was given to the mother. Modern Ashkenazi brit parties are often elaborate—families arrange for music, catering, and custom-printed balloons—but the meal is usually a brunch or light lunch. Smoked fish, bagels and lox, cheeses, salads, and chickpeas are often served. There's little flexibility in scheduling because these celebrations have to take place eight days after the baby is born (unless there is a health problem)—so they fall on workdays most of the time and people have to get to their jobs.

For Sephardim, the brit celebration is a culmination of a week of gatherings and there is a panoply of customs, rituals, and accoutrements that accompany it. Syrians place a large tiered tray in the center of the table, and guests deposit money and other gifts on it. When the circumcision is done, the tray is auctioned off to the highest bidder and the money is donated to the child. Moroccans put a dish of sand on the table to symbolize future fruitfulness (and to cover up the foreskin when it is removed). The throne of Elijah is given a prime position, reminding everyone that Elijah is in attendance. The infant is brought in, accompanied by musicians and dancers, on a special pillow that is elaborately embroidered and draped with colorful fabrics and lace. A group of women ululate—singing le-le-le-le-le in high-pitched voices—the signature sound of a Sephardi of both great joy and sorrow that sounds like a cross between a high-pitched howl and a stutter.

After the circumcision is done, the baby is given his name, and then a full meal is served, including all the layered flavors and spices that mark Sephardic cuisine. A sweet table, with cookies, cakes, spiced nuts, and fruit desserts, closes the meal, which may last for hours. One wonders who had time for all this cooking—but Sephardic women always come together to make sure that a new baby is given a proper welcome.

Sour plum sauce, called Avramila, is often served at a Sephardi brit in recognition of the fact that Abraham rested under a sour plum tree after the original *brit milah*. (According to legend, the prophet Elijah, who would not be born until several centuries later, visited him there. During his life, Elijah was an avid promoter of the brit, which is why a chair dedicated to him is often part of the ceremony.) Sometimes the sauce is served over fish in a dish called *gaya del avramila*, in which the flesh of the sour plums are boiled with oil, sugar, salt, and a little water. Sweet plums can be used as well, but the amount of sugar should be reduced. Another way to serve sour plums is in a tart like this one.

AVRAMILA, SOUR PLUM TART

The term Avramila means Abraham's fruit.

*Note: This recipe calls for vanilla sugar, which is more common in Europe and the Middle East than in North America. If you can't find it, slice a vanilla pod in half, scrape out a seed, and put it in a food processor with a cup of sugar; pulse a few times to chop and distribute it. Use it right away, or store in an airtight jar.

• • • • •

8 servings
INGREDIENTS

For the Dough:
2 to 3 tablespoons butter, plus more to grease the pie dish
1 cup all-purpose flour
1 teaspoon baking powder
¼ teaspoon salt
2 tablespoons vanilla sugar (*see note on previous page)
1 egg
½ teaspoon vanilla extract
whole milk, about ¼ cup

For the Fruit:
Several firm red plums, halved, and then cut into ¼-inch wedges or slices. Use
    enough to cover a 9-inch pan in a single layer
Brown sugar to taste—around ⅓ cup or vanilla sugar plus powdered cinnamon
3 tablespoons butter

   Preheat oven to 425°F.
   Grease a nine-inch tart pan or ceramic pie plate with butter.
   Sift together the flour, baking powder, salt, and vanilla sugar.
   Cut in two tablespoons of butter (use up to three, if needed), working it into the
dry ingredients until the mixture is like fine, crumbly sand. Set aside.
   Beat together the egg with the vanilla extract. Add enough milk to this to make
a half cup of liquid. Briskly mix this into the dry ingredients with a fork or wire
whisk, just until blended.
   Pour the batter into a well-greased tart pan, and level it with a spatula.
   Arrange the sliced plums in tight concentric circles on top of the dough. Sprinkle
liberally with the brown sugar (or with vanilla sugar and cinnamon), dot with the
butter, place on a baking sheet (to catch drips) and bake twenty-five minutes.
   Let cool before serving.

• • • • •

WHAT'S MY NAME?

During the brit, the father and sometimes the rabbi bestow a blessing on the child,
and the baby is named. Ashkenazim usually name the baby in honor of a relative
who has passed away and never after someone who is alive. Sephardim, however,

name babies after living relatives. This is sometimes a source of friction in families in which one parent is Sephardi and the other is Ashkenazi.

Sephardim have special customs for naming girls in a ceremony called a *brit bat* (sometimes *simchat bat*). In the first month of the baby's life, family and friends gather and the mother reads psalms and songs of thanksgiving; the names of women who were important to Judaism—Sarah, Rebecca, Rachel, Leah, Miriam, Abigail, Esther—are invoked to protect and welcome the baby as her new name is pronounced. Ashkenazi families usually announce the baby girl's name in a regular synagogue or temple service, or at a naming ceremony at home, and sometimes throw a *Kiddush* (a small gathering at which cake, schnapps, and wine are served) · to celebrate; sometimes the *Kiddush* goes further, with all kinds of Shabbat food. Recently, egalitarian Jewish families from all branches of Judaism have adopted the Sephardi custom of baby naming for girls, holding a big, food-full event to name the baby while they stress that she is just important to the family and to Judaism as she would be if she were male.

BAR AND BAT MITZVAH

When a girl turns twelve and a boy turns thirteen, they are considered old enough to think for themselves; their parents, in Jewish law, are no longer responsible for their actions. (Bat means daughter; bar means son.) This is noted in the *Mishnah* (*Ethics of the Fathers*, 5:21): "At age of [thirteen] one is obligated to observe the *mitzvot*." This means that the young adult must fast on Yom Kippur and can be called up to the Torah (though in ultra-Orthodox congregations, females are not called up to the Torah, no matter how old they are). In Ashkenazi families, it also means that it's time to call the caterers.

Coming-of-age rituals appear in many cultures; Bar and Bat Mitzvahs are certainly not the only ones or the strangest ones. In Kenya and Tanzania, young Masai boys drink a mixture of alcohol, cow's blood, and milk, eat a great deal of meat, and are circumcised when they become warriors. In some Ethiopian communities, naked children jump over castrated cows four times to prove they are adults. Boys in the Satere-Mawe tribe in the Brazilian rainforest show that they are mature by wearing special gloves filled with stinging bullet ants. There are rituals for girls, too. Latina girls celebrate adulthood with a quinceañera, at which they attend mass, renew their baptismal vows, and then wear flouncy dresses at a fiesta. American girls hold sweet sixteen parties to mark their transition from childhood to young adulthood.

The Bar Mitzvah as we know it today—a lavish party, attended by friends and relatives from near and far—is relatively recent, but there are hints of it from olden days. In biblical times, twenty was considered to be age of consent for taxation and ritual purposes; that changed to thirteen during the time of the Talmud. Still, until the twelfth century, marking a Bar Mitzvah (which means "son of the commandments") was just a way of deciding that a child was responsible for his own behavior and was allowed to put on *tefillin* (phylacteries) and read from the Torah for the congregation. The first mention of any rituals being performed around it came during the Babylonian captivity, when Rabbi Yehudah Gaon stood before his congregation and thanked God for absolving him from the punishments due his thirteen-year-old son.[2] This blessing is still read by the father (and/or mother) at traditional Bar and Bat Mitzvahs. In later years, the Bar Mitzvah *drasha*—a lecture composed and recited by the Bar/Bat Mitzvah boy/girl was added to the ceremony; it's mostly an orthodox custom today. Today, this coming of age event does not just indicate that a child has reached a chronological landmark; it means that he or she knows enough about Judaism to face the congregation, read from the Torah in Hebrew, and compose a meaningful essay. Rabbis in every branch of Judaism strive to make the experience one that will connect the child to his or her religion throughout life.

The first mention of Bar/Bat Mitzvah as a festive occasion came in the twelfth century, when a French man threw a birthday party for his son. In ancient times, birthday parties were reserved for kings; Ramses the Great for example, gave great birthday parties in Egypt. For commoners, celebrating oneself could be punishable by death. But, as the Middle Ages went by, more and more people added a celebratory element to their sons' coming of age.

In Europe, by the eighteenth century, many (not all) families created events around their sons' thirteenth birthdays. There would be a *Kiddush* in the synagogue and friends were invited for a full meal. In some communities, the Bar Mitzvah boy would visit all the homes of his neighbors, where he would be given a snack and a gift. The gala events of the twentieth century, though, were only in America, and most rabbis excoriated them. Rabbi Moshe Feinstein, the most respected Orthodox rabbi of his generation, wrote a paper in 1956 suggesting that Bar Mitzvahs be abolished because they pull boys away from Judaism rather than drawing them toward it.[3] Conservative Rabbi Harold Sapirstein of Temple Emanu-el in Lynbrook, New York, lamented the fact that these events had become more "bar than mitzvah."[4] Reform rabbis actually changed the Bar Mitzvah to a confirmation service that took place when the child was later in his or her teens, to give him or her more time to learn and mature (they later went back to the old way). As it became clear that the parties were no more than conspicuous consumption, people on every level tried to rein them in but were not entirely successful.

Sephardic communities never saw the need for lavish Bar/Bat Mitzvah shindigs. The child is called to the Torah, usually on a Monday or Thursday, some candy is thrown, there may be a table of sweets (*mesa allegra*) or a family dinner. But the hoopla that surrounds pubescent birthdays for Ashkenazim has never taken hold for Sephardim, except for those who live in America and are a minority compared to Ashkenazim.

According to archivists in Rome, Jewish girls were celebrating coming of age there over two thousand years ago.[5] Sephardim never lost this tradition, but the focus was more on boys than on girls until recently in Ashkenazi circles. But progressive European rabbis celebrated Bat Mitzvahs for their daughters in the nineteenth century. In the United States, the first recorded Bat Mitzvah was made for Judith Kaplan Eisenstein (daughter of Rabbi Mordecai Kaplan, an orthodox rabbi who later founded Reconstructionist Judaism) in Philadelphia in the early 1920s.

One aspect of the over-the-top Bar Mitzvah events that is commendable: At around the same time that they progressed to major events, they became egalitarian, and people held them for boys as well as girls. The Bat Mitzvah came to bloom at around the same time that the Bar Mitzvah became a major event. Nineteenth- and twentieth-century Sephardic sages from Baghdad, Aleppo, and Jerusalem (including Rav Yosef Haim, Rav Haim Sofer, and Hacham Ovadya Yosef) agree that the meal that is served to honor a twelve- or thirteen-year-old on his or her acceptance of the Torah is a *seudat mitzvah* and should be observed (just not with ice sculptures and sushi stations). They make a point of saying that a girl's coming of age is just as important as a boy's.

The elaborate catered affairs are just one aspect of the Bar/Bat Mitzvah celebrations. Whether or not a family springs for an evening event, there is usually a *Kiddush* served right after synagogue or Temple services. An array of dishes—from simple dips and spreads to kugels, cholents, and salads—is served. The one dish that is rarely absent is chopped liver.

Jews have been eating chopped liver since the early years of the Middle Ages in eastern Europe, particularly in Germany, when goose was the liver of choice; eventually they switched to chicken because it was easier to raise. In an effort to use every part of every animal, Jewish housewives looked for and found a way to prepare an organ that was usually discarded. Some forms of chopped liver were already included in non-Jewish German cuisine, but German Jews found better ways to breed and fatten geese, which resulted in bigger livers; in 1562, German poet Hans Wilhelm Kirchof wrote, "they say the Jews have good and fat geese . . . and further, they love the liver of the goose."[6] (Eventually, they found that force-feeding made the goose livers even bigger and tortured the geese to create paté de fois gras; fortunately, that practice is now abhorred and rarely practiced.) But Jews continued to serve chopped chicken livers on Shabbat and holidays. Most Bar Mitzvah buffets would seem incomplete without it, and it's sometimes molded into absurd shapes such as swans or the profile of the boy or girl being celebrated.

The laws of kashrut strictly prohibit the ingestion of blood, and livers are full of it. To make the liver kosher, the liver must be broiled over an open flame. If you're interested in doing this to the point where the liver is actually kosher, consult a rabbinical source—there are many restrictions. Or, buy pre-broiled liver from a kosher butcher.

Liver is full of many useful nutrients, including iron, zinc, folate, and vitamins A, B, and B12. It's also full of cholesterol and saturated fat; the jury is still out on whether eating liver causes high cholesterol levels in humans. There are many vegetarian substitutes for liver—string beans, chickpeas, tofu—and some people convince themselves that they taste just as good.

Jewish celebrations are communal affairs; neighbors and relatives don't just attend the catered event, they take an active part in creating it. Nowhere is this more evident than in food preparation for Bar Mitzvahs, especially in the earlier part of the twentieth century, before pre-packaged foods and catered events were the norm. Novelist Herman Wouk, in his semi-autobiographical book *Inside Outside*, writes about a yards-long kishke (stuffed intestine) that his mother made for his Bar Mitzvah; it had to be draped over furniture throughout the house, guarded by siblings (until it finally burst).[7] Children get together to stuff bags with candy (these bags are thrown at the Bar/Bat Mitzvah celebrant as he/she finishes reading from the Torah). Everyone who has a special recipe—Aunt Shirley's brownies, Cousin Yetta's sponge cake—brings it to serve at the *Kiddush*. And the baking of strudel, which is ubiquitous at Bar/Bat Mitzvahs and at weddings, is often a day-long affair, using the skills of many relatives, friends, and neighbors.

APPLE-NUT STRUDEL

Although some families make or buy it for Shabbat and holidays, strudel is too much trouble for most to undertake unless a major event is taking place. Strudel is one of those dishes that takes many hands to make properly—especially if you're making enough for a crowd—or maybe it's just that the patient stretching and rolling is more fun done with friends. In many towns in Europe—and in some Jewish neighborhoods in America, even today—roving bands of strudel-makers will show up a few days before a *simcha* to assemble this complicated pastry.

The strudels we know today originated in Austria or Hungary in the late seventeenth century (there's a handwritten recipe dated 1696). Baking was a Jewish profession in Austria at that time, and strudel was a part of their repertoire for all their clients. (Jews were known as the best bakers throughout Europe; a Christmas cookie that's popular in Denmark today is still called a "Jewish cookie" because it was first sold in early eighteenth-century Jewish bakeries in Copenhagen.) But thin, rolled pastry dates back much earlier, to nomads in Asia who, over a thousand years ago, would roll out unleavened dough so that they could transport it easily on their travels. Merchants on the Silk Road adopted this practice; they called their loaves of thin, rolled dough *yuvghah* and it became common throughout the Ottoman Empire before it reached Europe.

When the European bakers took over, they improved the fillings. The most popular fillings were cherries or apples, nuts, and cinnamon, but many other fillings were used. Today, creative cooks invent new sweet and savory fillings for their strudels: figs, apricots, orange marmalade, berries, as well as mushrooms and goat cheese, cabbage and caraway, even meat. Some Sephardi families have adapted the recipe to include their own spices and ingredients, such as using apricots and preserved lemons as filling and preparing a date-sesame strudel for Rosh Hashanah.

The part of strudel making that requires the most time is stretching the dough. This is not a roll-and-run operation; the dough is usually hand-stretched on a flat surface, and sometimes hung vertically (on a rack or oven door) to stretch some more.

• • • • •

Makes about 12 servings, so you may need to make 20 of them for a big crowd
INGREDIENTS

For the Apple-nut Filling:
4 to 6 (about 2 pounds) firm apples, peeled and grated or finely diced
¼ cup raisins
2 tablespoon liqueur, your favorite flavor
2 tablespoons butter or margarine
½ cup finely chopped or slivered nuts (almonds, walnuts, hazelnuts, pecans,
    or a mixture); reserve one tablespoon for the top
½ cup granulated sugar; reserve 1 tablespoon for top
¼ cup + 2 tablespoons brown sugar
1½ teaspoons cinnamon
Zest of one lemon
1 tablespoon fresh lemon juice
Pinch of grated nutmeg
½ cup breadcrumbs

For the Dough:
2½ cups flour, more for kneading
¾ cup warm water
3 tablespoons oil
1 tablespoon sugar
¼ teaspoon salt
3 tablespoons butter, melted

To prepare the filling: Place the peeled or grated apples in a sieve over a bowl and let them sit for about twenty minutes. Then squeeze them to remove as much water as possible. Save the juice to add to a shake or smoothie, and move the apples to the bowl.

Plump the raisins in the liqueur.

Melt one tablespoon butter or heat one teaspoon oil in a large skillet. Add the nuts and toss over medium heat for a minute or two until they begin to brown slightly—don't let them burn. Turn off the heat and keep tossing until they are cooled. Add them to the apples. Add the white sugar, a quarter cup of brown sugar, lemon zest, lemon juice, and nutmeg to the apples and stir well.

In a small bowl, combine the remaining brown sugar and cinnamon and set aside.

Heat another tablespoon of butter or oil in the skillet. Add the breadcrumbs and toss over low heat for about a minute until they are toasted. Add the crumbs and the raisins with the liqueur to the apple mixture and stir to combine.

To make the dough: Combine all the dough ingredients in a large bowl or the bowl of a food processor. If you're making the dough by hand, mix all the ingredients with a spoon until they form a shaggy dough, then turn onto a floured board and knead until it is very smooth—probably five minutes or more (this is where it's good to have extra hands). If you're working with a food processor, process for three minutes. A smooth, even dough is essential. If the dough is too dry, add a bit of water, a teaspoon at a time, and re-knead or process; if it's too sticky, add flour, a tablespoon at a time, and re-knead or process.

Shape the dough into a ball and place it in a bowl covered with a damp cloth or plastic wrap. Let it sit for about an hour. There's no yeast in this dough—it won't rise.

Now comes the hard part: Your ball of dough has to become a large (about eighteen- by thirty-inch) paper-thin sheet. You don't want any uneven spots, but you don't want any holes either. You might not get it perfect on the first try, but forgive yourself—it will still be delicious.

Spread a clean cloth on a table or board big enough to hold the dough when it's fully stretched. Flour the cloth lightly, and place the dough in the center. You can start with a rolling pin, and roll the dough as thinly as you can. Then, using your finger, starting at the center: pull and stretch a section, then roll it again. You may also want to pound it with your fists. Place your fingers below the cloth while you pull. If you tear the dough, patch it and roll some more. Repeat until the whole piece is stretched out.

Once your dough has reached the proper thinness, even out the ends with a knife so that it is a rectangle. Carefully lift the cloth and shake off any remaining flour. If you want to follow the traditional strudel-makers, hang the cloth, with the dough on it, over the top of an open door covered with another clean cloth, with the dough evenly balanced on either side of the door. This will stretch it a bit more. After thirty minutes, return it to the table, with the cloth.

Melt the rest of the butter. Preheat the oven to 375°F. Prepare a sheet of lightly greased parchment paper and a large cookie sheet.

Brush the dough with half the melted butter. Spread the filling over about one-third of the bottom of the eighteen-inch side, leaving a margin of about four inches on the bottom and two inches on either side. Sprinkle the reserved sugar-cinnamon mixture over the dough that is not covered with filling. Then gently roll in the filling, using the cloth to help you. When you have rolled about halfway, tuck in margins and keep going until it's all rolled. As you finish, roll the strudel onto the parchment, then lift and place it on the cookie sheet. Brush the top with the rest of the butter or oil and sprinkle on the remaining nuts and sugar.

Bake the strudel for twenty minutes, then reduce the heat to 350°F and continue baking until the top is brown and gooey and the apples are soft, about fifteen minutes more. Cool before serving.

• • • • •

TAYMANIM

Yemenite (Taymani) Jews are from the southern Arabian Peninsula and from one of oldest Jewish communities outside Israel. They retained many of the traditions, culture, and cuisine of the Jews who lived in Israel during the time of the Bible and were not influenced by the traditions of Spain or the rest of Europe, as were the Sephardic Jews. The first Jews to emigrate to Yemen were probably sent there by King Solomon in the sixth century BCE, to further the spice trade. There is some mention in the Bible that the romantic affair between King Solomon and the Queen of Sheba led to more Jews moving to the Arabian Peninsula, Sheba's home ground. The Yemenite Jews were welcomed by the tribal kings, and when the Jews were exiled from Israel after the destruction of the second Temple, many more Jews moved to Yemen. In the sixth century BCE, the Yemenite King Yûsuf 'As'ar Yath'ar, also Dhū Nuwās, converted to Judaism, which strengthened the Jewish Yemenite community. Later, they were persecuted and many moved to Israel; they were one of the first Jewish communities to establish footholds in Palestine in the nineteenth century. When Israel was declared a state in 1948, one the government's first efforts to gather Jews from all the corners of the world was to airlift all the Jews left in Yemen (see pages 179–180).

Yemenite food is frugal, but rich in taste. Yemenites rely on a slew of intricate spice mixes, including curry-based awayij; hilbeh, a mixture of fenugreek and other spices; and schug/zhoug (a chili paste). They also use harissa, a north African spice mix that includes kinds of chili peppers. Other than on Shabbat, holidays, and special occasions such as weddings, there is very little meat or dairy in Yemenite cuisine. Instead, there are many breads, including Jachnoon, salouf, and chuzbeh (for Shabbat), which is eaten with samneh (a clarified butter), schug, or other spice pastes. There are also many soups, for both every day and special occasions.

THE JOY OF BRIDE AND GROOM

Two elements run through the wedding traditions of all Jews: Everyone is very happy (we need to break a glass to remind us that the world is not absolutely perfect), and there's a lot of food. Starting with the decision to marry, everyone starts cooking.

For orthodox Ashkenazi families, the engagement party is serious business; there is a contract signed, with witnesses and rabbis, and then a *seudat mitzvah*, with challah and wine, but no specific kinds of food. Sephardi engagement parties are not as formal, and the usual assortment of fantastic mezze are prepared.

Sephardic weddings are week-long affairs, with several spectacular events. The first is usually a henna party, a journey to a different world, including costumes. It's held a week or so before the wedding day. The bride wears an elaborately decorated caftan, with a headdress and jewelry, including pearls. The groom wears a long white garment. There is much music—sometimes recorded, sometimes live—singing, dancing, speeches, and blessing. The food at a henna party is the pinnacle of Sephardi cuisine; only the best is served. Nuts, sweets, baked goods, borekas, dried fruits—all spiced and decorated to indicate that this is an important event. Trays of exquisite cookies are an integral part of the event, some of them made from fried strips of dough, some of them decorated with colored icings and sugar.

The high point of the night is the henna ceremony itself. Henna is a dye made from the leaves of *Lawsonia inermis*, a tall shrub that is native to north Africa and south Asia. Somewhere in antiquity—remnants have been found on six thousand-year-old mummies—someone discovered that grinding the leaves into a paste produced a semi-permanent dye that could be used to color hair and decorate bodies. Over millennia, incredibly complicated and beautiful henna patterns were designed; they are supposed to confer blessing on the body that wears them, and many cultures used them as a way to exalt and protect a bride on her wedding day. Henna was prized by Jews, but also by Muslims, Hindus, Sikhs, and Christians. Originally limited to the Middle East and Asia, it reached the West in the nineteenth century and many people, especially artists and entertainers, adopted it (Lucille Ball got her red hair from a henna rinse).

Henna was broken out to celebrate holidays, victories in battle, and new ventures; it is ubiquitous at weddings throughout the Middle East and Asia, and nowhere is it more prized than at weddings of Sephardi Jews. In Yemen, applying henna to a Jewish bride could take days. For most modern Sephardi brides, the henna party, with all its festivity, is a cherished tradition, but the application of henna to the bride and groom is mostly symbolic, with a patch of the dye painted on the palm of the hand. The dye fades slowly and faint traces can still be seen for about a month.

There's one more big event for the bride before the wedding, called *noche de novia*, night of the sweetheart. A few days before the *chuppah*, all the neighborhood women accompany the bride to the ritual bath, where she strips and dunks herself. Another full set of mezze is served, along with specially braided challahs that symbolize fertility. In Ashkenazi families, going to the ritual bath is a private affair, with only one or two attendants, usually the bride's mother. Some Hasidic families dance while holding a twisted challah (the Kollich Tanz).

The day of the wedding is a feast, from morning to night. As the bride and groom get dressed, dozens of small dishes are served to them and to all the people who come to visit.

In contrast, the lead-up to an Ashkenazi wedding is tame. On the Shabbat before the wedding, the groom is called to the Torah. Relatives attend, and when the groom finishes reading from the Torah, bags of candy are thrown at him, just as at his Bar Mitzvah. The bride and groom stay apart during the week before the wedding, and the bride's friends come to visit on Friday night or Shabbat which is called Shabbat Kallah. On the day of the wedding, bride and groom both fast— that's why they are given some time after the wedding ceremony to sit by themselves and have a snack—they are hungry from fasting all day.

After the marriage ceremony, someone breaks a glass, a reminder that all is not well, even on this happy occasion. We have to remember that the Temple in Jerusalem is still not rebuilt. This level of less-than-complete satisfaction is a hallmark of Judaism; though it's used to stereotype us, we can't deny that there is some truth in it, as seen in the breaking-the-glass custom. Around 2001, three well-received movies showed the difference between Jewish weddings and those of other cultures (and clarified this aspect of the Jewish personality). In *My Big Fat Greek Wedding*, a young woman falls in love with someone from outside her own community; though her family wasn't delighted with her choice, they accepted it in the end and love conquered all. In *Monsoon Wedding*, a young Indian bride initially rejects the groom that her family selected for her; the family agrees that she shouldn't be forced to marry him, but luckily she falls in love with the groom and everyone is happy. But in *Late Marriage*, when a philosophy student from the Georgian Jewish community falls in love with an older single mom, his mother insists that it is his responsibility to marry someone more acceptable; he relents and at his wedding it is clear that he will be miserable for the rest of his life. Of course, most Jewish weddings hold no such angst—but there's always just a bit of it in the background.

Once the marriage ceremony is over, and the couple joins the guests, the meal that is served is usually the best of the best. Fish is usually a part of it, because fish is a sign of prosperity and fertility. Some Balkan communities have a tradition of bringing a raw fish in a bowl to the wedding and the bride steps over it or dances around it. People throw rice and grains at the couple, remembering God's promise that humans would be as plentiful as seeds in plants—throwing rice at a wedding is an ancient custom that is used at weddings of all religions today.

The *Seudat Mitzvah* starts with *Kiddush* and challah. At Sephardic weddings, sutlach, a sweet rice pudding that is also served at many holiday meals, especially on Shavuot (see page 206), is the first course. Often, chicken dishes follow. In Morocco, there is a chicken with noodles recipe, called treya, that uses lemon, ginger, cinnamon, and cardamom pods. In the Moroccan-Jewish community in Paris, *La Pastilla*, a chicken pie made with cilantro, parsley, and almonds in phyllo dough, is a wedding favorite. Yemenite weddings are centered around an intricate soup called ftut, a beef stock spiced with turmeric, caraway, and cardamom and stuffed with chunks of bread. In Syria and Iraq, a molded rice salad called *arroz de bodas* (boda means wedding) is used as an edible centerpiece.

Sephardim, and many Ashkenazim, keep the wedding going for a full week, holding nightly parties called *Sheva Brachot* (seven blessings)—deferring a honeymoon or the chance to get used to married life. That means seven more meals, but they are usually prepared by someone outside the immediate family—a sibling, a cousin, a grandparent, a close friend—who has not been totally immersed in the wedding up to now. And finally, the wedding celebration is over.

COMFORT FOOD

The rule of thumb is that when a gentile dies, his family feeds you; when a Jew dies, you feed his family. Jews follow a formal death sequence that removes a lot of the tension and friction that can otherwise make grieving even harder. Everyone knows exactly what they are supposed to do. Jews who follow the rules don't have to worry about choosing a casket or burial clothes, about invitations, programs, or musical interludes. The funeral takes place immediately after the death, or as soon as possible thereafter. And once the funeral is over, mourners are given a week of intense comforting, called sitting shiva (shiva means seven), before they are expected to even think about getting back to life. The people around them also know what to do: They prepare the home, take care of transportation, and most of all, bring food. There is a specific meal that is served to mourners (known as the meal of consolation) when they return home after the funeral; it is prepared by friends, neighbors, and relatives, not by the mourners themselves. This meal provides needed sustenance, but also shows that there are still people around who care for those who are left behind. It's a simple meal, consisting of bread, wine, and round things—hard-boiled eggs, chickpeas, lentils, olives—to show that life goes round and round and that even if you are down today, the cycle will continue and you will be up tomorrow.

And for seven days, the comfort continues, as everyone who has any connection to the mourners or the person who died comes to visit and stays for a while—and brings some kind of food. Any kind of food is acceptable—breads, cakes, sandwiches, fruit platters, kugels, casseroles. A shiva house is usually filled with food, even if the mourners don't touch it. It's the final link in the Jewish connection to food.

LIFE CYCLE TRADITIONS AROUND THE WORLD

Morocco

At Sephardic circumcisions, people sniff spices and other things after the blessing over wine; rose petals are usually the fragrance of choice. This is to use the sense of smell to remind the baby and all assembled that (as written in the Zohar) God breathed into Adam's nostrils to give him a soul, and the baby is now connected to his own soul.

Iran

Legend has it that when the Pharaohs of Egypt ordered that all Jewish newborn boys be killed, midwives hid them in apple orchards. At circumcisions in Iran, a large platter of apples is served, to remember and honor those midwives. Apples have become a symbol of newborn safety.

Germany

In Germany, parents conducted an elaborate ceremony when naming their babies; this ceremony was used for both boys and girls, even if the boy had already been named at his circumcision. Parents would place a Bible in the baby's cradle. Then a rabbi would tip the cradle and announce the child's name, with a blessing. There is evidence that this ritual was used from the thirteenth to the seventeenth centuries, but by the end it was used only for girls.

Egypt

When babies in Egypt get their first teeth, they are served a cereal called belilah, which is made by cooking wheat with sugar, cinnamon, and raisins. There's usually a small ceremony with close friends, and everyone enjoys the sweet puddinglike cereal.

Jerusalem

Every year, thousands of boys celebrate their Bar Mitzvah at the Kotel, the last wall of the ancient Temple still standing. Because there is a steady stream of people who want to partake in the reading of the Torah in this sacred place, they must register in advance and they are given a time when they call the boy to the Torah to read and celebrate. Activists from an organization known as Women of the Wall are advocating for a similar privilege for girls.

Russia

In some parts of Russia, grooms give their brides a raw egg, which is a symbol of fertility and easy labor. In some families, the groom throws the egg at the bride, which is probably a symbol of future dry cleaning bills.

Syria

Three days before the wedding, the parents of a Syrian groom will send his bride three trays, called swanne, on the day she is to go to the ritual bath. The trays will contain everything she needs—lotions, perfumes, towels, and food. After her immersion, she, and the women who accompanied her, will eat the food. One item that is always included is Jordan almonds. In Turkey, el Dio de Bana (day of the bath) was held the day before the wedding. Guests brought gifts of soaps, perfume, and lingerie to the bride, as well as coffee and pastries that were eaten after the immersion.

Hungary

Sweet, fruity cakes were a staple of Hungarian Jewish bakeries before World War II. At weddings, *flodni*, a multi-layered cake studded with raisins, apples, walnuts, and poppy seeds, was a popular dessert.

Notes

INTRODUCTION

1. Pew Research Center: A Portrait of Jewish Americans, 2013. http://www .pewforum.org/2013/10/01/jewish-american-beliefs-attitudes-culture-survey/.
2. Ibid.
3. U.S. Holocaust Memorial Museum. Holocaust Encyclopedia. https://www .ushmm.org/wlc/en/article.php?ModuleId=10005161.
4. Yoskowitz, Jeffrey, and Liz Alpern. *The Gefilte Manifesto*. New York: Flatiron Books, 2016.
5. Sheskin, Ira M., and Arnold Dashefsky (eds.). "Jewish Population in the United States, 2014." *American Jewish Year Book* (Dordrecht: Springer, 2014), pp. 143–211.

CHAPTER 1

1. Cooper, Jack. *Eat and Be Satisfied: A Social History of Jewish Food* (Northvale, NJ: Jason Aronson Inc., 1993), p. 176.
2. Ibid, p. 180.
3. Ibid, pp. 177–78.
4. Levy, Esther. *Jewish Cookery Book,* first ed. (Philadelphia: 1871) (Facsimile edition: Carlisle, MA: Applewood Books, 2007).

5. Moses Maimonides, Moses. *On the Causes of Symptoms*, ed. by J. O. Leibowitz and S. Marcus (Berkeley: University of California Press, 1974).

6. Rennard, Stephen. "Chicken Soup Inhibits Neutrophil Chemotaxis in Vitro." *Chest* 2000; 118:1150–57.

7. Nadler, Allan. "Holy Kugel: The Sanctification of Ashkenazic Ethnic Foods in Chasidism." In *Food & Judaism*, ed. by Greenspoon, Lawrence J., Simkins, Ronald A., and Shapiro, Gerald (Lincoln: University of Nebraska Press, 2005), pp. 193–95.

8. Marks, Gil. *The Encyclopedia of Jewish Food* (Hoboken, NJ: John Wiley & Sons, 2010), pp. 127–28.

CHAPTER 2

1. Mowinckel, Sigmund. *The Psalms in Israel's Worship* (Rome: Gregorian & Biblical Press, 1962), 120ff.

2. Maimonides, Moses, *Hilchot Teshuva* 3:4.

3. Cooper, Jack. *Eat and Be Satisfied: A Social History of Jewish Food* (Northvale, NJ: Jason Aronson Inc., 1993), p. 112.

4. Siegelbaum, Rebbetzin Chana Bracha. "The Month of Tishrei: Rosh Hashanah's Physical Doorways into the Spiritual World." http://www.berotbatayin.org/wp-content/uploads/2014/09/TishreiRoshHashanah.pdf.

5. Ibid.

6. Kilgannon, Corey. "A High Holy Call for Lox, and Old Hands to Slice It, at Zabar's." *New York Times* October 9, 2016: A1.

CHAPTER 3

1. Rehren, Thilo, Belgya, Tamas, Jambon, Albert, et al. "5,000 Years Old Egyptian Iron Beads Made from Hammered Meteoritic Iron." *Journal of Archaeological Science* 2013;40(12):4785–92.

2. Cooper, Jack. *Eat and Be Satisfied: A Social History of Jewish Food* (Northvale, NJ: Jason Aronson Inc., 1993), pp. 11–12.

3. My Jewish Learning: Simchat Beit Hashoavah: The Water-Drawing Festival. http://www.myjewishlearning.com/article/simchat-beit-hashoavah-the-water-drawing-festival/2/.

CHAPTER 4

1. Wolters, A. "Halley's Comet at a Turning Point in Jewish History." *Catholic Biblical Quarterly* 1993;55:687–97.
2. Kalonymus ben Kalonymus ben Meir. *Even bohan* (facsimile Hebrew Edition). (La Jolla: University of California Libraries, 1865).
3. Tchernichowski, Shaul. "They Say There Is a Country," in Ruth Finer Mintz, *Modern Hebrew Poetry: A Bilingual Anthology* (Berkeley: University of California Press, second revised edition, 1969), p. 72.
4. Weingarten, Susan. "Medieval Hanukkah Traditions: Jewish Festive Foods in their European Contexts," 2010, https://www.researchgate.net/profile/Susan_Weingarten2/publications.
5. Ibid.
6. Marks, Gil. *Encyclopedia of Jewish Food* (Boston: Houghton Mifflin Harcourt, 2010), p. 272.
7. Leichman, Abigail Klien. "The Modern Olive-Oil Industry is Fairly Young, but Producers are Seeing Brilliant Results and Rising Recognition." *Israel 21c*, 2013, http://www.israel21c.org/israeli-olive-oil-comes-of-age/.
8. Fonda, Batya. *Food in Judeo-Sephardic Songs*, http://www.jewishfolksongs.com/en/Sephardic-food.

CHAPTER 5

1. The Kabbalah Centre website. https://www.kabbalah.com/what-kabbalah.
2. Brumberg-Kraus, Jonathon. "Kabbalah, Food, and Sustainability." http://wheatoncollege.edu/faculty/files/2011/05/KabbalahFoodsustainability_jbk.pdf
3. Hazon (the word means "vision") is a Jewish environmental organization that seeks to build a more sustainable, healthier world. Food is one of their core issues. For more information about Hazon, log on to www.hazon.org. For a PDF version of their Tu B'Shevat Seder guide, see https://hazon.org/wp-content/uploads/2012/08/2013-Tu-BShvat-Haggadah.pdf.
4. Sharon, Alina Dain. "Trees, Tu B'Shvat and the Jewish National Fund." 2017. https://www.algemeiner.com/2017/02/08/trees-tu-bshvat-and-the-jewish-national-fund/.
5. Kol-Kalman, Moshe. "The Blue Box." *The Israel Philatelist* 2009;LX(3):116–17.

238   *Notes*

6. Israel Ministry of Foreign Affairs. "Conservation of Biological Diversity in Israel." *Israel Environment Bulletin* 1997;20(4). http://mfa.gov.il/MFA/Press Room/1997/Pages/CONSERVATION%20OF%20BIOLOGICAL%20DIVER SITY%20IN%20ISRAEL%20-%20O.aspx.

7. Ben-Gurion, David, quoted in Cohen, Shaul Ephraim. *The Politics of Planting* (Chicago: University of Chicago Press, 1993), p. 61.

8. Gerber, Haim. "Modernization in Nineteenth-Century Palestine: The Role of Foreign Trade." *Middle Eastern Studies* 1982;18(3):250–64.

9. USDA Foreign Agricultural Service, Global Agriculture Information Network, 2015, p. 2, https://gain.fas.usda.gov/Recent%20GAIN%20Publications/ Citrus%20Annual_Tel%20Aviv_Israel_12-1-2015.pdf

CHAPTER 6

1. Koppelman, Lesli Ross. *Celebrate! The Complete Jewish Holidays Handbook.* (Northvale, NJ: Jason Aronson Inc., 1993), p. 298.

2. R. Yisrael Isserl of Ponevezh. *Sefer Menucha u-Kedusha* (Vilna, 1864), pp. 271–72.

3. Shurpin, Yehudah. "The History and Meaning of Hamentaschen." http:// www.chabad.org/holidays/purim/article_cdo/aid/2872815/jewish/The-History -and-Meaning-of-Hamantaschen.htm.

4. Montefiore, Judith Cohen. *The Jewish Manual* (facsimile edition). (Champaign, IL: The Book Jungle, 2009).

CHAPTER 7

1. Willems, Harco. "The First Intermediate Period and the Middle Kingdom." In Lloyd, Alan B. *A Companion to Ancient Egypt* (Hoboken, NJ: John Wiley, & Sons, 2010), p. 83.

2. Hoffmeier, James K. *Israel in Egypt: The Evidence for the Authenticity of the Exodus Tradition* (New York: Oxford University Press, 2005), p. 233.

3. Kahane, Rabbi Meir. "Burn Your Prides." http://meir-kahane.angelfire.com/ vayikra.html/.

4. Sturm, Ephraim, Passover Thoughts (privately published, in press, 2017).

5. Sheraton, Mimi. *1,000 Foods to Eat Before You Die* (New York: Workman Press, 2014).

6. Barber, Dan. "Why Is This Matzoh Different from All Other Matzohs." *New York Times*, April 15, 2016.

7. Sarna, Jonathan D. "How Matzah Became Square: Manischewitz and the Development of Machine-Made Matzon in the United States." Sixth Annual Lecture of the Victor J. Selmanowitz Chair of Jewish History, Touro College, New York,

8. Pew Research Group. "Attending a Seder Is Common Practice for American Jews," April 2014. http://www.pewresearch.org/fact-tank/2014/04/14/attending-a-seder-is-common-practice-for-american-jews/.

9. Beit-Arie, Malachi. "How Hebrew Manuscripts are Made." In Gold, Leonard (ed.). *A Sign and a Witness. 2000 Years of Hebrew Books and Illuminated Manuscripts* (New York: Oxford University Press, 1988), p. 36.

10. Cooper, Jack. *Eat and Be Satisfied: A Social History of Jewish Food* (Northvale, NJ: Jason Aronson Inc., 1993), p. 116.

11. Israel Faxx. "The Largest Seder in the World." April 10, 1998, Vol. 6, No. 67. http://www.israelfaxx.com/webarchive/1998/04/8fax0410.html.

CHAPTER 8

1. Jewish Virtual Library. "Establishment of Israel: The Declaration of the Establishment of the State of Israel." http://www.jewishvirtuallibrary.org/the-declaration-of-the-establishment-of-the-state-of-israel.

2. Shiloh, Yigal. "The Population of Iron Age Palestine in the Light of a Sample Analysis of Urban Plans, Areas, and Population Density." *Bulletin of the American Schools of Oriental Research* 1980;239:33.

3. Jewish Virtual Library. "Zionist Congress: First Zionist Congress & Basel Program." http://www.jewishvirtuallibrary.org/first-zionist-congress-and-basel-program-1897.

4. Kadary, Nili. "Herzl and the Zionist Movement: From Basle to Uganda—Background Text." Jewish Agency for Israel, 2002.

5. Wikipedia. "Demographic History of Palestine (region)." https://en.wikipedia.org/wiki/Demographic_history_of_Palestine_(region).

6. Jewish Virtual Library. "History and Overview of the Kibbutz Movement." www.jewishvirtuallibrary.org/jsource/Society_&_Culture/kibbutz.htm.

7. Facts about Israel. "Agriculture in Israel." www.factsaboutisrael.uk/agriculture-in-israel.

8. Quotter. http://www.quotter.net/water-is-the-blood-in-our-veins-quote-by-levi-eshkol_727951.

9. Seigel, Seth M. *Let There Be Water* (New York: St. Martin's, 2015), p. 16.

10. "Israel's Super-Sol Faces Antitrust Action." *Yahoo News*, June 1, 2009.

11. Wikipedia. "Tnuva."https://en.wikipedia.org/wiki/Tnuva#References.

12. Pimi Agro. http://www.pimiagro.com/index.php?m_id=3&if_link=0.

13. Rivka Elbaum's Lab. http://rivkaelbaum.wixsite.com/rivka-elbaum/research -topics.

14. Central Bureau of Statistics. Israel in Statistics 1948-2917. http://www.cbs .gov.il/statistical/statistical60_eng.pdf.

15. Jewish Virtual Library. "Establishment of Israel: The Declaration of the Establishment of the State of Israel." http://www.jewishvirtuallibrary.org/the -declaration-of-the-establishment-of-the-state-of-israel.

16. Central Bureau of Statistics. Israel in Statistics 1948-2917. http://www.cbs .gov.il/statistical/statistical60_eng.pdf.

17. Kramer, Jane. "A Feast for Jerusalem at the Met." *New Yorker Magazine*, December 4, 2016.

CHAPTER 9

1. Golinkin, Rabbi Professor David. "Why do Jews Eat Milk and Dairy Products on Shavuot?" http://www.schechter.edu/why-do-jews-eat-milk-and-dairy -products-on-shavuot/.

2. Ibid.

3. Kraemer, David. "Separating the Dishes: The History of Jewish Eating Practice," in Greenspoon, Leon J., Ronald A. Simkins, and Gerald Shapiro, editors. *Food & Judaism* (Omaha, NE: Creighton University Press, 2005), p. 235.

4. Magen Tzedek. http://www.magentzedek.org.

5. Arad, Dafna. "From the Tudor Table to the Bagel: Cream Cheese's Journey Revealed." http://www.haaretz.com/jewish/food/.premium-1.592697.

CHAPTER 10

1. Klein, Michele. *A Time to Be Born: Customs and Folklore of Jewish Birth* (Philadelphia: The Jewish Publication Society, 1998), p. 15.

2. Elper, Ora Wiskind. "Traditions and Celebrations for the Bat Mitzvah," in Brown, Erica, *The Bat Mitzvah in Contemporary Law and Jewish Practice* (Urim Publications: Jerusalem, 2003), p. 103.

3. Sherwin, Byron. *In Partnership with God* (Syracuse, NY: Syracuse University Press, 1990), p. 150.

4. The Jewish News of Northern California. http://www.jweekly.com/2005/04/29/too-often-there-s-a-lot-more-bar-than-mitzvah-in-our-coming-of-age-rituals/.

5. Pedians. *Judaism* (Pedia Press, 2005), p. 433.

6. Toaff, Ariel. "The Cuisine of the Jews of Italy. http://www.j-italy.org/ariel-toaff-on-the-cuisine-of-the-italian-jews/.

7. Wouk, Herman. *Inside Out* (New York: Little Brown, 1985), p. 38.

Bibliography

Amit-Cohen, Irit, translated by Jerry Aviram. *Zionism and Free Enterprise: The Story of Private Entrepreneurs in Citrus Plantations in Palestine in the 1920s and 1930s*. Berlin, Germany: De Gruyter Academic Publishing, 2015.

Angel, Gilda. *Sephardic Holiday Cooking*. Mount Vernon, NY: Decalogue Books, 1986.

Borowski, Oded. *Agriculture in Iron Age Israel*. Warsaw, IN: Eisenbrauns Publishing, 1987.

Brown, Michael P. *The Jewish Gardening Cookbook: Growing Plants and Cooking for Jewish Holidays and Festivals*. Woodstock, VT: Jewish Lights, 1998.

Brownstein, Rita Milos. *Jewish Holiday Style*. New York: Simon & Schuster, 1999.

Buxbaum, Yitzhak, *A Person Is Like a Tree: A Sourcebook for Tu BeShvat*. Northvale, NJ: Jason Aronson, 2000.

Cohen, Jayne. *The Gefilte Variations: 200 Inspired Re-creations of Classics from the Jewish Kitchen, with Menus, Stories, and Traditions for the Holidays and Year-round*. New York: Scribner, 2000.

Congregation Ohr VeShalom Sisterhood. *The Sephardic Cooks*. Atlanta: Author, 2008.

Davis, Mitchell. *The Mensch Chef: Why Delicious Jewish Food Isn't an Oxymoron*. New York: Clarkson Potter Publishers, 2002.

Dweck, Poopa. *The Aromas of Aleppo*. New York: HarperCollins, 2007.

Feeley-Harnik, Gilliam. *The Lord's Table: The Meaning of Food in Early Judaism and Christianity*. Washington, DC: Smithsonian Institution Press, 1994.

Fernandes, Edna, *The Last Jews of Kerala*. New York: Skyhorse Publishing, 2008.

Ferris, Marcie Cohen. *Matzoh Ball Gumbo: Culinary Tales of the Jewish South*. Chapel Hill, NC: University of North Carolina Press, 2010.

Fishkoff, Sue. *Kosher Nation*. New York: Schocken Books, 2010.

Fox, Karen L., and Phyllis Zimbler Miller. *Seasons for Celebration: A Contemporary Guide to the Joys, Practices and Traditions of the Jewish Holidays*. New York: Putnam Publishing Group, 1992.

Glezer, Maggie. *A Blessing of Bread*. New York: Artisan, 2004.

Goldstein, Joyce. *Cucina Ebraica, Flavors of the Italian Jewish Kitchen*. San Francisco: Chronicle Books, 1998.

Goodman, Matthew. *Jewish Food: The World at Table*. New York: HarperCollins Publishers, 2005.

Goodman, Philip. *The Sukkot and Simchat Torah Anthology*. Philadelphia: Jewish Publication Society of America, 1973.

Greene, Gloria Kaufer. *The Jewish Holiday Cookbook: An International Collection of Recipes and Customs*. New York: Times Books, 1985.

Greenspoon, Leon J., Ronald A. Simkins, and Gerald Shapiro, editors. *Food & Judaism*. Omaha, NE: Creighton University Press, 2005.

Greenstein, George. *A Jewish Baker's Pastry Secrets*. Berkeley, CA: Ten Speed Press, 2015.

Gur, Janna. *The Book of New Israeli Food: A Culinary Journey*. New York: Schocken Books, 2007.

Hilton, Rabbi Michael. *Bar Mitzvah: A History*. Lincoln, NE: University of Nebraska Press, 2014.

Horowitz, Roger. *How Coke Became Kosher and Other Tales of Modern Food*. New York: Columbia University Press, 2016.

Isaacs, Ronald L. *Every Person's Guide to the High Holy Days*. Lanham, MD: Jason Aronson/Rowman & Littlefield, 1999.

———. *Every Person's Guide to Shavuot*. Lanham, MD: Jason Aronson/Rowman & Littlefield, 1999.

———. *Every Person's Guide to Hannukah*. Lanham, MD: Jason Aronson/ Rowman & Littlefield, 2000.

———. *Every Person's Guide to Passover*. Lanham, MD: Jason Aronson/ Rowman & Littlefield, 2000.

———. *Every Person's Guide to Purim*. Lanham, MD: Jason Aronson/Rowman & Littlefield, 2000.

———. *Every Person's Guide to Sukkot, Shemini Atzeret, and Simchat Torah*. Lanham, MD: Jason Aronson/Rowman & Littlefield, 2000.

Kaufer Greene, Gloria. *The New Jewish Holiday Cookbook*. New York: Times Books, 1999.

Klein, Michele. *A Time to Be Born: Customs and Folklore of Jewish Birth.* Philadelphia: Jewish Publication Society, 1998.

Kraemer, David Charles. *Jewish Eating and Identity Through the Ages.* New York: Routledge Publishing, 2008.

Levy, Esther. *The Jewish Cookery Book,* first edition (Philadelphia: 1871). Facsimile edition: Carlisle, MA: Applewood Books, 2007.

Levy, Faye. *Faye Levy's International Jewish Cookbook.* New York: Warner Books, 1991.

———. *International Jewish Cookbook.* New York: Warner Books, Inc., 1991.

Lewando, Fania, translated by Eve Jochnowitz. *The Vilna Vegetarian.* New York: Schocken Books, 2015.

Machlin, Eda Servi. *Classic Italian Jewish Cooking.* New York: HarperCollins, 2005.

Mann, Vivian. *A Tale of Two Cities: Jewish Life in Frankfurt and Istanbul, 1750–1870.* New York: Jewish Museum, 1982.

Marks, Copeland. *Sephardic Cooking.* New York: Donald I. Fine, Inc., 1992.

Marks, Gil. *The World of Jewish Cooking: More Than 500 Traditional Recipes from Alsace to Yemen.* New York: Simon & Schuster, 1996.

———. *The World of Jewish Entertaining: Menus and Recipes for the Sabbath, Holidays, and Other Family Celebrations.* New York: Simon & Schuster, 1998.

———. *The World of Jewish Desserts: More Than 400 Delectable Recipes from Jewish Communities.* New York: Simon & Schuster, 2000.

———. *Olive Trees and Honey: A Treasury of Vegetarian Recipes from Jewish Communities Around the World.* Hoboken, NJ: Wiley, 2004.

———. *Encyclopedia of Jewish Food.* Hoboken, NJ: Wiley, 2010.

Merwin, Ted. *Pastrami on Rye: An Overstuffed History of the Jewish Deli.* New York: New York University Press, 2015.

Ottolenghi, Yotam, and Sami Tamimi. *Jerusalem: A Cookbook.* Berkeley, CA: Ten Speed Press, 2012.

Nathan, Joan. *The Flavor of Jerusalem.* New York: Little & Brown, 1975.

———. *The Jewish Holiday Kitchen.* New York: Schocken, 1979.

———. *Jewish Cooking in America.* New York: Knopf, 1994.

———. *The Jewish Holiday Baker.* New York: Schocken, 1997.

———. *The Foods of Israel Today.* New York: Knopf, 2001.

———. *Joan Nathan's Jewish Holiday Cookbook.* New York: Schocken, 2004.

———. *Quiches, Kugels and Couscous: My Search for Jewish Cooking in France.* New York: Knopf, 2010.

Rezny, Aaron, and Jordan Schaps. *Eating Delancey: A Celebration of Jewish Food.* Brooklyn, NY: Powerhouse Books, 2004.

Roden, Claudia. *The Book of Jewish Food: An Odyssey from Samarkand to New York*. New York: Alfred A. Knopf, 1997.

Sachar, Howard. *A History of Israel from the Rise of Zionism to Our Time*, third edition. New York: Alfred A. Knopf, 2007.

Sheraton, Mimi. *From My Mother's Kitchen*. New York: HarperCollins, 1991.

Siegel, Seth M. *Let There Be Water: Israel's Solution for a Water-Starved World*. New York: St. Martin's Books, 2015.

Solomonov, Michael, and Steven Cook. *Zahav: A World of Israeli Cooking*. Boston: Houghton-Mifflin, 2015.

Steinberg, Paul, edited by Janet Greenstein Potter. *Celebrating the Jewish Year: The Fall Holidays, Rosh Hashanah, Yom Kippur, Sukkot*. Philadelphia: Jewish Publication Society, 2007.

Sternberg, Rabbi Robert. *The Sephardic Kitchen*. New York: HarperCollins Publishers, 1996.

Waskow, Rabbi Arthur O. *Seasons of Our Joy: A Modern Guide to Jewish Holidays*. Philadelphia: Jewish Publication Society, 1982.

Wex, Michael. *Rhapsody in Schmaltz: Yiddish Food and Why We Can't Stop Eating It*. New York: St. Martin's Press, 2016

Yoskowitz, Jeffrey, and Liz Alpern. *The Gefilte Manifesto*. New York: Flatiron Books, 2016.

Zoloth, Joan. *Jewish Holiday Treats*. San Francisco: Chronicle Books, 2000.

WEBSITES

Aish Recipes: http://www.aish.com/f/r/

Busy in Brooklyn: http://www.busyinbrooklyn.com

Joy of Kosher: http://www.joyofkosher.com

Sephardic Food: https://sephardicfood.com

Tori Avery: http://toriavey.com

What Jew Wanna Eat: This Is Not Your Bubbe's Blog: http://whatjewwannaeat.com

Index

About the Authors

Lori Stein is president and director of Layla Productions, an award-winning book packaging/production consulting firm. She has contributed to the publication of over 200 books. Stein is co-author of *Recipes from America's Small Farms*, which has garnered outstanding reviews. As a volunteer, Stein has run an arts and crafts program at a pediatric hospital ward, tutored reading and other subjects, and taught gardening classes. For almost two decades, she has served as the site coordinator for the Carnegie Hill Yorkville Community Supported Agriculture food co-op in New York City.

Rabbi Ronald H. Isaacs recently became the *rabbi emeritus* of Temple Sholom in Bridgewater, New Jersey, where he was spiritual leader for forty years. He is currently rabbi of Beth Judah Temple in Wildwood, New Jersey. A prolific author, he has published more than one hundred books covering virtually all aspects of Judaism for diverse audiences. Among his titles are the *Every Person's Guide* series, the *How-to Handbook* trilogy, and the children's books *Farmer Kobi's Hanukkah Match* and *The Family (and Frog) Haggadah*. He blogs at *Thoughts from Rabbi Ron* and writes a monthly column for *The Cape May Herald*. "Rabbi Ron" is a popular lecturer and teacher. For additional information see his website www.rabbiron.com.